NIXON and the MEXICANS

How a Young Man Encountered the Diaspora of
1913–1930 and Made a Difference

HENRY M. RAMIREZ, Ph.D.

DEDICATION

For Maria Ester Gomez de Ramirez
My dear wife

ACKNOWLEDGMENTS

I hereby extend my hands in gratitude to so many. Firstly, to my wife, who tirelessly edited my drafts and recommended clarifications drawn from her own personal history and that of her parents, who were part of the Diaspora.

I also greatly appreciate the personal help, advice, and references provided by Elizabeth L. Uyeda, Los Angeles County Archivist and writer of the blog *Los Angeles Revisited*. She provided me the *sine qua non* information about Murphy Ranch, Leffingwell Ranch, Al Lemus, and Richard M. Nixon, when he lived as a youngster among the 200-plus Diaspora Mexicans of the ranches in rural East Whittier. That was the link between Mexicans and Nixon way back in the 1920s.

To all the "sons of the Diaspora" who shared their personal family histories in this book, I am very grateful. Their stories bring the experience of the Diaspora alive. I hope they will inspire other Mexican-Americans to treasure their own heritage as well.

Special thanks to Christian Alexa for distilling the message of hope into a beautiful painting for the cover.

Finally, I thank Mary Beth de Ribeaux, who guided this manuscript with her excellent editing skills and laudable sense of order, and along the way gained new appreciation for the heritage of her Cuban husband and Mexican children and Nixon's impact on their lives.

CONTENTS

FOREWORD

The term "paradox," according to the *Concise Oxford Dictionary*, means a statement contrary to accepted opinion, from Latin *paradoxum*, from the Greek word *paradoxon*, which means contrary to expectations, existing belief, or perceived opinion.

President Richard Milhouse Nixon is the greatest paradox in American history.

Everyone knows him for reopening diplomatic ties and commerce to China. But *we* Mexican-Americans know him for ordering the first U.S. census count of all the Spanish-speaking in the United States; for appointing over 100 executive-level Hispanics to the White House, the Cabinet, and departments, agencies, and commissions; for promoting generals and admirals in the U.S. Department of Defense; and for creating Hispanic millionaires during his watch with federal assistance to small businesses by his Department of Commerce and the National Economic Development Association (NEDA).

No President before or after him has done as much for us. Yet there was no hint of his connection to us initially.

I first heard of Richard Nixon as a staunch anti-Communist U.S. senator from California, then as vice president of the United States to President Dwight Eisenhower. When Nixon ran for president in 1960, I cast my first vote for him. *Mexicanos* were voting in droves for John F. Kennedy; to vote for Nixon was countercultural, and I caught hell from the Chicanos in Texas and Washington, DC, for doing that.

But since I was working for the *Washington Post*, I knew of Senator John F. Kennedy's record for absenteeism and his reputation as a ladies' man: a millionaire playboy. Nixon, on the other hand, was a hard worker. He used to kid that he became a lawyer by the seat of his pants—i.e., by studying hard. I knew what that was like.

Our childhood shapes our lives. From the sixth grade on up through graduation, our family spent the better part of the year migrating in search of work, from South Texas near the border all the way north to Michigan and west to California, as well as all points in between. We traveled each year from May to November, playing havoc with our schoolwork. I had to double-up, reading the day's assignment and doing past work for the months we were "up north." We worked side by side with Mississippi Blacks, Appalachian Whites, Puerto Ricans, and Mexicans from the old country, both legal and illegal.

So, when I first learned that President Nixon's parents had owned a little *tiendita* (grocery store) and gasoline station in East Whittier, and he'd had to work in the orchards and fields of Southern California, I immediately concluded that he had to have known us—

he had to have grown up with *mexicanos*. I also recognized he wanted to change history to include us in the destiny of this country when he became president. Dr. Henry Ramirez, originally from Pomona and Whittier, California, confirmed that in his first book, *A Chicano in the White House: The Nixon No One Knew.*

Before reading Dr. Ramirez's book, it was only a gut instinct that Richard Nixon knew us. But Henry, handpicked by the President as chairman of the Cabinet Committee on Opportunities for Spanish-Speaking People, knew that. He grew up in the same area as the President did. "He got to know us while we lived our culture in accord with our values: God, family, hard work, respect for the law, and an aversion to handouts," says Dr. Ramirez.

True. Our family, as South Texas migrant farmworkers, would travel over a thousand miles in search of work rather than receive government handouts, *el centavo*, unemployment checks.

This, Dr. Ramirez's new book, is a must read. It is both significant and timely. The rise of Donald Trump has signaled bullying and redneck power in the United States. The rhetoric against illegal immigration, especially from Mexico, is red hot. Further, the concerns around the Deferred Action for Childhood Arrivals (DACA) policy have added another layer of confusion and angst. However, this book may clear these issues for the reader. Dr. Ramirez's treatment of immigration in Part III includes ten stories of families that crossed the Rio Grande to help substantiate his thesis.

On immigration, I have a personal interest. My four siblings and I were born and raised in the United States, growing up on the border in South Texas. My father became a naturalized citizen of the United States. But my saintly mother, who entered the United States in 1908, before the laws on immigration were enacted, was "grandfathered-in." However, the feds at the local level, in their ignorance, required her to report annually as a resident alien. I know. I was the one that filled out "her papers" every year.

Besides my personal interest, I also spent two years interviewing and communicating with experts on immigration in Mexico and the United States.

Dr. Ramirez understands the nuances of the history of *mexicanos* in the United States. He instinctively knows the politics of skin color that divided social life in Mexico when Celestino Gorostiza wrote *El color de nuestra piel (The Color of Our Skin)*, a play about the Mexican government's practice of appointing light-skinned Spaniards (Criollos) over Mestizos and Native Mexicans *(indios)* to federal positions.

Dr. Ramirez knows about us being descendants of emperors, kings, and princes. He is both a philosopher and a historian. He spent ten years studying for the priesthood before receiving his Ph.D. His book reflects that knowledge. It is a great summary of the history of Mexico. I strongly recommend it for the *pochos* among us, those who do not know who they are. This book will help them. It is vitally important that they read it.

More importantly, Dr. Ramirez knows the nature and purpose of advocacy. Representing the political appointing power was one function of his job. Equally important was the need to represent the community that made his appointment possible, the Spanish-speaking— most of them Mexican-Americans, but also Puerto Ricans from the island of Puerto Rico as well as New York, New Jersey, Illinois, Florida, and throughout the United States; Cubans; and Central and South Americans. All were included in the public law that created the Cabinet Committee; all had to be represented to the appointing powers and their minions.

Dr. Ramirez was handpicked by Nixon to serve as chairman of the President's Cabinet Committee on Opportunities for Spanish-Speaking People. Presidents do not personally recruit candidates for high posts. They do "vet" candidates by calling on close friends for their recommendations, though, which is how Henry got selected. The reader will enjoy learning why Henry was reluctant to accept the position initially and how he finally arrived at agreeing to serve. For more details on this story, read his first book, *A Chicano in the White House*.

As for me, I attended the Georgetown University School of Foreign Service and worked for the U.S. Department of Commerce, U.S. Department of Justice, the agency named Action, and the Legal Services Corporation. I was a regional director for a Federal Regional Council (and the only non-lawyer director in the country). Later, I was selected as an associate director for the Cabinet Committee by the late John Bareno. Martin Castillo, the first chairman, was just leaving; it was December 1969. A flurry of pretenders vied to take Martin Castillo's place. I met the candidate for chairman Dr. Henry Ramirez on my way out. I was returning to Texas to run for the State Senate.

I later served as a senior staff assistant to Texas Governor Bill Clements, the first Republican governor of Texas in 104 years. I was an assistant to the campaign manager that got him elected in that one-party state. In 1979, Governor Clements called for action on the issue of immigration long before it became a national issue. Dr. Richard Rubottom and I wrote a position paper on the undocumented worker from Mexico. Governor Clements gave it to President Ronald Reagan, and it became the Simpson-Mazzoli Act. You know the saying: You do not want to see how sausage or legislation is made. Governor Clements, Dr. Rubottom, and I were not in favor of amnesty. I venture to say President Reagan wasn't either. You win some and lose some in the horse-trading on Capitol Hill to pass a bill.

I am one of the children of the Revolution that Henry writes about in this book. Both of my parents were members of the Diaspora, with our own story of suffering, hope, longing, wandering, struggle, and achievement. That is my personal connection to the topic of this book.

Our powerlessness and years of defeat are over. You will now find Spanish names in every field of endeavor in government and the private sector. And we owe a debt of gratitude to Richard Nixon for that progress and to my friend Dr. Henry Ramirez.

Mr. G. G. Garcia
Author, *Mercedes: Recuerdos de Ayer*
Amboy, IL

March 2, 2018

INTRODUCTION

"Why did you leave Mexico?" I still recall vividly the moment I asked my dad that question. We were having breakfast on a Saturday. At age 15, I was now working as an adult with a large crew of Mexicans in orange, lemon, and grapefruit orchards in Southern California. My life was no longer isolated in Pomona, California, where my family lived on the outskirts of town and where I went to school and church. My family didn't own a car; we walked or used a bicycle to get where we wanted to go, which wasn't very far. But now... Now I bounced along in medium-sized trucks with the rest of the crew as we traveled from grove to grove, meeting and working with so many other Mexicans. I became very aware that many Mexicans lived and worked in every town in Southern California, and some places had barrios where *only* Mexicans lived. I was the young one on the crew, silent, keeping to myself because I could not speak the Spanish of these hard-working, aging men who suffered pains and ailments due to the physical demands of the hard, dirty work of citrus picking. I heard them talk about Mexico continually. Yet none of them talked about *why* they left Mexico!

So, I asked my dad and waited while he struggled to answer. Finally, he spoke a few words that conveyed this thought: "I wanted a better life for all of you." And thus began the odyssey of a very young, inquisitive Mexican-American Mestizo. I yearned to know more. I thirsted for the deeper *why*. I have thought about and researched that question throughout the many stations of my life as well as the education, travel, and work I've experienced, and now, in the sunset of my life, I write what I have learned about the *why*.

Why did so many Mexicans and Mexican-Americans I knew from that era of my questioning come to live and work permanently in the Pomona Valley of California? Or, the larger question, why do so many Mexicans live in the United States in general? When did they arrive? How did they get from their little rural *ranchitos* deep in Central Mexico to the little railroad towns of the Southwest and other parts of the country?

Does the title of this book surprise you? How is the name Nixon associated with the story of Mexican-Americans? This book will reveal his highly significant and *sine qua non* involvement as well as open hidden doors to show *why* two million Mexicans, mostly landless and illiterate Mestizo peasants, fled their burning country from 1913 to 1930 to find work, security, and religious freedom in the land of the free. The Greeks have a word that describes this mass movement: *diaspora*, which means "scattering." Leaving behind all they knew, Mexicans scattered across the United States, found work, set down roots, and raised their families.

Generally, they did not speak much of their journey. As a result, few Mexican-Americans today know anything of their own heritage, legacy, and ethnicity. Total ignorance of their family history is common. Ask almost any young Mexican-American where their ancestors were born, but do not wait too long for the answer: They do not know! Part I of this book will help them learn about their heritage through a brief recounting of Mexican history and particularly the unfortunate sequence of events that led up to the Diaspora of 1913–1930, when their parents or grandparents (or perhaps great-grandparents) came to the United States.

While conditions certainly were more stable on this side of the Rio Grande, not everything was easy for the newly arrived Mexicans. The challenges they and their descendants experienced were real. But I have been privileged in my life to have had a close view of the man who spearheaded a great effort to right the wrongs that stood in the way of many Mexican-Americans, preventing them from fully enjoying the fulfillment of the American Dream. I participated in that effort myself. This is where President Nixon enters the picture. His long-enduring personal warmth toward Mexican-Americans dates to his own experiences of them in his youth and inspired him to action from the White House. Part II describes in detail the steps he directed to advance the civil rights of Mexican-Americans and, by extension, other Spanish-speaking Americans. Let this chapter of the Mexican-American story be made known, too!

Finally, Part III gives voice to Mexican-Americans directly. After sketching the horrific conditions faced in Mexico in the early part of the twentieth century, Part III presents ten family stories from real-life Mexican-Americans. I hope these stories will renew the appreciation that young Mexican-Americans have for the legacy of their parents and grandparents and help connect them with their own histories. May the path from my *"Why?"* illuminate theirs.

PART I

1. CHANGE COMES TO MEXICO

El Bajio (in English, "The Lowlands") is an extensive valley in the interior of Mexico. Surrounded by mountain ranges, the area is very fertile and well-watered and encompasses the present-day states of Guanajuato, Jalisco, Michoacan, Aguascalientes, and Zacatecas. Parts of the nearby states of Sinaloa and Durango will also be addressed in this book, although they are not part of El Bajio. At the time of the European invasion, many groups of people lived in these regions:

- The Otomi, Purepechas, and Guachichiles—in what is now Guanajuato;

- The Coca, Texcuexas, Guamares, and Caxcanes—in what is now Jalisco;

- The Otomi, Nahua, and Purepechas—in what is now Michoacan;

- The Caxcanes, Guachichiles, and Zacatecos—in what is now Aguascalientes;

- The Zacatecos, Caxcanes, and Guachichiles—in what is now Zacatecas;

- The Zuaque and Tehuecos—in what is now Sinaloa; and

- The Zacatecos, Tepehuenes, and Tarahumaras—in what is now Durango.

But three major changes were to sweep upon the people of El Bajio in the 1500s. First, Europeans arrived. Soon after Hernan Cortes invaded *El Reino de Megico* (the Kingdom of Mexico) in 1521, *los Conquistadores* (his generals) made further conquests in the interior of Mexico that included *El Reino de Michuacan* (the Kingdom of Michoacan), i.e., the region of El Bajio. By 1535, the expansive territories claimed by Spain became *Nueva Espana* (New Spain), which would eventually stretch from Oregon to Panama, including land that is now Nicaragua, Costa Rica, El Salvador, Honduras, Guatemala, and the Southwest United States. The Spanish monarchy via its representative, the viceroy, ruled by so-called Divine Right in a feudal system until 1821, when Mexico was granted independence from Spain through the Treaty of Cordoba.

It is a given and self-evident reality that armies change the daily life of those they conquer. The arrival of the *Conquistadores* changed daily life forever in El Bajio. They seized the lands and claimed everything in them—people, animals, and properties. They looted and got booty. They erroneously named the people "Indians," and the native languages of these "Indians" became dialects or even disappeared altogether. The people of El Bajio lost their freedom and independence, and instead they became subjects of the Spanish army.

A second major change arose as a consequence of the Spaniards' arrival. Unlike the Anglo-Saxon men who settled in Massachusetts and Virginia, the Spanish soldiers arrived without women. The Anglo-Saxons brought their Anglo-Saxon wives with them to the New World and raised their Anglo-Saxon children, but in New Spain, the Spanish soldiers started families with native women. This union of Spaniards and indigenous women produced children known as *Mestizos*; the outcome itself is known as the *Mestizaje*. This was a huge change, being entirely unknown before 1520. Now the Mexico of the sixteenth century was no longer inhabited by just two groups, the indigenous and the Europeans. A third group emerged, the Mestizos.

Father Jose Luis G. Guerrero observes in his book, *El Nican Mopohua:*

It is said that in its beginning, the Mestizaje was enthusiastically accepted, that it was promoted by the Indians, that they cheerfully delivered their daughters and sisters, but never did they anticipate the infamy in virtue of which, upon the birth of the children of those unions, the fathers would abandon them and consider their mothers with infamy by reason of being their mothers. As a result, both Spanish fathers and Indian mothers wound up rejecting the fruit of their union and created a 'sub-proletariat' due to the enormous number of abandoned Mestizo children (something that had never been seen in Mexico, where the children were a precious treasure).[1]

Regarding Father Guerrero's statement that "the Mestizaje was enthusiastically accepted," one wonders who really held that opinion. Was it the perspective of the *Conquistadores* or that of the defeated?

To understand more profoundly this change of the Mestizaje, it is essential to revisit the paradigms of morality and behavior during those years. The predecessors of the English colonists who crossed the Atlantic in the 1600s had been Catholics until not many years before, when Henry VIII broke from the Catholic Church (1530s). They still lived and comported themselves within the vestiges of Catholic morality. Possession of concubines was not practiced. On the other hand, the Spaniards had lived for seven centuries under the reign of Mohammedans, who had established the norms and acceptance of the possession of harems and concubines. The use and abuse of women was normal comportment for the Moslems. From that Mohammedan way of life, the Spaniards learned and acquired the practice of the *"casa chica"* for a concubine.

The third major change, which spread to El Bajio (and for that matter, eventually to all America starting with New Spain), was a remarkable and unexpected one of supernatural origin. Ten years after Cortes subdued the Aztecs in the capital city of Mexico, an awesome event occurred. By that time, the *Conquistadores* and the defeated Aztecs had abandoned their fighting and had commenced peaceful living, at least as best they could. No human

---

[1] Jose Luis G. Guerrero, *El Nican Mopohua* (Cuautitlan, Mexico: Editorial: Realidad, Teoria, y Practica, S.S. de C.V., 1998), p. 456.

being could have anticipated the direct involvement of God Himself, however!

Reader, know that this part of the story involves the supernatural. So, think about the birth of a Man, God Incarnate, in Bethlehem. His name was Jesus. He lived with His Mother, Mary, and his foster father, Joseph, in Judea. He was a teacher; He suffered on the Cross, died, and was buried. On the third day, He resurrected from the dead. He ascended into Heaven. Later, He also assumed His Mother into Heaven without her suffering the act of perishing.

In 1531, He sent his Mother to appear and talk to a man, a resident of Anahuac. (Anahuac was the area around what today is known as Mexico City.) The man was born in 1474, in Cuautitlan, a town near Mexico City. His original name was Cuauhtlatoatzin, which means "Talking Eagle." Upon being baptized a Christian, he chose a new name, Juan Diego. (Juan is the Spanish name for the Apostle John, and Diego, for the Apostle James.)

Mary, the Mother of Jesus, appeared to Juan Diego in December 1531 on a hill named Tepeyac, located in the northern part of Mexico City. Not coincidently, the Aztecs had dedicated that particular hill to the mother of their god Teotl, the one and only supreme god of the Aztec religion. Teotl was known by many names, each for a different aspect of his divinity.

Using Juan Diego's native language, Nahuatl, Mary identified herself as the Mother of God with the name Guadalupe. The indigenous people of Mexico realized that Mary's apparitions were of Divine origin and converted en masse to Christianity. Ten million of them converted in a few short years. It changed Mexico totally.

In addition, Our Lady of Guadalupe left an imprint of herself on Juan Diego's *tilma*, or cloak. A *tilma* is made of fabric woven from the fiber of a maguey plant and used by Mexicans of that time as an overcoat, poncho, blanket, carryall, and so forth. Juan Diego's cloak made of cactus (maguey) fiber is still fresh today, exactly as it was almost 500 years ago, when he used it for hundreds of chores. The image of Mary is still plain to see on it, too. Many, many people have looked at that image, studied it, and reflected upon it. Neither the *Conquistadores* nor the Catholic priests—Jesuits, Dominicans, Augustinians, and Franciscans—recognized her at first, nor did the indigenous peoples. She was different. She was neither a pretty, sweet European woman nor an Aztec girl. *Her face was without any doubt the face of a Mestiza!*

Today in the daily life of Mexico and Central America such a countenance is commonplace and totally normal, but back when Mary appeared and left her image on Juan Diego's *tilma*, that kind of face was not commonly seen.

2. MEXICAN DAILY LIFE

After the Spanish arrived, three groups coexisted in Mexico: the Europeans (or "Criollos"), the Native Mexicans, and the Mestizos. For several hundred years, a way of life evolved. How can we describe the daily life of these three groups? Numerous sources provide information on the European way of life in Mexico. The Europeans frequently wrote their version of events and the history surrounding their lives and perceptions. As one example among many, a reading of *Life in Mexico* by Fanny Calderon de la Barca (published 1843) will provide a rich myriad of insights into European opinions and observations.

We also know that the Native Mexicans "wrote" extensively in pictures and glyphs (or more accurately, "pictorially graphing"). One of the indigenous peoples native to what is now Michoacan, the Nahuas (pronounced "na-was"; the "hu" is pronounced as a "w"), designed pictures to communicate their history, philosophy, letters, and commercial dealings in the

Nahuatl language. (The Mayas and Otomi also "wrote" similarly.) People literate in Nahuatl had to "read" that a pictograph or glyph of a rugged, rocky hill meant just that: It was a hill, topped with rocks on rough terrain. It was a picture, not a series of letters. Almost all of the Mexican groups could understand the Nahuatl language to some extent, even though they used their own languages on a day-to-day basis. Thus, they enjoyed the faculty of communication by reading and grasping of the meanings of the Nahuatl graphics.

This ability to "read" a pictorial language lent an advantage when it came to the image of Our Lady of Guadalupe on Juan Diego's *tilma*. Every glyph, every stitch, every color, the light, her countenance, her clothing, all that and more carried a message, a lesson, a fact. She was indeed a pictorial book. "Reading" her symbols revealed supernatural lessons, which was something that, with few exceptions, the Spanish could not do. Thus, the story of her apparitions and the meanings and messages in the *tilma* of Guadalupe were known, understood, and transmitted by word of mouth to generation after generation of Native Mexicans in Anahuac and beyond.

After the *Conquistadores* arrived, however, a new language, Spanish, substituted for the native tongues. It was a language derived from another conquest: The Roman conquest of the Iberian Peninsula in the 200s B.C. The original language spoken in Iberia was Celtic, which was later replaced by Latin. Since most of the conquered people of Hispania were illiterate, they mispronounced and misspelled the Latin language into what is now known as Spanish.

The Mestizos and Native Mexicans needed to acquire the sounds of the new language, Spanish, as well as its letters. But reading and, especially, writing Spanish was not so easy. Those two skills were achieved in school. Good luck. Formal education was for the landed—i.e., the Europeans. Illiteracy was the world of the Mestizos and Native Mexicans.

And what do we know of the way of life of the Mestizos? Because of their illiteracy, very little. They did not write their history. However, one of the main purposes of this book is to illuminate a part of their unknown story. I, the author, enjoy an asset, for I am a Mestizo myself!

To round out the sketch of daily life for the three groups, however, I will compare them on several other aspects: housing, transportation, education, and religion.

Housing

Where did the people live? Almost all the Europeans in Mexico lived in towns and cities. Their houses occupied the areas around the public square, a location where they enjoyed the protection of armed police and the army. The owners of large estates (haciendas) lived in the residences marked by arches. So, if you lived in *"los arcos,"* you had the best address in town. Their homes faced the central park of the public square, a delicately landscaped area with well-trimmed bushes, lush green trees, and flowers. The public square also served as the civic center, since the local government seat and the church were located there as well. Landowners had convenient access, therefore, and other services were available to them in the nearby commercial establishments.

Some Mestizos and "uppity" Native Mexicans also lived in the towns and cities, but in areas removed from the center of town. In times past, there were towns and cities that actually prohibited residence for the indigenous. Jose Vasconcelos writes in his book *Ulises Criollo* that in the 1890s, Durango prohibited *"los indios"* from remaining in town once sunset merged into darkness.[2] Vasconcelos uses the term *"indio"* to refer to Native Mexicans. He does not bother to identify the Mestizos. It may be faithfully assumed that in his writings all non-Criollos (i.e., all non-Spaniards) were *"indios."* Vasconcelos was a lawyer and an ideologue of the Positivism of Auguste Comte. With his Spanish parents, he had lived in very close proximity to the *"indios."* His father had been a government bureaucrat assigned to different parts of Mexico. He got to know these *"indios,"* whom he never identified by their ethnicity: Yaquis in Hermosillo; Coahuilas on the Texas border; Otomi, Nahuas, and Mazanahuas in Toluca. In his first job as a lawyer, he was named attorney general for state of Durango. There he engaged in close contact with the Zacatecos, Tepehuenes, and Tarahumaras. Why was Vasconcelos not able to write about the Native Mexicans and Mestizos and identify them by their ethnicity? An inbred sense of superiority because of his Criollo heritage? I guess that is why I write from the perspective of a Mestizo!

Outside of town were the haciendas and smaller ranchos. Mestizos and Native Mexicans who lived there had huts for their housing. They lived under the complete control and supervision of the landowners. They were landless peasants living under a system of feudalism.

To give a specific example, in Salamanca, Guanajuato, the hometown of my parents, the original

---

[2] Jose Vasconcelos, *Ulises Criollo* (Mexico, D.F.: Editorial Universidad de Costa Rica, 2000), p. 251.

inhabitants were the Otomi. A relative of one of the *Conquistadores* established the village of Salamanca in 1605 over an Otomi pueblo called Xidoo. For years, the Otomi had their own church, cemetery, and housing just outside of the city in an area called Nativitas. (Today Nativitas is encompassed inside the city because of Salamanca's great growth.) On one visit, I spent half a day getting the "feel" for this church, the burial area, gardens, and neighborhood while imaging what life must have been like for my indigenous Otomi ancestors back into the many centuries.

According to the census of 1900, the number of inhabitants in Salamanca at that time was 13,583. This census also listed the names of 117 ranchos surrounding Salamanca and twenty-two haciendas. Of the ranchos, fifty-three of them housed about 100 inhabitants; twenty-five ranchos had fewer than fifty; and three had large populations of 700. Of course, the bigger haciendas offered a better quality of life than the ranchos. In the haciendas, population varied from a low of eleven to a high of 606. In total, the population of greater Salamanca (the city, the ranchos, and the haciendas) in 1900 was about 40,000 inhabitants.

Transportation

Taking Salamanca again as an example, it should help to comprehend the difficulties of everyday life by knowing that the average distance between the center of Salamanca and the haciendas surrounding it was two leagues (five miles). A second circle was developed later five miles beyond the first ring, and yet another and last circle was establishsed five miles beyond that one.

How did people travel those long distances between the town and the haciendas? If you were a Criollo, you went by horse or by horse-drawn buggies, carts, or carriages. If you were a Mestizo or Native Mexican, you would get to where you were going by walking or perhaps by means of a burro. For longer distances, you could travel by coach or train, if you could afford it. As we shall see later in this book, if you couldn't afford it but really wanted to travel by train to El Paso, Texas, for example, you would jump into an empty boxcar.

Education

What were the educational opportunities for those whose daily life was in the ranchos and haciendas with such distances separating them from each other and from the town? Not much. Of course, for city dwellers, the Spaniards (Criollos) and a few Mestizos, education was available—at a price. Thus, acquisition of education was a function of wealth. Offspring of landowners could acquire education in local private schools, in Mexico City, and for a few, in Europe. Is it any wonder that illiteracy for the indigenous and rural Mestizos was the norm?

Religion

It is well known that the Aztecs worshipped with human sacrifice. (They were not alone in this practice—Roman writers revealed that the European Druid religion also practiced human sacrifice.) What is not commonly known is that the Aztec religion was based on monism. That is, it had one supreme god (Teotl), who had many aspects, names, and characteristics. In this respect, the Aztecs were unlike the Greeks, for example, who invented their gods in the image of men and women who loved, played, warred, etc.

However, the appearance of Our Lady of Guadalupe in 1531 had a profound effect on the practice of religion in Mexico. As previously noted, about 10 million indigenous became Catholics as word of Juan Diego's encounter spread in the decade that followed. Why did so many Native Mexicans from so many groups (not just Aztec, but also Otomi, Nahuas, Mayas, Purepechas, etc.) become Christians? Why did they abandon their religion that had been so embedded in their way of life? Why did the Aztecs suddenly stop the practice of ripping out the hearts of sacrificial victims in adoration of their god?

In *Nican Mopohua*, Antonio Valeriano, an Aztec professor, wrote the narrative of the dialogues between the Virgin Mary and Juan Diego in his Mexican language, Nahuatl, in the 1550s. (In Nahuatl, *nican* means "here"; *mopohua* means "it is narrated.") Valeriano did not write in Nahuatl pictures as the Nahuatl language was written at that time, however. Instead, he used Roman letters. The first Nahuatl words in the *Nican Mopohua* read as follows: "*Nican mopohua, moteepana, in quenin yancuican hueytlama huizoltiea monexiti....*" Translated into English, the Nahuatl words mean: "Here it is narrated, it is listed, how very recently, appeared miraculously...."

Antonio Valeriano interviewed all persons who were directly involved with the apparitions: Juan Diego, his uncle, the bishop, the staff of the bishop, etc. He wrote a complete narrative of the events of December 1531 twenty years after they occurred. That narrative was copied in a few manuscripts and hardly circulated at all. Most probably that lack of circulation was providential, because it prevented the narrative from coming into the hands of the zealous Inquisition. One may well assume that the Inquisitors would have defined it as a heretical Indian cult. Besides, who in *Nueva Espana* at that time of the 1550s could read Nahuatl written in the Latin alphabet?

However, this absolutely extraordinary narrative of conversations with Juan Diego conducted by Mary, Ever Virgin, Our Lady of Guadalupe, the Mother of God, gradually became more widely known. The timeline unfolded like this:

1531: The events of the apparitions.

1551: Antonio Valeriano writes a few manuscripts of his *Nican Mopohua* in the Latin alphabet.

1649: Five hundred copies of *Nican Mopohua* of Antonio Valeriano are published, although no credit of authorship is given by the publisher except himself as author!

1886: About 350 years after the apparitions, *Nican Mopohua* is translated into Latin. My parents were born around this time.

1926: *Nican Mopohua* is translated from Latin to Spanish, although only ten percent of Mexicans could read Spanish. Ninety percent of Mestizos and indigenous groups were still illiterate.

1998: Close to 500 years after the apparitions, *Nican Mopohua* is printed in English! The Church in the United States begins to learn about Our Lady of Guadalupe.

The deep significance of this chronology is that the written word was not available to the Mexican illiterates, the Mestizos and the Native Mexicans. Nonetheless, devotion to, veneration of, and knowledge of Guadalupe became universal in Mexico almost immediately. An analysis of why millions converted to Christianity and abandoned their religion in a very few years yields an answer that is both simple and extraordinary: their language; their pictorial language! Here, they were highly literate. They had no need for *letters* written in any language, Latin or Spanish. They could look at the image left on Juan Diego's *tilma* and "read" all they needed to know. And how could the people hand down knowledge of the event century after century? The answer, my friends, is to be found again in their language-*pictures*.

The Spaniards, on the other hand, were illiterate when it came to words and ideas written in Nahuatl (even in letters, to say nothing of pictures), and for that matter, most of them were also illiterate in Latin. As the timeline shows, it wasn't until 1926 that they were finally able to manage the story of the event in Spanish, almost 400 hundred years after the apparitions.

The people of El Bajio, hundreds of miles away from El Tepeyac, knew the story. These forefathers of ours celebrated the apparitions throughout *Nueva Espana*. But the Criollo bishops and priests insisted on venerating Our Blessed Mary by other names. In Guadalajara, she was and still is "La Virgen de Zapopan."

3. CHANGE COMES AGAIN TO MEXICO

The previous chapters discussed three major changes that came to Megico (as the land was called before the arrival of Cortes): (1) European conquest; (2) creation of a new ethnic group, the Mestizos; and (3) the apparitions of Our Lady of Guadalupe and subsequent mass conversion to Christianity. Megico became known as *Nueva Espana*, a vast territory governed by Spain for 300 years. But name and borders changed again in the nineteenth century: Upon gaining independence from Spain in 1821, Mexico became a new nation. Swiftly so did Guatemala, Nicaragua, El Salvador, Honduras, and Costa Rica. Half of the remaining land of Mexico was swallowed up in a war with the United States under President Jimmie Polk.

More changes were yet to come, however, and these were in disastrous directions that would drown Mexico in misery. The roots of these changes were to be found across the Atlantic. In Europe, teapots of philosophies, ideas, and concepts were boiling. Today we can look back in history and shudder at the utter bankruptcy of those "modern yet pagan" ideas that have resulted in the deaths of so many millions of people around the world. Intellectuals have tried to describe the new age with a few words, such as "Militant Secularism." A less sophisticated person might express the age as that of "erasing Christianity."

The ideas invented in Europe were carried over the ocean waters and landed in educated circles in Mexico. The literate Criollo and Jewish intellectuals who absorbed them, primarily of the Mexican states of Sonora, Chihuahua, Coahuila, Tamaulipas, and Nuevo Leon, in turn began to boil with these European ideas. The educated class in Mexico City and Guadalajara were not far behind. These philosophies infected only ten percent of the Mexican population (the literate ten percent), but that was all that mattered. The Criollos held the power to impose their will on the nation and thus, on the remaining ninety percent of the population. Many of these Criollos and Hebrews were offspring of the hacienda class and had obtained higher education in France, Spain, and Italy. In those countries, so "advanced and civilized," they acquired ideas, concepts, and modern philosophies and returned to their "backward" lands deeply motivated with strong urgings to remake Mexico into a modern nation.

What were these ideas that captivated the Mexican Criollos? Over the course of the nineteenth century, various European nations contributed their own strains of thought. England contributed Masonry (a member of the Masons must believe in god, any god, but a personal God does not exist; only powerful forces in a "god"); Germany contributed the militant and godless materialism of Marxism and Socialism; eventually Russia contributed Bolshevism. France contributed the Positivism of Comte as well as the Jacobin leaders of the French Revolution, the Age of Enlightenment, the Age of Reason, the Scientific Method, and faith in God as mythology. The illumined French intellectuals invented encyclopedias where they could contain all known knowledge and even renamed history: The "Medieval Ages" became the "Dark Ages." How brainy and cute.

The French Revolution, which burst open in 1789, tried mightily to destroy the Catholic Church by bloody killings of nuns, priests, and faithful laypeople. Its principles dug deep roots in Mexico. In 1857, a new constitution for Mexico, modeled after the French Constitution, was promulgated as part of *La Reforma* of the Liberal government in power at the time, of which the future president Benito Juarez was a prominent member. Just as the French version authored by the infamous Jacobins brought about much bloodshed in France, so also would the Constitution of 1857 cause a similar upheaval in Mexico. Just as the French Constitution had called for the eradication of Catholics and the Catholic Church, so also would Benito Juarez and his political companions urge the same social changes in Mexico within a few years.

Lerdo de Tejada, an associate of Juarez, drafted a set of laws with stringent anticlerical measures, known as *Las Leyes de Reforma* (or *Las Leyes de Lerdo*), which became part of the Constitution of 1857. Mexico was Christian; but the government bureaucracy was fiercely anticlerical. The government now possessed the wherewithal for eradicating the mythology enjoyed by the peasants (i.e., Christianity). The Criollos and Hebrews educated in Europe or by Mexico City's professors who were socially advanced in the new European ideas could now apply and realize their "visions" of a new world with the use of arms, imprisonment, and killings authorized by the State.

All of this was bad news for the daily life of people in El Bajio. For well over 300 years, they had lived the principles of Jesus Christ. Now, the "enlightened ones" knew better and were ready to force radical changes.

However, before these folks of the Age of Enlightenment, or Age of Reason, could do too much damage, Porfirio Diaz was elected president of Mexico in 1877, twenty years after the Constitution of 1857. The Constitution and *Las Leyes de Reforma* were left in place, but with no enforcement. The new president did not bother the Catholic Church. He was more focused on initiatives to modernize and advance Mexico economically as it struggled away from the ancient feudal way of life. Although his handpicked successor served the next term as president, Diaz was reelected in 1884 and remained in office until 1911 in the face of a revolution. Under him, the country enjoyed peace, prosperity, and order and saw the rise of a middle class. The people of El Bajio, too, lived peacefully in an orderly society with strong money, modern mines, construction of thousands of railroad miles, agricultural advances, a petroleum industry, good wages, and full employment.

Yet the anticlericals held on to their European revolutionary principles and continued to fan their red-hot blazes. They demanded enforcement of the Constitution and *Las Leyes de Reforma* and worked feverishly to eliminate the Catholic Church because, as they saw it, the Catholic Church was the prime obstacle to progress. In their mind, only the use of Reason and Science assured progress! The author Jose Vasconcelos signals that the professors and intellectuals continued proclaiming the philosophies of Positivism of Comte,

Socialism, Marxism, and Militant Secularism. Two brands of Freemasons, the York and the Scottish Rites, also flourished in the circles of those in government and power. But President Porfirio Diaz permitted all these ideas provided they did not oppose his presidency and initiatives for advancing Mexico's economic rise.

In his book *Ulises Criollo*, Jose Vasconcelos illustrates this with a recollection from his school days:

> The fiesta of the Coronation of the Virgin in 1895 in Toluca was barely three days past, when one morning we were issued out of the classrooms with shouts. Reunited in disarray in the patio of the school, we were grouped by classes, and then the orders were given to march and make a manifestation against the clergy. For that end we were provided with banners. The parade commenced with several hundred students. Once in the street, the rearguard was taken by a group of nattily attired men. At the entrance to the city, we were joined by the dregs of the plebians and then the speechmaking started. We would stop at every intersection. Atop a carriage some orator would gesticulate; we would respond in unison: Death...! Death...! We were the flock that the Masonic lodges would release as admonishment to the Catholic population that had dared to content themselves on the day of the coronation. Shouting is all that we did because that is all the Porfirio Police would permit. And so, we would arrive at the mall *[Alameda]* shouting: May the *Leyes de Reforma* live...death to the priests *[curas]!*.... So little importance was paid to these manifestations that my mother would not be alarmed at my involvement and no one discussed the matter on days following. Everyone knew that Don

Porfirio let the dogs bark, from time to time, so long as they did not bite.[3]

The last statement by Vasconcelos, "Don Porfirio let the dogs bark, from time to time, so long as they did not bite," casts light on Mexico of 1895. Enforcement of the Constitution and *Las Leyes de Reforma* by the administration of President Porfirio Diaz remained lax, but the atheistic ideas and principles of the "enlightened" Jacobins of the French Revolution were kept alive by educators and intellectuals. And just who were these intellectuals who could read French, German, Russian, and English as well as converse in those languages? By golly, it was not the poor, uneducated Mestizos or the landless Native Mexicans. No! It was the powerful, landed, educated, well-to-do, and well-traveled Criollos, who made up only ten percent of the population. They were the military officers and government functionaries on all levels. They were the rulers and decision-makers. They were visible. In contrast, the Mestizos and Native Mexicans belonged to an invisible society. They were nothings!

For Mestizos and Native Mexicans, elections meant nothing, either. From the time of its independence in 1821, Mexico had been ruled by a variety of generals and dictators in rapid succession. Succession from one dictator to another was determined easily by use of an obsequious military or simply by use of a pistol. Even after the Revolution of 1910, although elections were held, the humble populace of Mestizos and Native Mexicans did not even know what the term meant. They

---

[3] Jose Vasconcelos, *Ulises Criollo* (Mexico, D.F.: Editorial Universidad de Costa Rica, 2000), p. 80.

only knew that the words "politics," "general," "mayor," "governor," etc., signified corruption, power, and force. The presidential election of Vicente Fox Quesada in 2000 was the first-ever authentic election. How refreshing. And he is a practicing Catholic, not an atheist.

But returning to the scene nearly a century before Fox's election, the ideas that had been circulating among the intelligentsia since Benito Juarez's time had reached a critical moment. Mexico, known as a land of volcanos, was about to erupt in violence: *La Revolucion* ignited in 1910.

4. *LA REVOLUCION*, 1920 TO 1920

A northerner from the border state of Coahuila, Francisco Madero sparked the Revolution against Porfirio Diaz by stirring up opposition to yet another reelection of Diaz in 1910 and running against him. Madero, a Spaniard with Jewish ancestry, was one of the wealthiest *hacendados*, if not the wealthiest, at the time. His education—typical among the well-traveled sons of *hacendados*—stretched from Mount St. Mary's College in Emmitsburg, Maryland, to France, Austria, and of course, California. And so, with all that a well-educated rich person could enjoy, why did Madero want to be president of Mexico? Why did he start a revolution, the most horrid in the entire history of Mexico? What did he want to achieve—more money, fame, or power? But he had all of that.

In reality, Madero's proclamations did reveal some honorable motives coming from an ideal of social justice. He declared that Porfirio Diaz had been a dictator for an excessive duration and now was the time for Mexico to have honest and authentic presidential elections. One can reasonably assume that he, along with others of the educated and land-owning class of northern Mexico, looked across the Rio Grande with envy at the U.S. presidential campaigns and our consistent, peaceful transitions of power. On the other hand, one may also speculate: Did Madero and his cohorts not comprehend the simple fact that ninety percent of the population did not vote and did not know what voting was about?

Madero succeeded in his demand for free elections. One has to wonder how many *indios* and Mestizos voted or even knew about it, but, following the fraudulent election of 1910 and the subsequent ousting of Porfirio Diaz in May 1911, Madero was elected president of Mexico. Diaz peacefully relinquished power and boarded a steamer bound for Europe to live out the remainder of his life with modest means. But during the two-plus years of Madero's presidency, the European ideologues left academia and surged into the public square. The advocates for the principles of the bloody anti-Catholic French Revolution, the Socialists, and the Bolsheviks finally gained power to change the centuries-old daily life of Mexicans for strange, foreign, and godless rules and laws.

Some of Madero's well-known supporters and ideologues included the agnostic writer Jose Vasconcelos (author of *Ulises Criollo*) and the Marxist lawyer Luis Cabrera (publisher of a journal in which he wrote very favorably of Lenin and the Russian system). They were assigned to Washington, DC, and instructed to operate a lobbying activity. A glimpse into the ideas of Cabrera will show what a dedicated revolutionary considered important. He proclaimed: "The Americans in Mexico constitute a national menace; we must deport them and take all of their properties."[4] As a dedicated Marxist, he was referring to American capitalists.

The Madero team also included former senators Venustiano Carranza and Alvaro Obregon and former governor Plutarco Calles, all from northern Mexico (like Madero) and all future presidents. Many, many others supported Madero as well, and they were Freemasons, ex-senators, ex-governors, and *hacendados* from the northern border states of Sonora, Coahuila, Chihuahua, Nuevo Leon, and Tamaulipas. They knew the North American way of life quite well. They admired the American political system, values, and Protestant religion. Most of them and their collaborators had studied and lived in the United States and even owned homes there. (Obregon and Calles each possessed a principal home across the border in Nogales, Arizona.) These Northern Mexicans felt superior to Southern Mexicans. The Southerners were deeply Catholic Mestizo and Native Mexicans, whereas the Northerners were Criollos and Jewish settlers and as such, perceived the Southerners as inferior. (Indeed, they had felt so much apart from their southern countrymen that in 1862, the governors of the northern states had pledged to join the Confederacy in forming a new country.) Now with the presidential powers of Francisco Madero, these men commenced the enforcement of their ideologies as authorized by the Constitution of Juarez and *Las Leyes de Reforma* of Lerdo de Tejada that had been suspended during Porfirio Diaz's rule.

---

[4] Senate Committee on Foreign Relations, *Investigation of Mexican Affairs: Preliminary report and hearings of the Committee on Foreign Relations, United States Senate, pursuant to S. res. 106, directing the Committee on Foreign Relations to investigate the matter of outrages on citizens of the United States in Mexico,* 1920, p. 797.

One of their first strange actions was the importation of Protestant religions from across the border! The Northerners entertained the conviction that the wealth and modern advances in the United States were due totally to Protestantism and, conversely, that the "backwardness" of Mexico was due totally to the practice of the Catholic religion. Thousands of Protestant ministers were escorted militarily into Mexico with armed protection for converting the Catholics. These "missionaries and their bishops" completely supported, aided, and abetted the anti-Catholic revolutionaries and published reports in favor of the revolution in U.S. newspapers and journals. Further, they actually participated in high-level government positions.[5]

Meanwhile, the Mexican lobbyists in Washington were ably supported by other lawyers who specialized in representing international clients and enjoyed the ideologies of Socialism and Marxism. These lawyers worked for the law firm of Sherburne G. Hopkins. It served the purposes of the Mexican Revolution to engage these lawyers for Washington representation. Carranza also purchased the services of this very powerful, very well-connected law firm. The Mexican lawyer-lobbyists, Cabrera and Vasconcelos, worked out of their offices. It was a very cozy relationship.

In hearings held by the U.S. Senate Committee on Foreign Relations, the U.S. Senate compelled testimony from Sherburne G. Hopkins under subpoena during its investigation of the Mexican Revolution. He testified that he was the American attorney that represented the interests of the Revolution from its inception under Francisco Madero. Further, he admitted his law firm

---

[5] Ibid., p. 93.

worked with the Mexican lobbyists and advocated their interests at the White House and State Department. Together, they directed and advocated the policies of the Mexican revolutionaries in the circles of official Washington. Attorney Hopkins was deeply involved in orchestrating and running the affairs in Mexico and getting the United States to militate unilaterally against Porfirio Diaz and later, Victoriano Huerta.[6]

How could a law firm influence official Washington to support the Liberals in Mexico whose clearly defined objectives were to eliminate the Catholic Church and to impose punitively *Las Leyes de Reforma* and the Constitution of 1857? Know! That is the way Washington works. Law firms employ lawyers whose main qualification is that they are former senators, congressmen, presidential appointees, ambassadors, etc. They operate within the secrecy provided by the law of confidentiality conferred on lawyer-client relationships and wield immense influence.

As it happened, Francisco Madero's presidency in Mexico was short-lived. In face of a military revolt against him in February 1913, he tried to flee to Europe in the same manner as his predecessor, Porfirio Diaz, but he never arrived at the Mexico City train station alive. A military officer assigned to the job of delivering him to the train shot him dead instead. Most writers, especially in the United States, assume (without proof) that General Victoriano Huerta was responsible. Facts are absent; assumptions are universal. At any rate, since Huerta was in charge of the military under Porfirio Diaz and enjoyed their loyalty, he declared himself *presidente* of Mexico, as was the custom.

---

[6] Ibid., p. 2412.

And thus ended *La Revolucion* under Francisco Madero. Historians write that the Revolution continued until 1930 under a series of presidents (in reality, dictators) who followed Madero. But, how can a revolution be waged by *presidentes*? It would be a revolt against themselves. No, the tragedies of killings, theft, fighting, rape, pillages, and a Diaspora of two million Mexicans must be understood under other labels.

5. HUERTA, CARRANZA, AND WILSON, 1913 TO 1920

Victoriano Huerta, president of Mexico after Madero, tried to govern. He was anti-Revolutionary and very pro-Catholic. Indeed, he was the *last clear chance* for the continuation of the centuries-old daily life of Mexico and the peaceful and orderly life of the people in El Bajio. But Mexican Liberals knew their control would slip away again as it had during the presidency of Porfirio Diaz if President Victoriano Huerta were not eliminated. Thus, a loose coalition of Liberal groups, led by Madero's former supporter Venustiano Carranza with his Constitutionalist Army *("Constitucionales")*, waged war against President Huerta and his army, known as the *Federales*.

The government of Victoriano Huerta did not last long. And who helped the Liberals topple it? Surprise! The newly elected U.S. President Woodrow Wilson, a progressive who heeded the recommendations of the Mexican revolutionary lobbyists in Washington.

Not long after his March 1913 inauguration, Wilson sent a special agent, John Lind, to Mexico to intervene in Mexican affairs while possessing authority surpassing that of the ambassador. Born in Sweden and raised in Minnesota, Lind was a naturalized U.S. citizen who neither spoke Spanish nor knew anything about Mexico. He was there simply to do the bidding of the U.S. president.

As a sidebar, it is intriguing to list the U.S. men who directly caused changes in Mexico. They were all rabidly anti-Catholic Presbyterians and Democrats: President James Polk, President Woodrow Wilson, and John Lind. On one occasion when John Lind heard the charge d'affaire of the American Embassy, Nelson O'Shaughnessy, mention he had received a report about Catholic priests being killed in Mexico, John Lind remarked, "That report carries good news, and when they kill even more priests in Mexico, all the more will it delight and please President Wilson."[7]

In August 1913, President Woodrow Wilson gave this mission to John Lind: "Tell Huerta to resign from the Mexican presidency or be forced out by the American military. Install Carranza as president." John Lind relayed the message faithfully to the Mexican Secretary of State, Mr. Gamboa: "Tell Huerta to resign the presidency, and if he does not, we will use military force."[8]

At the same time, Venustiano Carranza was seeking help against Huerta from another American source. Carranza's people made an agreement with the Communists of Baltimore, Maryland, who were organized under the name International Workers of the World

---

[7] Ibid., p. 2709.

[8] Ibid., p. 2708.

(IWW). In December 1913, Carranza's cohorts signed a contract with La Casa del Obrero Mundial, as the IWW was known in Mexico, in the port city of Veracruz. The Mexican signers of the pact were: General Alvaro Obregon, Ingeniero M. Rolland, General Salvador Alvarado, Gustavo Espinoza Mireles, General Maclovio Herrera, Rafael Nieto, Ingeniero Alberto Pani, General Gabriel Gavira, Jesus Urueta, Dr. Atl, Luis Cabrera, General Manuel M. Dieguez, and Rafael Quintero (who signed on behalf of Venustiano Carranza).[9] However, the terms of this agreement have remained secret. (In my observation, how clever are the workings of the Communists—lies and censorship!) It is known, however, that the persecution of the Catholic Church was part of the contract, as was the contribution of money and arms as well as the management of the war. Truth be told, American unions contributed to the persecution of Catholics and the Church.

One of the signatories, Dr. Atl, had made the arrangements for signing the pact with the IWW. He was a Communist from Guadalajara, Jalisco, and close friend of two famous Mexican painters, Diego Rivera and David Siqueiros, who were also his Communist buddies. In U.S. Senate hearings on the Mexican Revolution held in 1920, Wallace Thompson, editor of a newspaper called the *Mexico Herald*, was asked, "Do you know of an individual who goes by the name Dr. Atl?" Thompson replied affirmatively, adding, "His real name is Gerardo Murillo. I knew him personally in Paris in 1913, [when] he was passing himself off as an 'artist,' but he was in reality working as the head of the Constitutional Junta, *La Junta Constitucional*, which was the name Carranza called his

---

[9] Ibid., p. 1909.

rebel army. He was a prominent Carrancista and a Bolshevist. He proclaimed himself to be a Lenin-Trotsky revolutionary. The United States had deported him together with a Russian Communist, Emma Goldman."

Meanwhile, when President Huerta refused to obey the commands of Woodrow Wilson and would not resign his presidency, Wilson ordered the American Navy to invade Mexico at Veracruz in April 1914. This enabled Carranza to march to Veracruz under the military protection of the United States and declare himself dictator! At this point, President Huerta had little choice but to flee Mexico City and abandon the Mexican presidency. He had been so disobedient to the American president! He went into exile until arrested by U.S. agents in 1915. Shortly afterward, he died from lack of medical attention while imprisoned at Fort Bliss, El Paso, Texas. Thus, Woodrow Wilson got his way. He rid Mexico of the last clear chance for a Catholic president.

Since the U.S. president decided to intervene directly in the chaotic affairs of Mexico, whom did he select to follow Francisco Madero and Victoriano Huerta? He chose none other than Venustiano Carranza, the former senator and governor of the state of Coahuila well known for his corrupt political trajectory, the rebel leader who had worked with the Communists. Venustiano Carranza became a vicious egomaniac dictator. He gave the revolution a new purpose. His Constitutionalist army would reinstate *La Constitucion* and *Las Leyes de Reforma* with forceful vigor against the Catholic Church.

Carranza had the lawyers Jose Vasconcelos and Luis Cabrera, along with Rafael Zubaran, continue as his lobbyists in Washington, DC, under the new name, *"La Junta Mexicana Revolucionaria."* As Criollos (i.e., European Mexicans), the lobbyists felt comfortable with their ethnic cousins in Washington, the *americanos*, for they, too, were Europeans. Their countenances did not have any signs of being Mestizos or "Indians." Rather, as they worked in Washington, they might just as well be considered "*americanos*," except for their accents. Not only did they "fit in" ethnically, but likewise philosophically: President Wilson, along with his State Department presidential appointees, shared the same ideologies of these lobbyists from Mexico, including their bias toward Northern Mexicans and against Catholics.

For example, when John Lind was later subpoenaed by the U.S. Senate Committee on Foreign Relations in its investigation of the Mexican Revolution, he was asked what he knew about Mexico. Lind responded, "I think the Revolution was essential to eliminate the conditions of poverty, lack of education, and economic and social advances. The Mexican Northerners are more intelligent, more advanced, more like us; they have better schools and are better educated than the Southern Mexicans."[10]

Lind's anti-Catholicism is well documented, too. At a Pan American Conference, when Lind heard that the United States was not going to recognize Carranza as the new president of Mexico, he was noted by many witnesses to exclaim, "Oh my God! Poor Mexico, it will retrogress into the clutches of the Catholic Church."[11] Lind attributed all of Mexico's ills to the influence of the Catholic Church. He detested the Catholic Church intensely and contended it must be destroyed.

Thus, John Lind and President Woodrow Wilson determined the future of Mexico as we know it today, a secular and very corrupt government where the dominant

---

[10] Ibid., p. 2317.

[11] Ibid., p. 2361.

political party, the Institutional Revolutionary Party (*Partido Revolucionario Institucional*, or PRI) was spawned by the Liberals of the early 1900s. PRI is still in power nationally and in most Mexican states by means of voting irregularities. The roles of the Communists, the IWW, Woodrow Wilson, John Lind, the Masons, Socialists, and Positivists and the actions of the dictators Carranza, Obregon, and Calles have become conveniently unknown. The Mexican government controlled by the PRI has censored everything exposing that history. In the event that became known simply as *"La Revolucion,"* the *Federales* of President Huerta were the "bad guys" and the *Constitucionales*, Pancho Villa, and Emiliano Zapata were the "good guys," or at least the good rebels. A very famous book, *Los de Abajo*, written in 1914 by Mariano Azuelas, a medical doctor in Pancho Villa's army, depicts revolutionary war under the command of Pancho Villa against the *Federales*. Many movies have drawn their inspiration from this book, which depicts the simple ignorant peasant soldiers and the Revolution waged by Pancho Villa and the "good guys" against the bad, corrupt government.

Yet even the peasant children in the schools of Mexico knew that Carranza's "revolution" was a revolution sponsored by the United States and that the U.S. government had installed Carranza and empowered him to be dictator. What happened to Carranza in the end? He, too, tried to flee to Europe, but was killed on the way. It is well known that his successor, General Alvaro Obregon, ordered him "terminated" in 1920. Obregon held the presidency until 1924, followed by Plutarco Calles, who ruled until 1928. Under Calles especially, the anticlerical laws were strongly enforced, and a new wave of violence was unleashed.

During his presidency, Carranza had added Marxism and Socialism to the political caldron. This mix of old and new philosophies in the hands of the powerful fueled a war against the people of faith. It transformed the lives of the good and decent people of El Bajio! The people of El Bajio knew the truth. The Liberal adherents of the Constitution of Benito Juarez and *Las Leyes de Reforma* of Lerdo de Tejada waged war on them and against the Catholic Church. As one small, yet important example, to be in accord with *Las Leyes de Reforma*, the revolutionaries ordered that marriages now had to be conducted by a government agent and recorded in the Civil Register. Likewise, all births had to be recorded in the Civil Register. No big deal? But it was, because in doing so, the government was discouraging the sacraments of marriage and baptism, weakening the place of the Catholic Church in the daily lives of the people. It was another step toward annihilating the Church. To repeat: This was not a revolution; it was a war. And El Bajio was in the middle of the war zone.

The peasants of El Bajio, mostly Mestizos, who held their Catholic faith very deeply, faced stark choices in those tumultuous years of Mexican history: basically, fight or flight. Some could tolerate the attacks no longer and armed themselves as guerrilla fighters, becoming known as *"Cristeros"* and the war they were fighting, *"La Cristiada."* They knew the terrain of the valleys, hills, and mountains. They did not accept the assistance of city dwellers because they could not fight, survive, and live off the land. They did not ask hacienda owners for help; they knew the land owners would be more loyal to their possessions. Although the government would ensure that history would blame *them* for the murder, looting, and destruction of the period, they simply took matters into their own hands in reaction to the persecution instigated by the government against them, and many paid the price with their own blood.

Many other people from El Bajio chose flight, especially young Catholic families. They escaped to the north, crossing the border into the United States in desperate search of safety and religious freedom—the Mexican Diaspora. My parents were among them.

6. PERSONAL IMPACT OF THE DIASPORA

A historian, Jose Rojas Garciduenas, of the city of my parents, lamented in his book, *Salamanca: Recuerdos de mi tierra guanajuatense*: "As that period ended, in the decade of the 1930s, Salamanca become impoverished, languishing, terrified, and bitter, because of what it had suffered in those violent years of the Revolution, from 1913 to 1918 inclusive and then after a brief oasis of relative tranquility, again the violence, the blood, and the fear, from 1926 to 1929, because of the religious persecution and its consequences, the struggle that was named the *Cristeros*."[12]

The preceding chapters have traced the authentic history of the "Glorious Mexican Revolution" that led to the suffering of the *Cristeros* and the Diaspora families. The ideas that influenced the Revolution and the major personalities that acted in it have been named. Now I will

---

[12] Jose Rojas Garciduenas, *Salamanca: Recuerdos de mi tierra guanajuatense* (Mexico: Editorial Porrua, S.A., 1982), pp. 12–13.

bring the story to a personal level and write about how the Diaspora impacted me.

I was born in California of parents who came from Salamanca, Guanajuato, during the Diaspora, and I married Ester Gomez de Bernal, whose parents came from Ciudad Guzman, Jalisco. I was raised and educated in Pomona, California, along with hundreds of other families of the 1913–1930 Diaspora from El Bajio. I can recall their names: Cabrera, Blancarte, Trejo, Salado, Gonzales, Hernandez, Quintana, Banuelos, Marroquin, Lopez, Martinez, Calderon, Ortiz, Zuniga, etc. I can well imagine that other families hold similar remembrances.

Over the years, I questioned my parents, uncles, and other relatives, "Why? Why did you leave El Bajio?" Never did I get a knowledgeable reply. The best they could verbalize was, "*La Revolucion.*"

It was hard for me, a curious kid, to get answers to simple questions. With the passage of years in Pomona, I learned that my parents, four of my elder siblings, my grandmother, my uncles, and my aunt were all born in Mexico. I would ask questions repeatedly, trying to find out what it was like in Mexico. But I learned little about their daily lives over there (*alla en Mexico*). My dad, however, did tell me how they left Salamanca on the train for Juarez. The reasons, as far as I could tell at the time, dealt with religion and politics.

When I was ten years old, we moved one block away from Sacred Heart Church in Pomona. There I met hundreds more Mexicans and their Mexican-American children. I asked them a lot of questions, too. Their memories were sketchy, but I got a little more information. Several of them recalled stories of "*la batalla de Zacatecas,*" the bloodiest battle of the Revolution, a brutal clash between the forces of Pancho Villa and

President Victoriano Huerta in 1914. About Pancho Villa, they had spotty stories. But as to why and how they left Mexico, *"el porque,"* they did not know. For that they had no answers. Their conversations sometimes revealed the names of the states in Mexico from where they came. Rarely did they know the name of their village or hacienda, although often they recalled the name of the rancho. They simply knew they came from Mexico and that *"La Revolucion"* was the reason for their exodus.

Much later, I gained a wider view of Mexicans in this country. When the Civil Rights Commission recruited me out of my job at Whittier High School and appointed me Chief of the Mexican American Studies Division in 1967, I knew Mexicans were scattered primarily in the Southwest and some in the Midwest. I did not know how many there were, but I needed to find out in order to do good research. From the Census Bureau, I learned that the 1930 census counted Mexicans born in Mexico for the first time and accounted for about two million, thus finally revealing the size of the Diaspora. Travel and field work educated me further on the daily life of Mexicans exiled from El Bajio, which had changed dramatically for them; very importantly, I also learned about the daily life of their offspring, now Mexican-Americans, and the challenges they faced. In general, the emigres of the Diaspora living in the Midwest found religious liberty and abundant work in the steel mills and the factories dependent on steel. The emigres of the Diaspora who found their religious liberty and work in Texas labored in the cotton fields. And the emigres of the Diaspora who acquired their religious liberty and work in California picked fruit and vegetables.

My family was of the latter group. Here I present them in Figure 1, refugees of the Mexican Diaspora.

Figure 1. My family, c. 1929: Martin; Lupe (born in Salamanca); Manuel, Jesus (born in Salamanca); *mi mama*, Romana (pregnant with me, Enrique); Teresa, held in my mother's arms; *mi papa*, Pascual; Dolores; and Jose (born in Salamanca). (*Personal collection of Henry M. Ramirez*)

The photograph shown in Figure 1 depicts my family in Pomona, California, in early 1929. My parents left Salamanca, Guanajuato, in 1922 to start life anew in the United States. Since my parents had received a good education in Catholic schools in Salamanca, they could communicate via letters and telegrams with their kin back home. So, in 1926, my dad was able to arrange for the departure of his mother, siblings, and their several offspring from Mexico. Figure 2 shows my grandmother and some of my father's family who joined us and found their new home in Pomona, California, with us.

Figure 2. My grandmother, Nazaria Guerero de Ramirez, with my uncle Elias; my cousin Luis Jr.; my uncle Rosendo; and my uncle Alfonso. (*Personal collection of Henry M. Ramirez*)

Around the same time, my wife's family left their home in Jalisco, Mexico, and settled in Claremont, California, a town just a few miles away from Pomona. Figure 3 shows her father and two oldest brothers, who had both been born in Jalisco. Figure 4 shows my wife's mother, Dona Jesusita Bernal de Gomez, together with Rigoberto and Ramiro again, as well as their sister Esperanza, also born in Jalisco. The rest of Don Marcelino and Dona Jesusita's children—Raul, Ester (my wife), Ramon, Ruben, and Ricardo—were all born in Claremont.

Figure 3. My wife's father, Don Marcelino, with two of his sons, Rigoberto and Ramiro. (*Personal collection of Henry M. Ramirez*)

Figure 4. My wife's mother, Dona Jesusita Bernal de Gomez, with three of her children, Rigoberto, Ramiro, and Esperanza. (*Personal collection of Henry M. Ramirez*)

As the numerous children of the Diaspora families grew, many of them served their new country in uniform during World War II and in Korea and Vietnam. No information exists that can pinpoint the exact number of veterans (since Mexican-Americans were not specifically counted in the census until 1970), but it appears common for five sons from Diaspora families to be drafted, and most of them served in the infantry. In my family, five of us served; in my wife's family, five men also served. Rigoberto, the eldest brother of my wife, served in India as a radio technician. The next brother, Ramiro, a college graduate, tried to enlist in the Army Air Corps, but when it became known he was born in Mexico and was not a U.S. citizen, officials denied his entry into the Air Force. He had no choice but to return to his country of birth. The next four sons, all born in the United States, served.

It was from this context that my life's trajectory emerged. A son of the Diaspora, growing up in California picking fruit, surrounded by family who worked hard and served honorably, nourished by the faith they handed on—these characteristics formed me and prepared me for my life's work, first in education and then in government service. I was blessed in that work to be able to make a difference in the lives of other Mexican-Americans, from assisting struggling students, for example, to identifying civil rights issues. Eventually—and significantly—my life would intersect with someone else's, a person who also grew up in California, only about 20 miles or so from where my family settled. That person was Richard M. Nixon, who would become the thirty-seventh president of our country. In his youth spent in Whittier, California, where his family ran a grocery store, Nixon encountered many Diaspora families. And that fact, too, turned out to be so significant that, at the point where my life intersected with his, great strides were able to be accomplished for Mexican-Americans and other Spanish-speaking Americans thanks to his initiatives.

7. NIXON AND THE MEXICANS

How was it that several hundred Diaspora families working at the Murphy Ranch and Leffingwell Ranch near the town of Whittier, California, changed the lives of other Diaspora families and their descendants—indeed, not only Mexican-Americans but all Spanish-speaking Americans throughout the entire country? It was because they were the families that a young Richard Nixon (class of 1929) got to know while working at his family's grocery store. The impression they left on that young man carried through his lifetime and had far-reaching effects.

The Murphy Ranch workers shown in Figure 5 are among the Mexicans that Richard Nixon came to know. According to Al Lemus, son of Remedios Lemus (one of the workers in the photograph), his family had fled from a hacienda in Penjamo, Guanajuato, Mexico. At least four other men in the photograph had fled from the same hacienda located in the heart of El Bajio: Evaristo Diaz, Jesus Ponce, Cesar Diaz, and Felix Duenas. They were all part of the 1913–1930 Diaspora escaping persecution and violence from the so-called revolution, which we now know as a war against the Catholic Church. They lived in company-provided housing and got groceries at the store run by the Nixon family.

Figure 5. A group photo of workers at Murphy Ranch, September 1941. Remedios Lemus is in the top row, third from the right. *(Photo courtesy of Al Lemus)*

The Nixons and the Mexican families of Murphy Ranch and nearby Leffingwell Ranch lived in two societies. One was Protestant; the other Catholic. One was European with light skin; the other Mexican Mestizo, of darker skin. One spoke English and was literate; the other spoke Spanish and was illiterate. The schools in California were segregated at this time. And in this social milieu, the Nixons and the Mexican Mestizos developed and nourished a strong and lasting mutual respect. (We Mexican-Americans also consider it highly significant that Richard M. Nixon celebrated his honeymoon with a drive to Acapulco, Mexico, in 1940!)

Ed Nixon, the President's youngest brother, has related corroborating stories of the interaction of the Mexicans and the Nixon family-owned business. "They would buy 100-pound bags of pinto beans, potatoes, and flour," Ed Nixon has recalled.[13] A Whittier High School teacher offered another perspective with this remembrance: "My grandmother, who lived at Murphy Ranch, would comment on how nice a person Richard Nixon was; he would give us credit readily."[14]

When I was a teacher at Whittier High School, I learned from various sources that due to deep poverty, Richard Nixon worked in the groves and fields along with the Mexicans. I had done the same type of work, and I knew that very, very few Anglos except the poorest did that. Much later in my career, when I had just been appointed chairman of the Cabinet Committee on Opportunities for Spanish-Speaking People, I marveled as President Nixon recalled how he had worked picking oranges. Later, he even joked with me about how many boxes of oranges we had each picked per day. It was that day, as I met with the President in the Oval Office for nearly an hour, that Nixon affirmed his connection to Mexicans, discussed his knowledge of them, and instructed me on what he wanted me to do for them. He showed he deeply cared for the people he had known and worked with at Murphy and Leffingwell Ranches.

I listened as President Nixon reminisced about what he had learned from these men and their families. He observed, "They are hard-working, honest, law-abiding family men and deeply Catholic." The President elaborated on all of these judgments and by extension applied them to the Mexican community. He stated in careful words, yet with a strong tone, that he tired of his administration being concerned only for Blacks. He was aware that no one in Washington, DC—or over the entire

---

[13] Ed Nixon, telephone interview with the author, June 1, 2016.

[14] Interview with the author, July 2016.

Atlantic seaboard, for that matter—knew Mexicans. So, he reiterated over and over, "You and I are going to change that." He said we were going to "knock down that invisible wall of discrimination we gringos have built in the Southwest against you Mexicans!"

Let it be known. Richard M. Nixon learned about simple, unlettered Mexicans who lived the Commandments and practiced the Beatitudes. He admired them and realized that they faced societal blocks to participating in the American Dream. When he became president, he did not forget those noble Mexicans of the Diaspora. On his own initiative and without advocacy from screaming people, he determined what had to be done! What a blessing. *No other president before or after his time in office has done the same.*

Part II of this book goes into detail about what President Nixon ordered be done and how I came to be in a position to have a great role in doing it. This is the story of what he realized so that we, the Mexican-American children of the Mexicans of the Diaspora of 1913–1930, could participate in the American Dream. No sooner had he given this order than he also included other Spanish-speaking people, the recently arrived Cubans and Puerto Ricans. In summary, President Nixon accomplished the following:

- He decided to employ me to be in charge of all matters dealing with Mexican-American affairs;

- In the Oval Office, he swore me in as chairman of his Cabinet Committee on Opportunities for Spanish-Speaking People; he also discussed with me his knowledge of and admiration for Mexican-

Americans and what he wanted to accomplish for them;

- He conducted a meeting of the Cabinet Committee on Opportunities for Spanish-Speaking People and directed his Cabinet officers on what he expected from them to accomplish his defined objectives for the Mexican-Americans;

- He ordered the Census Bureau and other government agencies to count Mexican-Americans;

- He ordered conferences in all regional offices serving the Spanish-speaking people;

- He ordered equal employment opportunities for Mexican-Americans;

- He ordered high-level appointments of Spanish-speaking people;

- He ordered business opportunities from government procurement;

- He invited a Spanish-speaking Catholic archbishop to celebrate a Sunday service in the White House;

- He approved advocacy with the Vatican for ordination of Spanish-speaking bishops;

- He ordered paperwork for his signature to grant amnesty to Diaspora Mexicans; and

- He proclaimed National Hispanic Heritage Week.

PART II

1. NIXON SELECTS A CHICANO

Soon after Richard M. Nixon was inaugurated President of the United States, he took action in February 1969 to include the Mexican-Americans of the Diaspora in the American Dream.

His first action was to appoint a Los Angeles lawyer, Martin Castillo, to be in charge of the Inter-Agency Committee on Mexican-American Affairs and deputy director of the U.S. Commission on Civil Rights. At that time, I was employed at the Commission as chief of Mexican American Studies. Since I had a large office and was involved with Mexican-American matters, Martin Castillo decided to move in and share my office. This action gave me a front-row seat on the Mexican-American initiatives of the new administration.

Whereas President Lyndon Johnson tried to assist the needs of Mexican-Americans with a committee he created by means of a presidential memorandum,[15] President

---

[15] The White House memo to establish the Inter-Agency on

Nixon did a lot more with a law passed by Congress. It was one of the most significant actions he accomplished.

After serving honorably for almost two years, Martin Castillo returned to his law practice, and it came time to appoint a new chairman to lead the Cabinet Committee on Opportunities for Spanish-Speaking People (CCOSSP), as the Inter-Agency Committee on Mexican-American Affairs became known after President Nixon signed Senate Bill 740 in December 1969. President Nixon personally selected me to do the job. Here's how events leading up to my selection unfolded.

The first figure in the chronology is Roy O. Day, publisher of a local California newspaper, the *Pomona Progress Bulletin*. He and I go way back to the days when my family lived on Gordon Street next to downtown Pomona. As a little adventurer in the 1930s, I came to know the merchants on Second Street, including Mr. Day. I didn't know until much later that Mr. Day maintained an interest in my career from the poor little Mexican boy who attended Catholic schools to the seminarian in Los Angeles and Camarillo, California, then soldier in the Army during the Korean War, teacher with the Whittier High School District in Whittier, California, and then government official at the U.S. Commission on Civil Rights in Washington, DC. He knew a lot about me. It helped that I had been getting newspaper ink since my teaching days at Whittier High School and even from national newspapers when I went to Washington, DC.

Soon after President Nixon appointed me, Mr. Day invited me to have lunch on my first visit to Los Angeles. We met in September 1971 at the Hyatt Hotel, where he happily shared the following account with me:

Mexican-American Affairs is dated June 9, 1967.

"You know," he started, "Nixon and I go way back to the Pomona of the '40s after the war. I was in charge of his first campaign for Congress. We have kept in close touch over the years because we had a poker-playing group with Harris, the Whittier car dealer, the Whittier Bank of America manager, and one more. Last year, when a vacancy occurred at the agency where you are now, Nixon spoke to us at a poker game in a troubled manner. He wanted and needed a Mexican-American to fill that vacancy. 'That person,' he said, 'has to possess sterling qualities. He has to know Spanish, be a conservative, have a good philosophy, look "Mexican," etc.' I blurted out and stated in no uncertain terms, 'The man you want is here in Washington. He works but a few blocks away from the White House at the U.S. Commission on Civil Rights. He holds a high-level, responsible position there. Get him!'" With a deep sense of accomplishment, Mr. Day added to me, "So you see, I recommended you!"

Indeed, he had. Years later, I received a blind copy of a letter dated May 25, 1973, written by Mr. Day addressed to "Dear Friend and President Richard Nixon." Among other items, Mr. Day wrote, "You will recall I recommended this man very highly to you prior to his receiving his present appointment."[16]

There is no way to know whether what happened next was caused by Mr. Day's poker game recommendation. My research, however, points to causality initiated by the President. In the Nixon Presidential Materials Archives, I found a significant report that attests to the discovery process preceding my selection by the President. It appears that he had asked his former law partner, Tom Bewley (a practicing attorney in Whittier, California), to

---

[16] Roy O. Day to President Nixon, May 25, 1973.

check me out. The report of this action is contained in a memo sent to Robert Finch, counselor to the President, dated May 18, 1971.

The memo cites names of public figures in Whittier and surrounding towns who knew me personally and states what reputation I held with them. Since I was able to obtain only one page of the memo, I do not know more specifics. Of course, it is interesting that Nixon himself wanted to know what the people he personally knew thought of me. Suffice to say that the part I read showed that his friends thought I was okey-dokey.[17]

Another event happened in mid-December of 1970: A Congressman invited me to lunch. This is a rarity. Ranking Congressmen do not just pick up the phone and personally call a mid-level bureaucrat—and not for lunch! But Congressman Chuck Wiggins from El Monte, California, called me personally! He gave the details and address of an exclusive restaurant up on Capitol Hill. I was surprised and elated. That call was momentous.

Years before, I had worked for Wiggins' election as a precinct worker in Whittier. I knew the Congressman, but only slightly. In no way did I comprehend why the man I helped get elected would call me for lunch! In years to come, I would get to know him a lot more. At this lunch, however, initial rapport was understandably awkward. It started with small talk and then quickly progressed to the topic of the vacancy at the CCOSSP. The Congressman wanted to know which candidates Nixon should consider for appointment to the chairmanship of the "Cabinet Committee," as he simply called it.

---

[17] George Grassmuck to Bob Finch, memorandum, May 18, 1971, "Henry M. Ramirez—Report from Tom Bewley in Whittier." National Archives, E.O. 12356 Section 1.1.

I suggested about ten names and outlined the pros and cons of each. He did not engage or respond; his disinterest in those names was patent. "You did not include yourself," he firmly stated. "Why not?"

He listened patiently to my rather lengthy explanation of my plan to return to my home state. I should add that I had also rejected the possibility of entering the heated maelstrom of partisan bickering. I had my profession in education, and that was where my future beckoned.

Lunch was over. We parted cordially with no suggestion of future follow-up. For my part, I gave no further thought to the implications of our discussion, nor did I search for other reasons for his call. I went on my merry way back to work on the education reports I was creating for the President and Congress. Today, I describe my mental exercises as those of a noninquisitive dummy. At that time any Washington neophyte would have asked himself: "What is going on here?"

Of course, I hadn't known about Roy Day's recommendation and Tom Bewley's investigations in December 1970. I considered the lunch with Congressman Wiggins an effort on his part motivated purely by his desire to contribute what was best for the Mexican-American community. Quite truthfully, I perceived absolutely no White House involvement. The White House? No way! That thought never, but never entered into my brain. That ramification was way beyond my pay grade.

Then, a few weeks after the lunch, the cryptic hands of the White House emerged. My boss, the staff director of the U.S. Commission on Civil Rights, Bill Taylor, received a call from the White House. Presidential counselor Robert Finch wants to talk with Ramirez, I was told. I asked Bill why I was being summoned, but he did not know.

After receiving instructions about where to go, how to enter the grounds, what door to approach, etc., I visited the West Wing of the White House and was escorted to the office of the counselor. Every aspect and detail of this visit was novel and strange. I did not know why I was there. All I knew was that Robert Finch had summoned me to a meeting. His assistant, Dr. George Grassmuck, was the one who had called my boss, Bill Taylor.

As I approached the door to the West Wing, an alert Marine saluted smartly and briskly opened the door. I identified myself to the receptionist. She nodded, asked me to be seated, and announced my arrival. Dr. Grassmuck showed up, identified himself, and took me to the counselor's office. Finch's secretary, Carol, greeted me warmly, and Dr. Grassmuck then escorted me into the large and well-decorated office and remained. Robert Finch arose from his imposing desk and joined us. I was quite nervous but tried to remain composed.

This was big-time stuff! I was in the presence of a person who was frequently in the news. Robert Finch was the former lieutenant governor of California and had previously served as Secretary of the agency then known as the U.S. Department of Health, Education and Welfare (HEW). He spent no time on pleasantries or small talk. He spoke directly and calmly, in total control.

"Since you excel at the Commission doing national studies, we want you to do a study for us," he announced. "We want the study to dwell on what the Mexican-Americans think about this administration. What are their perceptions of this presidency? What do they feel about the Cabinet Committee? What qualifications should the new chairman for the Cabinet Committee have?"

"Mr. Counselor, that is a big job," I whispered. (I was taken aback, yet felt no suspicion that the summons to the White House was about anything other than the study he mentioned.) "Do you really mean what you are saying? You really want to know what they think about Republicans, about this White House and this president? You want to know what they want out of this government? Do you want it straight or watered down?"

"Yes, we want to know what is really going on out there in the Southwest," he answered. Elaborating further, he said, "People in this town, and for that matter, all along the Atlantic seaboard from Maine to the South, do not know who Mexican-Americans are. This town knows only African-Americans and Whites. Official Washington does not know Mexican-Americans, so the government does not worry about their concerns. You have been active in the civil rights movement as it affects the Chicanos. You travel and converse with leaders all over the Southwest. You do research and know what is current in the communities there. Give me three proposals on what research you will do to respond to my request."

I agreed and asked for temporary assignment to the Executive Office Building (EOB) across the alley from the West Wing of the White House. Outsiders consider EOB part of the White House, but insiders knew the West Wing was the White House and the EOB was simply for support staff, though still very important. But Washington rides on perceptions. I knew that news of my presence in the "White House" would spread swiftly throughout the Spanish-speaking world; this would assist me greatly in acquiring information, opinions, thoughts, and experiences from leaders. Most important, my association with the White House would assure that my telephone calls would be answered with celerity. My request was granted; Dr. Grassmuck showed me to a third-floor office that would become my working home in the "White House."

Several days later, I returned to the West Wing to present Counselor Finch with three outlines for the proposed study. One was for a quick memo; another was for research on the literature; a third was for a thorough compilation of research, interviews, and opinions of key persons that would require travel to gather.

He opted for a 20- to 30-page memo based on my experiences, telephone interviews, and knowledge of the Mexican-American civil rights movement. As a safeguard for my professionalism, I pointedly announced that I was going to write factually and objectively, without reservation or worry about hurt feelings. Robert Finch expressed no reaction to this statement, either facially or in words.

I was already deeply aware of how Mexican-Americans perceived this White House. Many older Mexicans I knew in Pomona, while greatly appreciative of Roosevelt for bringing jobs and ending the Depression (which they blamed Hoover for starting), knew nothing about partisan politics, Democrats, Republicans, Nixon, or the White House. Those were all meaningless terms to them. They knew about the corrupt and thieving government in Mexico, and that was enough. But some Mexican-Americans were happy to know that I was working in the "White House." These included the very small group of Mexican-Americans involved in civil rights and the many Mexican-Americans who had achieved a college education and were social workers or teachers (often politically active as liberal Democrats). Despite political differences, they were glad to have me, a former high school teacher who had won his reputation as a very relevant civil rights protagonist, positioned at my level. They expressed their support with hundreds, if not thousands, of telegrams, letters, and phone calls. Robert Finch was later to call me to say, "OK, we get the message; now turn off the spigot!"

I adamantly stated that my work in no way should be construed by Finch or anyone else as a bid to be considered for the position of chairman of the Cabinet Committee. I'll never forget it. He retorted happily, "Do not be concerned; that is not in the cards. We do not want a civil rights activist."

Sometime in March 1971, I submitted a fifty-page study, "An Overview of Spanish-Speaking Affairs for White House Perspectives." (It was not dated.) Counselor Finch thanked me with a gracious letter. And then, I heard nothing further. My adventure into research for the White House had ended, or so I thought, with relief.

A year later, I discovered that my study had been reviewed by the White House Political Office in the hands of Chuck Colson. The study had been refined to include presidential actions and to frame political tactics and strategies for the pending presidential reelection campaign.

Meanwhile, Washington was abuzz with the names of those campaigning for the coveted position of chairman. My name began to surface, even though I was not even a candidate for that position. And sure enough, Counselor Robert Finch again summoned me. In wonderment, I made the now-familiar walk up the driveway to the front door of the West Wing. It almost seemed as if the squirrels had lost their apprehension of me.

The several minutes of processing and walking through the West Wing gate and up to the White House gave me a bit of time to reflect on my actions. They were now affecting me in my professional—as well as private—life. What did these visits to the White House represent for me and my family? Some events seemed beyond my control. I had completed what Finch wanted. I had declared my vigorous disinterest in politics, my plans to return to California to pursue a position as a superintendent, and rejection of any consideration for the position at the Cabinet Committee. Finch himself had assured me that it was "not in the cards." So, what did he want this time?

At his office, Finch again thanked me for my latest report. In his lawyer-like manner, he went straight to his purpose for summoning me to the West Wing and offered me the position of chairman. I do not recall him reciting any whys or wherefores. It was a simply stated request. I reacted slowly and with dismay. I deliberated for a prolonged while, wrestling with the offer's implications for my family and myself. This would disrupt the career ladder I was on in the field of education: next, superintendent and then university professor. It would place me into a cauldron of partisan politics, competing ethnic and racial interests, a presidential campaign, and huge expectations for achieving civil rights aspirations. Oddly, I cannot pinpoint the date Finch offered me the position. The truth was, I did not like the offer. I had forewarned him in February of my deep disinterest in high-level politics.

Finally, I responded to Counselor Finch that I would accept the position, subject to three conditions. His countenance showed his dislike for my phrasing, but he asked me to explain. I did. My conditions were: (1) a permanent office in the White House EOB; (2) tangible support from Chicano leaders in the form of letters and telegrams to the White House; and (3) the recognition of my power to fire and hire at the Cabinet Committee.

As best I can now recall, I conveyed this supporting rationale for my conditions:

1. An office in the White House (EOB) would immediately place the Mexican-Americans on a par with the Blacks. Robert Brown, who was in charge of all matters dealing with Blacks, already had his office in the EOB.

2. Further, the rubbing of shoulders and face-to-face daily contact in the halls of power would enhance the advancement of the civil rights agenda of the unknown Mexican-Americans.

3. The need-to-know power movers in the White House had to know that I had gained my spurs as a known and respected civil rights leader. I had to be reckoned with.

4. The personnel in the Cabinet Committee were loyal to others. I had to have my own loyal team. That is a rule of Washington. I would fire without concern for who had been that person's politically powerful "rabbi."

"You have got to be kidding," Finch immediately reacted. "There is no way we will meet those conditions." I was dismissed abruptly and with disdain. So, I was not the popular kid, but I was relieved that I could go on with my plan to return to California.

But wouldn't you know it! Two weeks later, again I am summoned and again offered the chairmanship. Finch added, almost parenthetically, that two conditions were acceptable, but an office in the EOB was out of the question. I quickly rejected the offer. This reaction seemed to provide Finch a sense of comfort. He commented, "That suits me fine. We have been concerned with your civil rights attitude, so forget it."

Feelings were surfacing, and the situation was becoming uncomfortable. "I did not call you; you called me," I retorted. I remained adamant about having an EOB office. I had come to realize that White House staffers divided people into "us" and "them." The "us" were the White House personnel, while they saw political appointees who had "gone native" as outsiders (i.e., those who had been captured by the interests of the agencies and people they serve). Given the nature of these relationships, I knew that to do an effective job for the President and Spanish-speaking Americans, I would have to be one of the "us." Anything short of that would diminish the stature and power of the chairmanship over time. After all, the chairman would be a member of the Cabinet and would deal with the President's Cabinet officers—and where better than in the hallways of the White House?

Counselor Finch was dismissive once more. Whatever the future held for both of us, matters clearly were not going to be warm and fuzzy. But I had defined the role and function of the position.

Several weeks later, while vacationing in Williamsburg, Virginia, with my family, Finch again called me to the White House urgently. He insisted on meeting as soon as possible. I was puzzled. What had happened? Was he going to accept my remaining condition? I flew to Washington on the next available plane, interrupting my vacation.

From the airport, I took a taxi directly to the West Wing gate. The Secret Service guards were becoming very familiar with me and processed me perfunctorily and quickly. The West Wing receptionist also knew me quite well by now. Miss Shelley, who later married Pat Buchanan, was always proper and correct, without any sign of warmth. Her words and gestures were economical; she never uttered "hi" or "how are you." She did not ask me why I was there this time, either, but merely waved me on to Counselor Finch's office.

As usual, Finch opened the meeting directly. There was no talk about my vacation, my family faring alone in Williamsburg, or anything of that nature. He simply stated, "We have met all three conditions. Now will you take the chairmanship?" They had me; I was finished. Before I could respond, he thundered, "When the President personally wants you and asks you to serve, you do not refuse." At that revelation, I was elated and humbled. At any rate, I chose that moment to define my relationship with the counselor by stating clearly and slowly, "I thought *you* had selected me for the job. I had no idea the President himself wanted me to head up the agency." Then I said, humbly and simply, "I accept." Tensions evaporated, and Dr. Grassmuck took a photo (Figure 1).

And that ended the last step leading to my appointment. The President, Richard M. Nixon himself, had chosen me to be his right-hand man on all matters dealing with Mexican-Americans and later, by extension, with other Spanish-speaking groups. The President would now meet the needs of the children of the Diaspora.

May Roy O. Day (1900-1986), who started the chain of events, rest in peace.

Figure 1. Dr. George Grassmuck took this photograph of me and Robert Finch (right) to celebrate my acceptance of the President's offer of the Cabinet Committee chairmanship. *(Courtesy Richard M. Nixon Library)*

2. NIXON DIRECTS HISPANIC AFFAIRS

August 5, 1971: The White House staffers had choreographed the drama of the day for optimal impact. Only they knew the contents of the day's program. All I knew was that I was going to be interviewed by the President. Several big surprises lay in store for me.

Meanwhile, President Richard M. Nixon was achieving a dream he must have formed in his teens while living a life of poverty with an exiled group. Now as president, he was finally able to incorporate the hitherto unknown, invisible, and forgotten members of the Mexican Diaspora of 1913–1930 into the American Dream. Although the atmosphere in the country, especially in Washington, was defined by the continuing Vietnam War at that time and the President was under heavy pressure from his critics both on the Left and on the emerging Right, Nixon nonetheless relished this moment; this day, he would focus his full attention on the civil rights struggle of Mexican-Americans. At this point, only he and I understood and appreciated what we were about to accomplish, but after August 5, 1971, recognition that the U.S. population included a group identified variously as Mexican-Americans, the Spanish-speaking, Chicanos, Puerto Ricans, and Cubans—and in a lesser way, Hispanics—would begin. Mexican-Americans would become visible for the first time.

In detail, here is what happened on that awesome day.

Upon arrival inside the West Wing, I got my first big surprise of the day when I met a group of persons who greeted me and revealed why they were there. These nine people were going to be my advisors!

Counselor Robert Finch was our master of ceremonies. In the latter part of 1970, Finch had already gathered a database of information on the status of efforts and programs in the federal government supporting the Spanish-speaking population. With the assistance of his aides, he oversaw every detail of this historic day.

Counselor Finch escorted my advisors and me to the Oval Office, where the President greeted us as we were introduced. The White House press photographers were allowed to photograph us with the President as a group (Figure 2), and then the President himself swore us into our new offices: I as chairman of the Cabinet Committee on Opportunities for Spanish-Speaking People (CCOSSP); they as my presidential advisors.

Figure 2. From left to right, the just-appointed members of the Advisory Council to the Chairman of the CCOSSP: Jorge Tristani, Edgar Buttari, Manuel Gonzalez, Manuel Giberga, Hilda Hidalgo; to the right of President Richard M. Nixon: Dr. Henry M. Ramirez, Ted Martinez, Ed Yturria, Eugene Marin, and Ignacio Lozano. *(Courtesy Richard M. Nixon Library)*

Counselor Finch then escorted the nine advisors to an initial meeting with the Cabinet officers in the Cabinet meeting room. However, I remained in the Oval Office, alone with the President. He told me to pull my chair next to his desk. It was a huge desk, devoid of clutter, and he sat comfortably behind it. I felt warmly welcomed. I quickly formed a first impression: In his dark suit, the President appeared physically trim and strong, with a vibrant voice and focused, penetrating eyes. He spoke without any notes, without hesitation, and with a strong sense of confidence in his knowledge.[18] I was very

---

[18] I write here from contemporary notes, my memory refreshed by tapings acquired from The Cutting Corporation (Bethesda, Maryland). Unfortunately, someone deleted parts of the conversation the President and I held (Tapes 6, 7, 8, and 9). The deleted

surprised at his profound experiential knowledge of Mexican-American issues and personalities.

He opened with a lengthy monologue on the state of affairs for Mexican-Americans and the panorama of issues confronting them. He outlined his experience with our civil rights struggles. He recalled his contacts with the famous Leo Carillo, with Judge Gerardo and Judge Velarde of the Whittier courts, and with Danny Villanueva, the former Los Angeles Rams football player. He reminisced about the days when Mexicans were integrated into the Whittier schools. He mentioned the Mexican barrios known as Jim Town, Canta Ranas, and Murphy Ranch. He recalled his experiences picking oranges and lighting "smudge pots" in freezing weather, and how he had come to know the people firsthand and prize their value systems, hard work, close-knit families, and Catholic religion.

Richard Nixon is the only U.S. president born and raised in California—and with Mexicans! Years later, I wanted to find out more about how he had come to possess such closeness to us Mexicans, so I interviewed his brother, Eddie, several times and read his book, *The Nixons: A Family Portrait*. It was then I realized just how close he and his family really had been to the Mexican barrios. After their father failed in the citrus business in Yorba Linda, the Nixon family established a small grocery

---

discussions were on these topics: the prejudice in the Southwest against Mexicans; how to get Mexican-Americans to vote in higher numbers for President Nixon; how our studies at the Civil Rights Commission had proven that the socioeconomic status of parents was both cause and effect of students' good grades; and how I was to get around Nixon's "palace guard" via his valet. (The latter may have been in the tapes, but the audio is so bad, it is hard to understand.)

store with a gas station in front near the intersection of Santa Gertrudes Avenue and Whittier Boulevard in the unincorporated part of Los Angeles County, almost adjacent to the Orange County line. Their business catered to the nearby ranches, Murphy and Leffingwell, where Mexican families resided and worked. Richard Nixon picked oranges and field crops with members of these families and attended schools in Whittier with a few of them, too. There are people still living in the Whittier area who are grandchildren of the Mexicans who knew Richard Nixon when he worked in the store and remember stories of him granting credit to poor Mexicans.

I am quite familiar with that area, although it has greatly changed since the 1940s when the Nixon family lived there. In 1958, my wife and I purchased acreage for a new home that had been part of the Leffingwell Ranch at the intersection of Santa Gertrudes Avenue and Leffingwell Road. The entire area formerly encompassed by Murphy Ranch and Leffingwell Ranch became the upscale "East Whittier."

But back to that August day in 1971. As the President continued his monologue, he lamented that Mexicans do not lobby for their rights. He made the usual references to the effectiveness of Blacks in lobbying. The crucial importance he attached to this activity quite surprised me and caught me unprepared to react or think about it. He encouraged me to make the point a priority at the Cabinet Committee and added, "They should raise as much hell as they can." At that, I went through mental gyrations. Surely, he meant lobbying by the community, not by me in my role and function as a high-level presidential appointee, soon to be confirmed by the Senate. But I was beginning to sense he was not going to engage in a discussion. He was going to be the commander-in-chief.

"I have assigned Bob Finch the job of riding herd on Mexican-American matters in this administration," he went on. "The Cabinet Committee is now Bob's responsibility." He then listed the areas the Cabinet Committee would pursue: jobs, discrimination, bilingual education, government appointments, administration of justice, and lobbying. He wanted progress reports and reports to Congress on Committee actions. He pledged full staff support and comprehensive cooperation from the Cabinet.

The President did not mention any other Hispanic group during our Oval Office meeting. He noted that his orientation to the needs of Mexican-Americans was derived from his interaction with them in California, from his early years in Yorba Linda to later times in Whittier. He and his wife, Pat, had attended Whittier High School, and he noted that Pat had taught business courses there. He added, "In fact, it was where you also taught." He gave a general sense of the Mexican kids he had known at school from the barrios of Jim Town in West Whittier, Canta Ranas in Los Nietos, Murphy Ranch in East Whittier, and even Pico Viejo in Pico Rivera.

I wondered, as he reviewed his salient contacts with the Mexican community, just how few people there were in my life who could match his personal knowledge and experience of those in my community. I knew he and Pat had even honeymooned in Acapulco, Mexico. Few Southern California Anglo couples did that in those days.

He then delved into the area of discrimination. In his years as a poor, young White in Yorba Linda, he picked tomatoes, cucumbers, and oranges alongside the Mexicans. He spoke specifically of his experiences in picking oranges at Murphy Ranch in East Whittier. I knew Murphy Ranch well from my work with the mayor of Whittier, Jack Mele, who had asked me to help relocate the Mexican families living there so that land developers could clear the land for the construction of a fancy golf course and expensive housing along the fairways. I was amazed to hear Nixon talk about his work at Murphy Ranch back in its days as a working citrus ranch. I knew of few Anglos who had done that type of low-level, dirty, nasty labor. His discussion reflected deep awareness of the discrimination Mexican-Americans endured.

Following these comments, he sat back, looked at the ceiling, placed his fingers around his jaws, and waxed eloquent: "We in the Southwest have built an invisible wall of discrimination and have kept the Mexicans away from the opportunities this great country has to offer." He continued to compare "a Southwest wall of discrimination" with the Great Wall of China. As he ended on this topic, he thundered: "It will be our job to knock down that wall of discrimination!" (In retrospect, China must also have been very much on his mind, for soon after that day, his visit to China was announced.)

During our time in the Oval Office, the President's scheduler, Stephen B. Bull, kept coming in to remind him that he was falling far behind and that the Cabinet Officers had been waiting for quite some time (as had some ambassador). Dr. Grassmuck had prepared me to spend only a few pro forma minutes with the President, but we had already spent what seemed almost 20 minutes—and yet he wasn't finished!

The President was enjoying our meeting. He seemed to kick back visibly, choosing to neglect his schedule. He began ruminating about his past campaigns in California and how the Mexican-Americans participated. In the course of reviewing names and events, he repeated a question Republicans often voice: Why are Mexican-Americans Democrats?[19] They are not liberals; they are conservative in lifestyle. It puzzled the President.

The President then veered into a related topic in an offhanded way, which made it appear that he attached only incidental interest. He lamented that all he could gather from Mexicans was five percent of their vote. Then he moved his chair closer and in a stronger voice rephrased the statement. This time, it sounded important to him. He repeated, "Five percent. That is all I get. I do not understand why such a low number. It is not for lack of effort. I have participated in Sixteenth of September East L.A. parades, ridden on horses for Cinco de Mayo parades, worn sombreros and sarapes, attended fiestas eating tacos, enchiladas, and tamales. This time, I want fifteen percent of the Mexican vote. I want to do a good job on civil rights for Mexican-Americans. I want to help you do a good job, so that we can get to that goal." He

---

[19] A year later, in 1972, then-governor Ronald Reagan spent a lot of time on the same topic during my visit to his Sacramento office. He mentioned many Spanish-surnamed Americans who fitted that mold perfectly. He spoke admiringly of state Senator Ruben Ayala from San Bernardino. Governor Reagan got to know Ruben at close range and remarked, "I just do not know why Ruben is a Democrat." I tried to explain but am sure he did not follow my rationale. Reagan was a Midwesterner from a small town, and his traditions and knowledge were based on his European background. While living in California, he came into some limited contact with Mexican-Americans, but he and they lived in two separate worlds. They knew of each other but did not know each other.

asked me what I thought about that and whether I thought the target of fifteen percent was feasible.

In my eagerness to impress and please, I assured him that we could achieve it. In fact, I modestly suggested the goal should not be fifteen, but twenty-five percent! I knew Mexican-Americans were basically conservative, and I felt sure they'd respond to those who would reach out to them with respect and understanding. Surely, they would respond to presidential initiatives and efforts that were authentically substantial and transformative.

He smiled and gave forth a hearty belly laugh. He sat back on his large, comfortable black leather executive chair, twirled around, and pulled forward close to me. He pontificated, "You are a Latin teacher with no political experience, and you tell me twenty-five percent! You do not know what you are talking about. I am the politician. How will we get to that level?"

At that, I reached into my shirt pocket, withdrew a neat, crisp three-by-five card, and gave it to him. He read it intently. I wish I had made a copy of that card in the morning before departing from my office. I never got it back, but I had typed on it five sentences that represented my vision for the new job that went more or less like the following:

1. Hold high-level government meetings at federal regional centers to promote these goals at the local level.

2. Count Spanish-surnamed Americans by employment and contract/grant participation.

3. Appoint 100 Hispanics to supergrade positions (i.e., positions above a GS 15).

4. Adopt and enforce a systematic program to assure federal employment of Spanish-surnamed Americans.

5. Include us in White House activities to create a national awareness of the conditions of Mexican-Americans.

I proudly reiterated that the President would get twenty-five percent of the Mexican-American vote if he were to get these goals implemented and enforced. "Good service has its own reward," I recall stating with a great deal of conviction. I knew that Mexican-Americans would be responsive to the achievement of these goals and find the President most *"simpatico."* I could tell he liked that word.

He examined the card again and pushed a button. Someone came into the Oval Office. The President handed him the card and ordered, "Give this to [so-and-so]." (I never got the name clearly, but it sounded like Haldeman.) "Have him read it, and tell him I want those things done." He remarked to the functionary that I had said he would get twenty-five percent of the Mexican-American vote if he took those actions, then added with some nice Navy-style words (he was wont to use them in our interview and also in a later Cabinet meeting), "Well, doggone it,"—and so on—"we are going to do them."

History shows that President Nixon actually received over thirty percent of the Mexican-American vote in the next election! The Committee to Re-elect the President gathered voluminous reports describing how Mexican-Americans voted in November 1972. One of them was an exit poll done in the Boyle Heights area of East Los

Angeles, and another was done in San Antonio. I have not been able to garner copies of these reports (although I did have some once), but I did read them. Among the many newspaper articles that floated about at the time, I was able to retain one from the *Washington Post*: "According to a CBS analysis, President Nixon received 49 percent of the Spanish-speaking vote in Texas and Florida and 31 percent of the Spanish-speaking vote nationally."[20]

So, the Latin teacher with no political experience turned out to be right after all, and the President later acknowledged my work on his behalf.

The President had some advice for me before bringing our meeting to a close. He got quite close and whispered that it would be almost impossible for me to inform him of progress toward the goals I had outlined on the note card because of the system of "palace guards." He advised me to use the avenue of his personal valet, Manolo Sanchez. Through Mr. Sanchez, I would be able to get information to him on how we were doing. "You know Manolo?"

"Yes," I affirmed.

"Well, then, get to him and tell him what you want me to know!"

---

[20] Tony Castro, "Texas Chicanos Voted GOP; New La Raza Unida Got 6%," Washington Post, November 13, 1972.

Figure 3. First Cabinet Meeting of CCOSSP. Clockwise around the table, left to right: Secretary of the U.S. Department of Housing and Urban Development, George Romney; Secretary of the U.S. Department of Agriculture, Clifford N. Hardin; Assistant Secretary of the Treasury, Charls Walker; Counselor to the President, Robert H. Finch; vice chairman of the Committee and Attorney General, John Mitchell; Secretary of the U.S. Department of Labor, James D. Hodgson; chairman of the Civil Service Commission, Robert Hampton; director of the Office of Economic Opportunity, Phillip V. Sanchez; special assistant to the president, Fred Malek; Undersecretary of U.S. Department of Housing, Education and Welfare (HEW), John Veneman; Assistant Secretary of HEW, Patricia Reilly Hitt; chairman of CCOSSP, Dr. Henry M. Ramirez; President Richard M. Nixon; executive director of CCOSSP, Antonio Rodriguez; administrator of the Small Business Administration, Thomas Kleppe; special assistant to the chairman of the Equal Employment Opportunity Commission, John Oldecker; and intern, Louie Cespedes. Seated to the left are members of the Advisory Council to the CCOSSP; Edgar Buttari and Ted Martinez are visible. Seated by the windows: director of Spanish Speaking Programs, Civil Service Commission, Fernando E. C. de Baca; and assistant to Counselor Finch, George Grassmuck. *(Courtesy Richard M. Nixon Library)*

After that momentous (and for me, emotional) exchange, the President took me by the arm and escorted me into the Cabinet Room for the first meeting of the CCOSSP. I was amazed! The room was filled with Cabinet officers, along with my newly appointed presidential advisors, Counselor Finch, and staffers. To my surprise, the President took me to a chair, personally seeing to it that I was seated to his right (Figure 3).

Counselor Robert Finch opened the first-ever meeting of the CCOSSP. The President asked Mr. Finch to say a few words regarding the organization and progress of the Cabinet Committee for the benefit of the members present. Counselor Finch then thanked the departments for their reports on the status of their respective outreach to Spanish-speaking people. He said that the name of the game was to upgrade federal activity for the Spanish-speaking in all areas.

Then the President addressed the committee. His tone was very serious, unlike his relaxed composure just minutes before in the Oval Office. The minutes of this Cabinet meeting are in my private collection, but here is a transcript of the President's words:

I have said before around this very Cabinet table—that there has not been enough follow-through in our efforts for Spanish-speaking Americans. There has not been enough pressure from the media, from Congress, and from within Spanish-speaking communities themselves compared to the pressures exerted by other minority groups. In government, only those groups that raise hell and threaten, "You either do something or we will blow the place up" get any attention. This has been particularly true during the sixties and the early seventies. Let me be very candid about this. I am not suggesting that any group that has not had an equal chance should be disorderly. We do not suggest that individuals under any circumstances roll over and be nice guys and not complain. The political reality is that whether dealing with Congress or federal agencies, we should make an all-out effort to rectify our record.

The President then turned to me and commented that we had both started out at the bottom in the Whittier area. He reminisced about his days working in the California orchards, and he and I traded quips on who was the best orange picker. I said that I had picked a hundred boxes of oranges per day. The President said, "You can't afford to be in government!" Everyone laughed.

The President became quite serious again, and his mood permeated the room as he continued:

What has happened here is this: Mexican-Americans, Puerto Ricans, etc., are an important factor in our total economic output, and considering what they can do, they are not getting their fair shake with regard to other groups.

This is going to change. It can only change if the members of the Cabinet get off their duffs. I don't want this administration to be one that only responds to those that only tear up the place and pound fists. It just happens that in recent times we have had some very disturbing experiences in Los Angeles and other places.

I am speaking now to the Mexican-American community; for when I lived in Whittier, I had very close ties with this group. They were family-oriented, law-abiding people. Although they did need attention, the wheel was not squeaking much. This has to change. We owe it to all groups in society to see they get an equal chance, especially those who have been law-abiding people.

You have not had an effective lobby. I told Henry that you need a lobby. You should have it, but we should not wait until a lobby is set up. In terms of jobs, we must urge agencies to fill their slots with Spanish-speaking people. We have to search for openings—we should go out and find good slots and fill them. We must find the applicants—they don't apply because they think it is hopeless.

The thing I want to get across to those who are non-government is that I urge all minority groups—women, Blacks, Mexican-Americans—to use your capabilities and improve them. We aren't providing opportunities just as a favor to you. We must keep America competitive. We are pricing ourselves out of the world markets. Twenty-five years ago, we were first in everything—today the world is totally changed. Our former enemies are now our major competitors in the free market. The players are new—Western Europe, Japan, China, the Soviet Union, and potentially Latin America and Africa.

Twenty-five years from now, whoever is sitting in this chair will be representing the second or third strongest country unless we develop all our resources. We must develop our human resources. I would like for every American in this country, whatever his background, to have an equal opportunity to develop to the fullest of his capacity. We cannot afford to have any group in this country not have an equal opportunity to develop their capabilities. The government must assume this responsibility—private business does not move as fast in developing opportunities. We must provide opportunities not presently available where there is a great need for new talent.

The Mexican-American does not have that chance now. That is going to change or the people in the personnel offices in every department are going to change.

At this point in the meeting, the President became agitated and angry at the Civil Service Commission's lack of progress in promoting and fostering the employment of Mexican-Americans. He pointed out in detail how he had ordered the Commission to adopt the Sixteen-Point Program developed by the Cabinet Committee with the sole purpose of boosting employment of the Spanish-speaking in the federal government. He had been informed that the Sixteen-Point Program was on schedule, but he had been truly flabbergasted to learn that absolutely nothing had been accomplished. He raised his voice and pointed at Robert Hampton, chairman of the Civil Service Commission, who was seated at the far end of the huge oval table. The President read him the riot act and warned him that if the Sixteen-Point Program was not adopted forthwith, he, the President, would have to replace Hampton. Needless to say, some action took place soon after.

The President then concluded:

Don't wait until the wheel squeaks—or something is blown up in Los Angeles. Provide opportunity until there is not one scintilla of suggestion that we are not only not discriminatory but are making positive moves to rectify the situation. Everyone has a better chance in this country to get an equal break. In government, we have an ever-greater opportunity.

I want Bob to follow up, and Henry, too. It is the only way to work in the future. I want quarterly reports from both of you concerning the progress of each agency—and also their failures.

And the President left the room.

For people used to the strong leadership of President Nixon, these were tough words but not unusual. He had always been precise and direct in dealing with his inner staff members and advisors. This meeting showed clearly that President Nixon had a deep and real concern for the problems and progress of Mexican-Americans. No one can suggest that he was playing to the public or the press on that day, because there were none present. The meeting was private, and there is no need for histrionics when one speaks to confidential aides and advisors. Charm belongs in the reception line. In the Cabinet Room, you tell it like it is.

At the conclusion of the Cabinet Committee meeting, however, Robert Finch took me to the White House Press Room. I could not believe it. From the stage, I recognized reporters seated in the front row—Sarah McClendon, Sam Donaldson, and others frequently viewed in the evening news. And yes, Finch exposed me to a White House press conference. Publicity for the new kid on the block was intense, particularly in the Spanish-language media from the United States, Latin America, and Spain.

Then I joined my little family, who were being greeted by the President as he walked from the West Wing to his working office in the EOB. To conclude this day filled with surprises, I had my first meeting with my presidential advisors.

President Nixon finally had his ducks in a row. He was now getting the right people to lead the charge for the Spanish-speaking, something he had yearned to accomplish since day one of his presidency.

As for me, I was inspired with deep awe. In moments of solitude after these inaugural meetings, I analyzed their significance and profound implications, mentally and emotionally processing my observations of the President himself, analyzing the emergence of this new American group and how the President had ordered his staff to assure equal opportunities for Mexican-Americans. Within a government that was just now discovering the existence of this new group crying out for justice, recognition, and inclusion in the *res publica,* the President had placed the power of the incumbency at our disposal. We were to use it with profound prudence and energetic firmness. We had now become official emissaries of President Nixon's vision to include Mexican-Americans and other Latinos in the mainstream of American life.

For me, now was the time for decision-making and action. I was no longer an outsider, I was now a doer! By this time, the White House was in reelection mode, so my every action would be evaluated against its impact on reelection. Yet for myself, I weighed my own achievements and accomplishments against how much they advanced *la causa*—the betterment of living conditions for Spanish-speaking people.

3. NIXON ORDERS CENSUS BUREAU: "COUNT THE MEXICANS"

There's an axiom in government: "In order to count, you must be counted." Prior to 1970, however, Mexican-Americans were not counted. We were still unknown or overlooked, and therefore, we did not "count" in politics. How did it come about that Nixon ordered Mexican-Americans be included for the first time in the U.S. census of 1970? This chapter unravels the string of events leading to that presidential mandate.

The very first effort to count Mexicans in the population actually took place during the census of 1930. That census counted Mexicans who were born south of the U.S.–Mexico border as belonging to the "Mexican race." Any Mexican-American children born in the United States of parents who were born south of the border were also counted as part of the "Mexican race."[21]

---

[21] Census of 1930, Census Bureau, Department of Commerce,

However, this attempt was problematic. Recall from Part I that a totally new and different group of Mexicans, named Mestizos, was formed after the conquest of Mexico as a result of unions between Native Mexican women and European men. Their appearance was distinct from Native Mexicans and likewise from Europeans. It is reasonable to surmise that government officials at the U.S. Department of Commerce's Census Bureau tried very hard to define this group of people. They formulated a questionnaire designating Mestizos as a separate race, the "Mexican race." Yet most Mestizos in the United States at that time were refugees living in isolated poverty and unable to answer census questions in English. It is highly probable that the official census count of 1,422,533 people of "Mexican race" was very inaccurate.

Furthermore, the Mexican government objected to the use of "Mexican race" as a designation. This fact causes me to chuckle—after all, the ruling class in Mexico were descendants of illiterate European peasant *conquistadores* looking to gain land and riches. Evidently, they had overlooked the fact that almost all other citizens of Mexico were either Native Mexican or Mestizos. In the 1930s, the ruling, literate, and landed class in Mexico were of *sangre pura*—pure blood—and they knew it. Marriage certificates were required to identify the blood purity of each party to a conjugal contract: *sangre mezclada* (mixed blood) or *sangre pura*. Hence, the European Mexicans knew that they themselves were of the White race, even several centuries after *la conquista*. Moreover, they were the government.

Washington, DC.

In a move that pleased the Mexican government, the U.S. government discontinued designating Mexicans as a race.

The 1940 census did not count the number of Mexicans living in the United States and their Mexican-American children at all. Instead the 1940 U.S. census included persons of Mexican birth or ancestry in the racial definition for White, even though most were Indian or Mestizo, with only a few having European ancestry. As a result, because Mexican-Americans were counted in the White category, not separately, they became the "forgotten Americans," the "forgotten people," and the "invisible minority."

Meanwhile, other events were occurring in the country as Blacks began to demand their civil rights. We Mexican-Americans, however, were not participants in the surge to secure civil rights along with them. Because we were not counted, we did not exist! To be counted became an absolute necessity.

In 1957, President Eisenhower established the U.S. Commission on Civil Rights, giving it authority to conduct research, document discrimination, and hold public hearings with power to compel testimony under subpoena. The commissioners delegated authority to their staff to perform studies, write reports, gather testimony, and conduct hearings on discrimination in education, housing, voting, administration of justice, employment, banking, and so on against the Black population. The information gathered on practices of discrimination was made public and submitted to the president and Congress.

As a result of the extensive and exhaustive documentation of widespread discrimination against Blacks, the Civil Rights Act of 1964 was enacted, which improved the government's ability to enforce civil rights. Prior to this, the Commission could only study the problem of discrimination. Now, every government agency would have staffing and resources, and new offices were created for civil rights, equal-opportunity employment, federal contract compliance, community relations service, desegregation, and voting rights. In addition, Congress increased the federal budget for enforcing civil rights.

The federal government had been gathering census data on Whites and Blacks for over two centuries—since the first census in 1790. And, because of the work of the Commission, it also had extensive data on discrimination against Blacks in every aspect of American life and in most geographic areas.

In 1964, President Johnson inaugurated the Great Society. The federal budget was increased greatly to finance the "War on Poverty." Distribution of funds to the very poor became of paramount interest, and funds began to flow into all kinds of local organizations newly formed to fight poverty. Official Washington knew a lot about the conditions and positions of American Blacks. The data showed large disparities between them and European Americans, so many of the War on Poverty efforts were directed to eradicating poverty among Blacks.

However, Washington was overlooking another very poor group: Mexican-Americans. This group did not count, because it was not counted. It was, in fact, *invisible* since the census had decided Mexican-Americans belonged to the White race. Further, most of this "invisible minority" did not live in Washington or New York, which were the national media centers, but in that far-off region called the Southwest. Thus, the media disregarded their existence or, when they did notice, they did not even have a consistent name for the group. Some called them Latinos or Spanish or Mexicans; still others called them Chicanos.

The children of the 1.4 million Mexicans counted in 1930 were now U.S. citizens, even veterans of foreign wars. They were very much Mexican-Americans. But by this time, discrimination against Mexican-Americans was causing them to be restless. Embryonic rumblings of protest were audible. Student walkouts had occurred in Southern California and would soon erupt in Texas and Colorado. Groups had protested against the Equal Employment Commission for excluding Mexican-Americans. Chicanos had protested in November 1967, marching in front of the Shoreham Hotel in Washington. We Chicanos, just regular folks, were beginning to get national awareness of our existence.

Fortunately, one agency had the volition and responsibility to find out about this little-known group of Americans. In 1968, the U.S. Commission on Civil Rights established the Mexican American Studies Division to determine and document discrimination against this group of people. The Commission hired me, a Chicano from California, to be chief of this new division. I was never told why the Commission established the Mexican American Studies Division, and I never asked what discussions and decisions led to its creation, but it must have been included in the Commission's budget request after the findings of a newly opened field office in Los Angeles caused a stir in Washington. The Commission's leadership had previously been as totally unaware of Mexican-Americans as had official Washington. But that would change. And once the Commission found us, we would no longer be unknown.

Sometime in very early 1968, the Commission decided to conduct investigations on discrimination against Mexican-Americans. The Mexican American Studies Division began its studies in mid-1968 focusing on discrimination in education. The Commission staff commenced investigations by visiting and interviewing civic and community leaders in southern Texas, from El Paso to Brownsville. The commissioners and staff learned a great deal about systematic discrimination in education, employment, administration of justice, and housing. The trip was succeeded by extensive research and interviews. This initial exploration culminated in a weeklong 1968 hearing in San Antonio; the report of this hearing extended over 1,000 pages.

When I took the position as chief of the Mexican American Studies Division in 1968, I left my dearly loved job teaching Julius Caesar, Cicero, Virgil, Horace, and the Greek philosophers and dramatists. I had always enjoyed associating their thoughts with the humanities and the course of European history from antiquity to the present. For my new post, I was handed a job description and told to read it carefully. I had been teaching Latin, Spanish, American literature, and humanities and had coached baseball and tennis. Now, all of a sudden, I had the awesome responsibilities of a social scientist and a researcher expected to do national studies.

The staff director, William Taylor, instructed me to submit a plan of action for the commissioners' review. I realized that the Commission's mission was to document discrimination and denial of equal protection of the law. From my own life experience, I was very aware of how Mexican-Americans were discriminated against, especially in the area of education. The task ahead was seemingly so great that I could not even guess whether I was capable of performing it. As the saying goes, "In the world of the blind, the one-eyed is king."

I conceptualized and designed research to see what impinged on the education of Mexican-American students from grades one to twelve. I was given a budget and authorized to hire staff. I quickly set out to gather personnel smarter and more knowledgeable than I and hunted for young, smart college graduates cum laude with the background and personal understanding of the subject matter. Together, we formulated questionnaires for superintendents, principals, and teachers on issues affecting Mexican-American students. The U.S. government, however, had no norm for visually identifying Mexican-Americans. The only time it had identified Mexicans was in 1930, and that was with a simple question: "Where were you born?"

Our first order of business was to create an identifier: Who was a Mexican-American student? We defined the students we targeted as "persons considered in school or community to be of Mexican, Central American, Cuban, Puerto Rican, Latin American or Spanish-speaking origin." We noted that this group is also often referred to as "Mexican, Spanish American, or Latin American; local usage varies greatly," and that for the purposes of the questionnaire, the terms "Mexican-American and Spanish-surnamed American were used interchangeably." We included this definition in the research methodology of the Mexican American Education Study as part of the instructions for determining ethnic and racial groupings. Wherever ethnic and racial data were requested, the instructions suggested visual means of identification; individuals were not to be singled out or questioned about their racial or ethnic lineage in any way.

The questionnaires were sent to educators in Arizona, California, Colorado, New Mexico, and Texas in the spring of 1969 with instructions for their return by May 9. The response rate was extremely high. We were deeply surprised and welcomed this outcome. I don't know why it was so high, but perhaps our protocol helped. My boss, Eunice Grier, and I visited each school superintendent of the five states in the study. We explained the purpose of the study, its hypotheses, its methodology and schedule, and possible benefits. We asked them to write a personal letter to each school district superintendent to encourage their participation. Approximately ninety-nine percent of the district forms and ninety-five percent of the school forms were returned. Arizona had a 100-percent response rate, but a few districts in the other states did not respond: Houston Independent School District (it was involved in a lawsuit at the time); Silver City District in New Mexico; the districts of Lucia Mar and Kingsburg, California; and North Conejos, Colorado.

It is highly significant that almost all of the thousands of questionnaires were returned. The study could now be characterized as a census of students in the Southwest in 1969. It was the first time in history that so many Mexican-Americans—1.4 million students in grades one to twelve—were counted. The Mexican Americans Studies Division of the U.S. Commission on Civil Rights had accomplished what no other entity in the federal government had. Mexican-Americans were no longer an invisible minority! In 1930, almost 40 years prior, Mexican-Americans were counted for the first time. In this Mexican American Education Study, Mexican-Americans were scientifically counted again, albeit only a fragment of the group, since the study only considered students in grades one to twelve and only in five states.

In another step forward, I met with Leon Panetta, director of the U.S. Department of Health, Education and Welfare's Office of Civil Rights, to discuss how his office could use my identifier of who is a Mexican-American. He then used it to count the Mexican-Americans in all primary and secondary schools in America.

But a further, gigantic step to change Mexican-Americans from being invisible was yet to come.

A national election had produced a president who was from California. He knew who Mexican-Americans were. He had been raised among them and had gone to school with them. He had worked as a poor Anglo with them, gathering crops in the fields and orchards. Whereas Mexican-Americans were an invisible group to most European Americans living in a large part of the country (i.e., in the South, Midwest, and, of course, the Northeast from Maine to the Mason-Dixon Line), Mexican-Americans in the Southwest were well known to President Nixon as fellow Americans.

Recall from Part II, Chapter 1 that Martin Castillo, deputy director of the U.S. Commission on Civil Rights, had adopted my office as his office as well. As a result, I had a prime opportunity to tutor the "top Washington Mexican, The Honorable Martin Castillo." Castillo reported to President Nixon. He was connected. So, I decided he should approach the President with a highly urgent and needed action: Count the Mexicans in the 1970 census.

The biggest hurdle and battle in getting Mexican-Americans counted awaited at the Census Bureau. By then, the Bureau had already finalized its 1970 census forms, and of course, Bureau officials had no plans to count Mexican-Americans. Nothing new there! They had not counted us in forty years, so why start now? Little did they know to what extent matters had changed.

Now we had a president who knew and liked Mexican-Americans. Capitalizing on that fact, I energized my allies and urged Marty Castillo to take leadership on getting us counted. Now was the time for action! With advances in civil rights for minorities and billions of dollars being spent on the War on Poverty, we could no longer wait to become visible participants in the national community. But only presidential action would change the plans at the Bureau. Marty understood and went into action to get the President to order the Census Bureau to count us.

History now records: President Nixon ended the practice of neglect. In 1969, even though the Census Bureau had already printed questionnaires for the 1970 census, the President nonetheless ordered the Bureau to count Mexican-Americans and they did. As a result, about nine million Americans of Mexican origin or descent (as well as our fellow Americans of Spanish-speaking origin or descent) became "visible." Thus, Nixon ended the applicability to Mexican-Americans of the axiom, "If you are not counted, you do not count."

4. NIXON ORDERS FEDERAL GOVERNMENT TO REACH OUT TO MEXICAN-AMERICANS

To prepare for job interviews, I have developed the habit of writing out what I would do on the new job. Back in 1964, when I was being interviewed for a change in my teaching position at Whittier High School, California, school principal Seabron Nolin asked me how I was going to help students improve their education. In anticipation of that query, I had written out a detailed plan during the summer prior to the incoming school year for fundamental changes to the way a high school was managed. The plan called for starting a novel club, to be named New Horizons. After I got the job, I reviewed the files of students, predominantly Mexicans, and selected 100 underachieving but high-potential students for this extracurricular effort to improve their academic outcomes. It was essential to measure improvements in the education of the selected students to know whether my new position was a success. The vision I had outlined over the summer included measurements of five outcomes of education before and after the program (reading, daily school attendance, grade point averages, participation in extracurricular activities, and graduation). The results showed that the New Horizons Program was highly successful and benefited the students greatly. (All seven schools in the Whittier Union High School District have incorporated it into their schools, and on September 16, 2014, the program's fiftieth anniversary was celebrated with fanfare from California state legislators, local mayors, and school board officials.)

Similarly, in early 1968, William Taylor, executive director of the U.S. Commission on Civil Rights, had asked me what I proposed to do as the chief of its Mexican American Studies Division. I answered, "I know how the schools in Southern California discriminate against Chicanos. We need to document whether that situation also exists in the rest of the Southwest and make recommendations to Congress and the President on how to change that with the laws available."

And then, in 1971, at the critical moment of my meeting with President Nixon in the Oval Office, I was ready when he asked how I thought he could get twenty-five percent of the Mexican-American vote. He gestured with his hands thrust up and his eyes lifted in search of an answer. Recall from Part II, Chapter 2 that I had handed him an index card with five ideas typewritten on it. The five action items on that index card synthesized my vision of what I would do as chairman of the Cabinet Committee on Opportunities for the Spanish-Speaking People (CCOSSP), but only if he so ordered it. He did. President Nixon gave orders to execute my five visions.

One of the five action items on the card was regional conferences. Why regional conferences?

My blend of experiences, studies, and travel gave me a foundation for conceptualizing objectives and methodologies for transformational activities—in this case, transforming the nation to include Spanish-speaking people in its mainstream at the local level. In the Oval Office, I had stressed the fact that the U.S. government tends to assume the habits and character of the regions in which it functions. So, to reach out to Cubans, mainland Puerto Ricans, and Mexican-Americans, we had to visit them where they lived. Changes had to be made at the local level. A user-friendly government reaches out and does not make people come to Washington for relief.

President Nixon had already been working on the same idea. He wanted government services available at the local level, so he reorganized the major federal agencies into ten regional offices to bring government closer than far-away Washington, DC. In January 1971, he directed the federal regional directors (or representatives) in the major agencies to convene themselves as Federal Regional Councils. Later, in February 1972, by Executive Order 11647, President Nixon included more agencies and further defined authority given to the ten Federal Regional Councils. The regional directors were delegated authority to employ and contract for services and products. In turn, the ten Federal Regional Councils were subdivided into District Federal Offices, and they, too, were delegated authority for employing and making contracts for services and products.

On the index card I had handed President Nixon, I had written that we should hold high-level government meetings at federal regional centers (regional conferences) to promote our goals at the local level. Now was the opportune moment for accomplishing changes close to where the people lived. Now was the historical moment when the federal government would reach out to Spanish-speaking communities where they lived—in the Southwest, the Midwest, the Northeast, and the Southeast. The Spanish-speaking would no longer remain a neglected group. President Nixon had verbalized his own vision in the private meeting he had with me as well as at the first meeting of the CCOSSP and had clearly pronounced on the outcomes he wanted. He had given us marching orders and authority through his counselor, Robert Finch. How much closer could we get to real power?

But there was one big obstacle that had to be removed so that regional conferences could be planned and started: It was the presidential promise of a White House conference on Mexican-American issues. I recommended the White House conference should be replaced by regional conferences. Dr. George Grassmuck (White House staff executive assistant to presidential counselor Robert Finch), Tony Rodriguez (executive director of CCOSSP), and I met on August 18, 1971. We agreed that the regional conferences would take the place of the White House conference that Nixon had promised in his first presidential election campaign. Most presidential campaign promises of lesser importance are soon forgotten. This promise held latent use as a negative in a reelection campaign. But the idea of close-to-home U.S. government regional meetings was even better, surpassing by far in importance a White House conference.

Another obstacle was overcoming negative stereotypes. As I interfaced with people in government with whom my staff and I worked, they gave me the distinct impression that they still viewed us through the lens of Hollywood stereotypes. Hollywood had invented a cast of Mexican characters who demonstrated the ineptitude of low-life inferiors through decrepit clothing, poor diction, and an unpleasant, swarthy appearance. The characters were unshaven, ugly, toothless, and illiterate. They were brigands, peasants, sex-driven Latin lovers, or dictators who salivated involuntarily. They were poorly armed, awkward gunmen who rode to battle on reluctant mules and burros. And, oh yes, they could not shoot straight. Only European Americans like John Wayne could take out two of them with one bullet.

Even the President's staff were still unaware of the affairs of Spanish-speaking people. The truth is that they were no different in their modalities toward us than the staffers had been under Kennedy or Johnson. I knew from conversations in my office with Marty Castillo just how ill-informed he found the White House staffers to be. A memo found in the Nixon Materials Section of the National Archives about programs for Spanish-speaking peoples, dated October 17, 1970, confirmed the low level of information. It was written by Dr. George Grassmuck, a Midwesterner, for Robert Finch's signature and addressed to the White House special assistant on Black affairs, Robert Brown.[22] What? Robert Brown was responsible for Black Americans, yet he was receiving memos on programs for the Spanish-speaking?! The contents exposed the regressive mentality in the White House that existed before President Nixon vehemently made known that he wanted Mexican-Americans to share

---

[22] Robert H. Finch to Robert Brown, memorandum, October 17, 1970, "Administration Programs for Spanish Speaking Peoples (P599)." National Archives, Adelphi, MD, FO 12958-4-3-08.

in the good of this country and before I presented my five visions.

Although the task seemed almost insurmountable, I was firmly entrenched in my vision of a transformed country that included us. The President had spoken, and party loyalty demanded adherence to his policy. He had bellowed out that it would be our job, his and mine, to destroy the invisible wall of discrimination the European Americans had erected in the Southwest against the Mexican-Americans. I felt buoyed. Only the President could fire me as I went about this arduous task. And arduous it was. I already knew the personal sacrifices demanded from a visionary because of my previous efforts to transform the educational system at Whittier Union High School District. It is all uphill, with few plateaus. (I've often felt that Ravel's "Bolero" would be a good soundtrack for my crusades.) The President had asked me how long I thought it would take to make the needed changes. I had replied, "A generation."

But step by step, we made forward progress. Planning for the first regional council meetings for the Spanish-speaking soon gained top priority. As an initial step, early in my tenure as chairman, I reviewed and explored the essential need to acquire ethnic data. I reminded my staff that Washington only knew us as members of the White race. The White House, Congress, the press, think tanks, and foundations did not know us as Mexican-Americans. I counseled the staff that we were embarking on a whole new voyage. We were going to compel the bureaucracy to count how many of us were employed by the government because the President ordered counting to be done by ethnicity, not color, under our authority. I warned my staff that assistant secretaries would raise hell and charge them with using heavy-handed tactics, but I told them to proceed and not worry. They would be backed up and supported. The assistant secretaries did raise hell, but my staff got the job done.

My staff and I designed two projects. The first, "Project Blue," was created for federal headquarters in Washington, and for it, I instructed my staff to prepare questionnaires that asked for an ethnic and racial count of all employees in each agency, as well as an account of all contracts awarded by race and ethnicity. They also had to develop action plans with timetables, goals, and targets to assure that the newly recognized ethnic group would get jobs and federal resources on parity with others. Quarterly reports would also be required.

Concurrent with Project Blue was "Project Alpha," developed for the regional offices. It was the most comprehensive effort ever initiated at the local level to assess what was being done for the Spanish-speaking. When the President's representatives visited a region, each regional director (RD) was to present findings and timetables. In preparation to kick off the visitations and reports, RDs were instructed to:

1. Communicate effectively the President's genuine concern to federal officials and regional community leaders.

2. Develop action plans with goals and timetables to assure Spanish speakers' participation in each region's employment programs, contract compliance, and procurement.

3. Acquire discretionary monies for funding interagency programs with high visibility and high impact on Spanish-speaking communities.

4. Manage data collection, retrieval, and analysis for a comprehensive assessment of delivery of services to Spanish-speaking Americans.

With the development of task forces, timetables, goals, and targets, we anticipated that we would very significantly influence the federal government to assist the Spanish-speaking over the next five years.

My vision was to have the entire federal government and all the functions it regulated (train and airplane travel, banks, and so on) count participation by, outcomes for, and anything pertaining to the Spanish-speaking. Of course, the entire matter of determining who was a Spanish-speaking person, a Spanish-surnamed American, a Chicano, Mexican-American, mainland Puerto Rican, Cuban, Latino, Latin American, Central American, Hispano, or Hispanic was a puzzle. It seemed prudent to accept that reasonable people would encounter handicaps in counting.

Greatly aided by the advent of computers, statistical data concerning Mexican-Americans and other Spanish-speaking Americans began to grow, making the unknown known. Recall that before the 1970 census, Mexican-Americans were counted as Whites. This means that unlike Blacks, who could prove discrimination with census results that showed disparities across every field of life, the Spanish-speaking, who did not exist in the data before 1970, could not. No one had data on the disparities in our lives, as explained in the previous chapter.

As chairman of the CCOSSP, I expanded the data on Spanish-speaking people exponentially. All federal agencies were required to count Mexican-Americans, mainland Puerto Ricans, Cubans, and other Latinos by ethnicity and the dollar values of the contracts and grant awards they were issued. The count by ethnicity in the federal government began in its regional offices. The presence of Mexican-Americans, mainland Puerto Ricans, Cubans, and other Latinos in the military was also computed. From there, it would be a snap to know, for example, how many Mexican-American colonels and captains were in active service and ready for promotion to general or admiral and how many had been promoted.

In fact, I asked that exact question when I discovered that many Blacks were being elevated to the rank of general. Robert Brown, White House special assistant on Black affairs, had proudly boasted that during Nixon's first term, the number of African-American generals and admirals had increased from two to fourteen. So, when the answer to my query turned out to be zero, I complained to the President. His response was quick: "Go make one."

I called the White House military liaison and informed him of the President's order. I told him, "We want the best full-bird colonel now serving." They found Colonel Richard Cavazos, and he quickly became the first Mexican-American general.

Several years later, on a business trip to Mexico City in 1976, I visited my friend, Ambassador Joe Jova. I met a one-star general in the hallway outside Joe's office. The general gave me a genuine *abrazo* (hug), all the while shedding wet tears on my shoulder. As I looked up quizzically, he proudly pointed to his star and said, "Thank you. I am the one they chose." He retired a four-star general. The Pentagon could promote Blacks during the President's first term because they knew the names of the African-American colonels and captains, but they didn't know the names of the ranking Mexican-Americans. Now they could do the same for Mexican-Americans.

Once the counting started, people in other areas of government also started taking an interest in the previously unknown minority. For example, in May 1972, I received a memo from a White House staffer, Tony McDonald, about Spanish-speaking Medal of Honor winners. The U.S. Department of Veterans Affairs had compiled a list of twenty-six Medal of Honor recipients with Spanish surnames. Eleven had been in World War II, seven were from the Korean War, and eight had served in Vietnam. What a discovery! If place of residence defines ethnic origin, then five were Puerto Rican and the other twenty-one Mexican-American. Eleven of them had died in the years 1943 to 1945; it is highly probable that they had been born in Mexico and were illegal aliens. How good that their ultra-brave patriotism had been noticed and honored.[23]

Meanwhile, Counselor Finch was gathering a high-level team to plan and implement visits to six of the ten Federal Regional Councils. The six chosen regional councils were all located close to Spanish-speaking populations: New York, Atlanta, Chicago, Dallas, Denver, and San Francisco. President Nixon had already assigned Finch, his dear friend and former lieutenant governor of California and former secretary of the U.S. Department of Health, Education and Welfare (HEW), as counselor in charge of all matters affecting the Spanish-speaking. He was particularly instrumental in reorienting the regional offices to count and include the Spanish-speaking.

---

[23] Tony McDonald to Henry Ramirez, memorandum, May 12, 1972, "Spanish Speaking Medal of Honor Winners."

The team Finch organized included top-level representatives of Cabinet Committee member agencies and staff from the Office of Management and Budget (OMB). He added clout to the presidential team with Frank C. Carlucci, deputy director of OMB. Frank Carlucci organized and directed the regional directors to advance the President's special emphasis on programs for the Spanish-speaking: He issued memoranda to the respective chairmen of the targeted federal regional councils, charging them to comply with the implementation of the regional Spanish-speaking programs. The individual agencies responded with proposals of projects for funding and reported how they had utilized advice from representatives of the diverse Spanish-speaking communities from the states served by the regional offices in drafting final plans of action.

The coordinator of all the Federal Regional Councils was the President's close friend and political ally from his first campaign, Patricia Reilly Hitt, Assistant Secretary of HEW. In Washington, however, mere titles do not reveal the real power that those connected to the source can exercise where or when needed. Assistant Secretary Patricia Hitt was well connected indeed and an awesome center of power and influence. She was very close to her mentors, Finch and Nixon. In fact, as a native of Whittier, California, she and her husband had been in the small circle that launched Nixon's political career.

Figure 4. Counselor Robert Finch, Assistant Secretary Patricia Hitt, Chairman Henry M. Ramirez, and others receive an orientation to the procedures for the regional agency directors' presentations on how they would implement the President's orders. *(Personal collection of Henry M. Ramirez)*

The regional directors met with Counselor Finch, the assistant secretaries, and me to report on their progress toward the goals and objectives set by the President (Figure 4). It was rewarding to observe that their data on contracts and personnel included Spanish-surnamed Americans as well: In 1971, we were counted at the regional and local level for the first time. For the first time in history, the federal government was truly focusing on this new and emerging group of Americans, the Spanish-surnamed. The regional offices could now use demographic data on Spanish-surnamed populations in the states they served by analyzing the results from the 1970 census. The agencies would also now know where this new group lived and how many there were, so they could deliver programs where needed.

The first regional conference meeting took place in Chicago on October 14 and 15, 1971. I could have selected San Francisco, Dallas, Denver, Atlanta, or New York, but my first choice was the Midwest. My motive was to address Mexican-Americans living in the Midwest—who were not only invisible but unknown. Hardly anyone knew they existed. They had not even undergone the experience of being forgotten! But over one million Spanish-surnamed Americans lived in Illinois, Indiana, Michigan, Minnesota, Ohio, and Wisconsin (states served by Region V offices). A cluster of vibrant, vocal, and voting mainland Puerto Ricans lived in northern Chicago, but Mexican-Americans were scattered among rural, urban, and suburban places.

Recall that in the wake of the Mexican Revolution of 1910, there was disorder, lawlessness, and bloody religious persecution in Mexico. Many innocent and hapless Mexicans suffered under Marxist strategies for destruction of the Catholic Church and murder of its adherents. Young families fled their primitive, rural living conditions (primarily from the states of Guanajuato, Michoacan, Zacatecas, Aguascalientes, Durango, Jalisco, and Queretaro in central Mexico, an area known as El Bajio) to resettle not only in the Southwest United States, but also Chicago and the upper Midwest.

Historian Jose Rojas Garciduenas, who had grown up with my parents in Salamanca, Guanajuato, was an eyewitness of the town's refugee exodus. In *Salamanca: Recuerdos de mi tierra guanajuatense*, he wrote, "The poor refugees went to California or the Midwest. The middle class and professionals fled to San Antonio, Texas, or similar places in the United States or Mexico City. The well-off and landed class went to Europe."[24]

Those poor refugees he wrote of tended to be indigent, illiterate, landless Mestizo peasants; at the time many of them were young married couples with small children. For them, railroad freight cars often provided their escape to the north. Railroads were used by the revolution to transport horses, arms, and war material from the United States to the warring sections of the country, including El Bajio. On their return to the United States for more supplies, the trains would stop to replenish water for their steam engines, and poor refugees would climb aboard the empty freight cars for their journey north. Of course, the few refugees who could afford a ticket rode in passenger cars, but the Mestizo peasants had no money.

Crossing into the United States was no big deal, and once there, the poor Mexican exiles encountered labor recruiters in the border towns busily trying to attract them to the flourishing citrus industry in California or to the thriving Great Lakes. Labor agents processed tens of thousands of workers and placed them on trains with money to travel to their new jobs. Families separated as some members chose the Midwest over the West. I personally knew families in Pomona, California, whose cousins and uncles had separated after they crossed the border. The Topeka and Santa Fe Railroad transported workers from El Paso, Texas, to Argentine or Emporia, Kansas, and from there, workers decided: California or Chicago or elsewhere.

---

[24] Jose Rojas Garciduenas, *Salamanca: Recuerdos de mi tierra guanajuatense* (Mexico: Editorial Porrua, S.A., 1982), p. 13.

But from the perspective of the CCOSSP in 1971, we realized we were dealing with the *children* of these Mexican Revolution refugees. They were born in the generation of World War I and many served in World War II. They were now middle-aged, educated, bilingual, and married with families of their own, and they demanded inclusion in the American Dream. Whereas their refugee parents had been born into and raised in a feudal society—that is, in haciendas or rancherias each about five miles away from the next hacienda or small town—these war veterans were returning to school on the GI Bill, getting educated to live in a capitalist society. Spanish had become a second language. (I am a prime example of the loss of fluency. I had to spend the summer of 1951 in Mexico trying to acquire fluency in the skills of speaking and listening to spoken Spanish.)

As I planned for the Chicago regional conference, I realized I had no personal knowledge of who was who among the Hispanic leadership in the Midwest, so I hired Roy Fuentes, a longtime Midwesterner. Roy was a Michigan educator involved in the civil rights movement in the Midwest; he knew the Mexican-American leaders and community organizers personally. He became our ambassador to and from the Midwest Mexican-American communities. The Puerto Rican community was represented by a well-known minister with whom I had worked on prior events, but whose name I do not now recall.

In early September 1971, in advance of the Chicago regional conference meeting, member agencies of CCOSSP dispatched trained personnel to Chicago to teach members of community organizations how to apply for government grants and how to deal with the federal contract and grant regulations.

Just prior to the meeting, we issued a press release dated October 12, 1971: "Committee Chairman and White House Officials to Meet in Chicago with Spanish Speaking Community Leaders from Six States." It was subtitled "Washington Delegation to Present Demands of Community Leaders to Regional Directors of 7 Federal Agencies," while one of its statements noted: "Mr. Ramirez emphasized that he and Counselor Finch arranged the trip, at the request of the President, to discuss the problems of the federal government toward alleviating and eliminating the problems of the Spanish speaking."

Despite our best efforts and planning, however, the Chicago trip got off to a rocky start: In the evening prior to the regional conference, community leaders were invited to meet with the personal representatives of President Nixon to discuss their concerns. The meeting was the first time anything like this had taken place in Chicago. Unfortunately, the leaders arrived a little tipsy and belligerent. Disregarding the intent and purpose of the meeting, they used rough language, some bad gestures, and unacceptable behavior. I was told later that they had been loyal to "the" mayor.

Nevertheless, a productive meeting of some duration took place the following day with all the directors of the federal agency members of the Federal Regional Council. The reports from each agency showed that they were including Mexican-Americans and Puerto Ricans and reaching out with government services. Later that evening, the Federal Regional Council hosted a large reception that was very well attended and very nice.

Overall, the Chicago regional conference was highly successful (Figure 5). Due to the diligent work of the government grant and contract specialists, who had reached out for the first time and showed community groups how to apply for grants related to education, training, housing, health, and more, about $75 million was awarded to Spanish-speaking organizations that had never participated in government programs before.

Figure 5. A small segment of the crowd of Mexican-American and mainland Puerto Rican leaders at the first regional conference in Chicago of eleven federal agencies, mobbing Counselor Finch in this corner. *(Personal collection of Henry M. Ramirez)*

Further benefits and outcomes of our regional conference would manifest themselves in time by way of profound systemic improvements. Some improvements were realized in counting for the first time how much money was awarded in contracts and grants to Mexican-Americans and Puerto Ricans. Just as significant, the number of Mexican-Americans and Puerto Ricans employed in the federal regional agencies was established for the first time. It was of paramount importance that the Mexican-Americans and Puerto Ricans of the Midwest be included in the nearby services of their federal government. That a Republican president was directing the show was, for me, absolutely irrelevant.

Despite our success, however, the conference in Chicago showed me how the media worked concerning President Nixon. Chicago was a media town. It operated under the iron rule of the big-boss Democrat Mayor Richard J. Daley. While the Spanish-language media handled their job in a very positive and informative manner, the English media manifested their traditionally liberal, biased, pro-Democrat side. They looked for angles and phraseology to present prejudiced misinformation to their public. I did a half-hour interview on Spanish-language TV's *Oiga Amigo*, which went very well. In contrast, on October 14, 1971, *ABC Eyewitness News* aired this report by Fahey Flynn:

A fact-finding committee from the U.S. Department of Health, Education and Welfare visited a settlement house in a Chicago Spanish-speaking community this afternoon...but there was some reported reluctance to permit news coverage. Frank Agraz reports: "Casa Atzlan was one of the spots toured today by presidential counselor Robert Finch; Dr. Henry Valmedes, chairman of the Cabinet Committee on Opportunities for the Spanish-Speaking; and recently appointed HEW regional director, Richard Friedman. Even though press releases heralded the visit to Chicago, there was an unexplained hesitancy to allow Channel Seven News to film the official sight-seeing trip. Director of Casa Atzlan, Molly Cabildo—while happy to show off her three-story, brightly painted building—never got around to asking why the group was there—and no one told her. The tour and some meetings tonight with Latin American community leaders was described by a news release as the first in a series of conferences in seven cities to acquaint the federal government with the problems of the nation's fifteen million Spanish-speaking residents. It would appear that the government wants to do its homework on the nation's second largest minority in private. If only everybody would leave them alone."[25]

Let me clarify. Mr. Flynn, a professionally trained wordsmith, had a copy of our press release in his hands and could not read the name "Ramirez" correctly. He pronounced it *"Valmedes."* Then he identified the community leaders as "Latin American." But he worked in Chicago. Did he not know that they were Mexican-Americans and mainland Puerto Ricans? And, of course, for a liberal, it is *de rigueur* to finish his report not with a fact, but with an editorial opinion.

In contrast to the television media, most newspapers in the six-state region reported on the conference in a straightforward manner without stinging or emotional verbs, adjectives, and adverbs. The newspaper *El Informador*, catering to Mexican-Americans, wrote a lengthy, comprehensive, and informative story. The opening line in the article reads in my English translation: "Eleven agencies of the federal government convene for the purpose of executing the orders of President Nixon relative to Spanish-speaking Americans."[26] The publisher of *El Informador*, Charlie Gomez, was not a puppet of Mayor Daley.

---

[25] Fahey Flynn, WLS-TV, Chicago, IL: October 14, 1971, 10 p.m. Radio TV Reports, Inc.

[26] "Henry M. Ramirez Estara en Chicago el dia 14 de Octubre," *El Informador*, October 17, 1971.

On the other hand, the Puerto Rican paper, *El Puertorriqueno*, used negative, anti-Mexican, and evil-spirited verbiage. The headline translated as "President Nixon Hunts for Votes."[27] That is hardly news. In a democracy, the number-one job of any politician is to get votes. The reiteration of that basic reality did not provide information or political education to a population hungry for it, nor did it offer any insight into what the associated article contained. What a loss to the people for the arrogant satisfaction of Mayor Daley's buddies.

Likewise, the *Chicago Sun-Times* also did an extensive report giving its liberal European American readership a stereotype of unruly and childish Mexican-Americans and mainland Puerto Ricans. Their reporter discovered the most important and salient aspect of the regional conference to be that it was a stormy session of U.S. officials and Latins. Media work of this genre showed they did not know who we were, but my understanding of the English-language media was growing rapidly.

The trip to the information-gathering bowels of Chicago taught me that I was not going to get much fair and objective treatment from the media in my efforts to educate and inform Spanish-surnamed Americans on the federal government's new Nixon-era interest in knocking down walls of discrimination. On the contrary, they would follow the example of longtime White House reporter Sarah McClendon: They would bear false witness. They would play the game of advocating for their side of the story: liberalism as defined by Nietzsche.

As I write these lines, my retrospection on the first regional conference elicits opinions, thoughts,

---

[27] Fernando J. Fernandez, "Presidente Nixon BUSCA VOTOS," *El Puertorriqueno*, October 7–13, 1971.

observations, and conclusions. During my three years of work at the U.S. Commission on Civil Rights, I had come into contact with various people involved in the civil rights arena. Yet I did not know the extent to which Mexicans of the Diaspora had settled in the Midwest. Further, I had no understanding of the acculturation undergone by their Mexican-American children, who were now World War II veterans with their own children. I had no studies on their political standings, practice of religion, educational attainment and achievement, or employment patterns.

Fact is, I was naïve. You might wonder whether I held the perception that we "Washington big shots" were going to teach the Mexicans of the Midwest and bring them up to-date. Well, no! I honestly wanted to share the good outcomes that President Richard Nixon wanted for us. I truly expected to find a warm welcome in Chicago. But that was not to be! I had not factored the possible involvement of the mayor of Chicago and his total control of all around him. I knew in the 1960 presidential race of Kennedy and Nixon that Mayor Daley had stolen that election by fraud in Cook County. Our regional conference in Chicago took place merely ten years later.

One action I took upon my return to Washington was to start a monthly newsletter to counteract misinformation in the unreliable media and make sure Nixon's message got out. The newsletter, called *Hoy,* was under the direction of its editor, E. B. Duarte, from Brownsville, Texas. A list of 20,000 people received monthly copies, including congressmen, senators, key government officials, Washington movers and shakers, and leading community figures in the Spanish-speaking world. *Hoy* presented the administration's achievements—not promises—for the Spanish-speaking people in simple, declarative sentences without colorful or emotion-laden adverbs and adjectives.

Besides my crash course on the media, what were other takeaways from the first regional conference? The federal agencies serving the six states of Region V began to collect data on employment and contract awards under the category of Spanish-speaking people. Mainland Puerto Ricans and Mexican-Americans would no longer be uncounted and unknown. And no longer would the Region V Latinos vent frustrations over their conviction that Washington had ignored them. Importantly, this was the first time any president had really addressed himself directly and personally to the regional problems and conditions of Spanish-speaking peoples abiding in the Midwest. President Richard M. Nixon was the first, and he did this through two close personal friends, Bob Finch and Pat Hitt, and me, his Chicano assistant.

Soon after the Chicago conference, Finch led the way to New York City on behalf of the President and the CCOSSP, where the next regional conference was held on December 9, 1971 (Figure 6). This meeting was closed to the public and was conducted in the mode of a very high-level governmental conference. Its emphasis was almost entirely on what plans the various federal regional agencies would implement for mainland Puerto Ricans.

Frank J. Groschelle, chairman of the Federal Regional Council for Region IV (based in Atlanta, Georgia), sent Counselor Finch a copy of the action plan for his region on March 22, 1972. In his letter, he noted that the Region IV Council had tapped the advice from representatives of the Spanish-speaking communities in Miami and Tampa in drafting this final plan of action. Groschelle also wrote to another member of the presidential team, Frank C. Carlucci, who chaired the Undersecretaries Group for

Regional Operations in the Executive Office of the President at OMB, informing him of projects identified for funding.

Figure 6. Regional conference in New York City, December 9, 1971. *(Personal collection of Henry M. Ramirez)*

Counselor Finch personally launched the follow-up work with instructive letters for the regional directors on how they were to continue implementing the action plans presented at the regional conferences. In a very short time, the vision expressed by President Nixon in August 1971 was being actualized.[28] Presidents Kennedy and Johnson had talked a good talk and snookered the Mexican-Americans, but they did not walk the talk of their famous speeches. With President Nixon, efforts to

---

[28] Nixon Presidential Materials, "Accomplishments of CCOSS," National Archives, Adelphi, MD, FO 12958-4-3-08.

include Mexican-Americans, mainland Puerto Ricans, and other Spanish-surnamed Americans in the mainstream of American life at all levels of the federal government were bearing fruit. A popular Mexican dictum is *"hechos, no dichos"* ("deeds, not words"). And President Nixon complied with *hechos*.

Washington has another dictum: "Personnel are policy." The next step called for appointments of Spanish-speaking personnel as federal regional directors of agencies. The first highly visible evidence of changes, in addition to the internal work of data gathering, would be well-publicized appointments of Latinos to powerful positions: the directors of six regional and district offices.

5. NIXON APPOINTS HISPANICS TO HIGH-LEVEL OFFICES

The regional conferences discussed in the last chapter were one of the five visions I presented on a note card to President Nixon in the Oval Office in August 1971. Another one of the visions on that card called for the appointment of 100 Mexican-Americans to executive positions in his administration. My concept for this vision rested on the practices of large corporations. They appoint board members to help run them, so why not bring in new "board members" to help run the federal government? We Chicanos had served in the military as officers of high rank. We owned successful businesses. We were emerging in the sciences, higher education, local and state government, and corporate management. We were ready for inclusion in federal government decision-making. President Nixon was responsive to this desire. He vowed to include us in the decision-making process and in the ranks of government workers. Since he had direct control over the assignment of high-level government executives, he made it happen—and it was hugely successful. This is how it came about.

In the first meeting of the Cabinet Committee on Opportunities for Spanish-Speaking People (CCOSSP) on August 5, 1971, President Nixon had ordered a nationwide recruitment drive to bring more Spanish-speaking Americans into government decision-making positions. He directed department heads to open top jobs for Mexican-Americans, and actions to carry out his direction started shortly after the first Cabinet meeting. (The President's awareness of Mexicans arose primarily from his knowledge of them in his youth. But because the conditions of the Puerto Ricans and Cubans were also rising in awareness by 1971, the CCOSSP also thereby included them.)

Counselor Finch had already reorganized the Office of Presidential Personnel. Fred Malek was put in charge. Under him, Barbara Franklin was given the mission of identifying women for top jobs, while William "Mo" Marumoto was to recruit the Spanish-speaking. With Counselor Finch thus staffing the White House with "his" team, Washington would finally "get it." The executive search process to identify, recruit, and appoint Spanish-surnamed Americans to high-level executive positions became a hectic rush.

William Marumoto scheduled weekly meetings in his White House office to review high-level vacancies to see if they could be filled with Spanish-speaking executive talent. He gathered four persons to participate in the process: me, the chairman of CCOSSP; Carlos Conde of the White House Communications Office; Tony Rodriguez, former executive director of CCOSSP on loan from his employment at the State Department; and Alex

Armendariz, a staffer on the presidential reelection committee.

Conde was assigned to assist Herb Klein, the director of the White House Communications Office. His job was hugely important: to inform the Spanish-speaking population of presidential actions and assure them that their needs were being met in employment, grants, and contracts. As for Tony Rodriguez, we decided that he would be able to vet prospective high-level candidates from a private, secure location with limited access. Thus, Marumoto assigned an office for Tony Rodriguez and his secretary in a separate building, the New Executive Office Building. (People in the New Executive Office Building still enjoyed the privilege of saying they worked "in the White House" and could use White House stationery. For recruiting purposes, it was impressive.)

The White House's nationwide executive search caused a never-before-seen excitement in the hearts and minds of Mexican-Americans, mainland Puerto Ricans, Cubans, and other Latinos. Men and women were being called and recommended, their resumes requested, and many were interviewed in the White House. For me, the experience was incomparable and unique. I was an observer of history in the making, even while being a vital participant. On my frequent trips around the country, I was besieged by persons with resumes or those recommending their friends. In the White House, the five of us involved in implementing the White House executive search for Hispanics were nicknamed "the Brown Mafia" (I was called "the Godfather").

I also led a small group of Hispanics who met from time to time with a small group of Blacks headed up by Robert J. Brown, White House special assistant on Black affairs. In an upstairs establishment on 14th Street, we studied a list of high-level positions the White House Personnel Office was working on that had been marked for "minorities." We discussed amicably which should go to Browns and which to Blacks. Our agreements also meant our candidates received our mutual support.

The undreamed-of results of our work following President Nixon's orders were soon demonstrated: A report dated January 7, 1972, stated that the President had made twenty-six presidential and supergrade appointments of Spanish-surnamed Americans, a mere five months after he had verbalized his wishes.[29] Of additional significance was the fact that the regional conferences were also bearing fruit. Seven Spanish-surnamed persons were appointed as regional directors for the first time in history!

Monthly reports kept Counselor Finch and Fred Malek informed. Barely ten months after the presidential orders for the Hispanic executive search were issued, a report noted that Nixon had made thirty-three presidential and supergrade appointments to date, and "it appears we will have more within a matter of weeks."[30] Remarkably, by the following November, the number had grown to a historic fifty-four. An equally high number of appointments to boards, commissions, and advisory committees were also recorded.[31] Figure 7 shows some of them.

---

[29] White House Office of Presidential Personnel, "Spanish Surnamed Presidential and Supergrade Appointees Under the Nixon Administration as of January 7, 1972." National Archives.

[30] White House Office of Presidential Personnel, "High-level Spanish Speaking Appointments, June 20, 1972." National Archives.

31 White House Office of Presidential Personnel, "Spanish Surnamed Presidential Supergrade and Key Appointees Under the

Figure 7. October 27, 1972, photograph of presidential appointees in the Cabinet Room with President Richard M. Nixon. Left to right, clockwise: William "Mo" Marumoto, special assistant to the president; Carlos Villareal, administrator, Urban Mass Transportation; Ray Telles, commissioner, Equal Employment Opportunity Commission; Joseph Jova, ambassador to the Organization of American States; Louis Nunez, deputy staff director, U.S. Commission on Civil Rights; Bert Gallegos, general counsel, Office of Economic Opportunity (OEO); Carlos Conde, White House staff assistant; Antonio (Tony) Rodriguez, on loan from the U.S. State Department; Rudy Montejano, commissioner, Interstate Commerce Commission; Dr. Henry M. Ramirez, chairman, CCOSSP; the President; Romana Banuelos, U.S. Treasurer; Phillip Sanchez, director, OEO; and Senator Robert Dole. *(Courtesy Richard M. Nixon Library)*

One U.S. Commission on Civil Rights appointment was that of distinguished lawyer Manuel Ruiz. To the press, it was just another presidential appointment and

Nixon Administration as of November 1972." National Archives.

received very little play. A Mexican Mestizo born in Mazatlan, Ruiz had been the first Latino graduate from the University of Southern California Law School in 1930 and was considered the "California dean" of Mexican-American lawyers. He authored numerous works, including *Mexican-American Legal Heritage in the Southwest*, and was one of the founders of the Mexican-American Political Association (MAPA). Commissioner Ruiz had been well known since the 1930s as a civil rights activist for Mexican-Americans.

Manuel Ruiz was not the first Mexican-American commissioner, however. The first was Dr. Hector Garcia, a Corpus Christi medical doctor appointed to the U.S. Commission on Civil Rights by President Lyndon Johnson (and, in contrast to Ruiz's appointment, that one act was heralded highly in the media as of huge significance for Mexican-Americans). Yet, the fact that the first Mexican-American commissioner, Hector Garcia, did not display interest in the Commission's own Mexican American Studies Division disappointed me and my staff of Chicanos and Chicanas greatly. Precisely at that time, we at the Mexican American Studies Division were designing our vast study of educational practices in the Southwest. He never asked for any kind of report, and he never visited our beehive. He never learned my name nor even of my existence, and yet I was the designer of the Mexican American Education Study. So, imagine how I reacted when I was summoned to the office of the executive director of the Civil Rights Commission (who was himself a lawyer) and instructed, along with several other employees, to "put the touch on" people who had received contracts from the Commission to pay for a going-away party for Dr. Garcia, as his term as commissioner had expired.

Some years later, however, when the Reagan White House asked me, along with Henry Zuniga of El Paso, Texas, and Alex Armendariz of Washington, DC, for a list of three Mexican-Americans to consider for the Presidential Medal of Honor, Dr. Garcia's name arose. Henry Zuniga pushed hard for Dr. Garcia, and Alex seconded him. It was only reluctantly, and for the sake of unity, that I acquiesced in recognition for his dedication and work as the founder of the American GI Forum, a Hispanic veterans and civil rights organization. He got the medal.

Dr. Garcia was an enigma. He was deeply partisan, almost to the point of being irrational. He was born into a family of landowning Criollos (Spaniards) in northern Mexico and raised in a privileged society that lived by strict behavioral criteria regarding class differences. But the Revolution of 1910 caused the extended Garcia family to hustle out of their lands and head for the nearest towns across the Rio Grande. There in Mercedes, Texas, they set up a retail business to serve the starving, naked, poor, and illiterate Mexican Mestizos fleeing from the horrors of that Mexican Revolution. Young Hector attended the University of Texas at Austin during the Depression and became a medical doctor in 1940. He encountered no discrimination. He was, after all, a European American. He looked no different from his European American classmates and university society. His only salient differences were that he spoke Spanish, had a Spanish surname, and had come from Mexico.

My source for many details of Dr. Garcia's life was Mo Garcia, who was my personal assistant and confidant during my tenure as chairman. Dr. Garcia and Mo were first cousins; their fathers were brothers. In Mexico, these brothers had attended a teacher's college at a time when the philosophy of scientific Positivism was sweeping Mexico, the French ideology that inspired the Mexican Revolution in 1910. This godless philosophy says that Reason is the only worthy driving force of humanity and that the Catholic religion is a tool of human retardation. I think the Cartesian system of epistemology won the day in Mexico in the brains of the rebellious intellectuals and educated classes. Mo Garcia was raised in a separate town. He became an agnostic.

There is a vivid similarity between Dr. Garcia's life and that of his contemporary, Henry B. Gonzalez, a Democratic congressman from Texas. The Gonzalez family, too, were educated Criollo landowners from northern Mexico who had come to Texas. A *National Journal* article by Jonathan Cottin with quotes from Gonzalez clearly shows how fierce the opposition was to Nixon's achievements for Mexican-Americans.

Cottin first wrote: "President Nixon has ordered a nationwide recruitment drive to bring more Mexican-Americans into government policy-making positions. Mr. Nixon directed department heads to open top jobs for Spanish-speaking Americans during an August 5 meeting of the Cabinet Committee on Opportunities for the Spanish Speaking People. 'He used very firm language,' recalled Henry M. Ramirez, committee chairman. 'He put it to them.'"

But then Mr. Cottin balanced his nice reportage on Nixon's efforts with these statements: "Representative Henry B. Gonzalez (D., Texas) said Mr. Nixon has 'merely continued' programs designed to help Mexican-Americans started by Presidents Kennedy and Johnson. 'I don't think he's improved it,' said Gonzalez. 'The President has done things to get headlines,' Gonzalez added. 'But the appointments have been political hacks lacking any particular knowledgeability or clout.'"[32]

In my view, it seems that neither Henry B. Gonzalez nor Hector Garcia could rid themselves of their European sense of superiority over the Mexican Mestizos that President Nixon and I were bringing to high-level government positions. Of course, they were also deeply partisan Democrats, and blindly so.

Yes, 1972 was a challenging and cognitively difficult time for partisan Democratic Mexican-American politicos. Their hopes and wishes had vanished under Kennedy and Johnson. President Richard M. Nixon advanced the Mexican-American community with unexpected "first time evers."

---

[32] Jonathan Cottin, "Republicans Woo Mexican Americans," *National Journal*, September 25, 1971.

141

6. NIXON ORDERS EQUAL EMPLOYMENT OPPORTUNITIES

With emotion and deep urgency, President Nixon told me man to man that he wanted his Cabinet officers to include Mexican-Americans in the federal government, as already described. And we at the Cabinet Committee on Opportunities for Spanish-Speaking People (CCOSSP) set out to accomplish that goal.

This was not a new desire for Nixon. Soon after the Second World War, then-Congressman Nixon and his cohorts started including Mexican-Americans in California government. Beginning in the 1950s, a visionary congressman named Pat Hillings persuaded Nixon and his friend, Robert Finch, to get the Republican Party in California to begin a serious outreach to young Mexican-Americans, who were urbane and sophisticated ex-GIs. Two persons exercised hands-on leadership: Stu Spencer and Robert Finch.

Both of these men had first-hand familiarity with Mexican-Americans. A native of Phoenix and son of an Arizona legislator, Finch graduated from Occidental College in Eagle Rock, California, which lies between downtown Los Angeles and the Rose Bowl in Pasadena; he raised his family in that area. By virtue of his upbringing and early adulthood, he got to know his Mexican-American contemporaries. In 1966, he was elected lieutenant governor of California on the same ticket that brought the governorship to Ronald Reagan.

Stu Spencer was raised in Alhambra, California, and went to school with East Los Angeles Mexican youths, whom he knew as "Chicanos." Further, Spencer attended colleges in their backyard: East Los Angeles Junior College and California State University, Los Angeles. Spencer was one of the first, if not the first, very successful political campaign managers and consultants in California. His company enjoyed outstanding success and became famous for managing the presidential campaigns of Nixon in 1968 and 1972 as well as two gubernatorial campaigns for Ronald Reagan. Spencer is also well known for overseeing both of Reagan's presidential campaigns in 1980 and 1984. He worked closely with Denny Carpenter, also from Southern California, who was the California Republican Party chairman in the sixties.

Denny Carpenter knew Mexicans very well. As an FBI agent, he had been posted in Mexico City for ten years and had married a Mexican woman. As chairman, Carpenter trained and hired young men like David Gonzales, a former student of mine, to host hospitality rooms at the organizational conferences, meetings, and conventions of Mexican-Americans. These men reached out to the nascent, rising voices of young activist Chicanos who had returned from World War II and the

Korean War and were exiting the barrios, pursuing their GI college education benefits, and entering the ranks of the middle class.

To grasp the national significance of this Nixon-GOP outreach to young Chicanos, one must compare the history of the Kennedy-Democrat overtures to the same set of young Chicanos. Did Kennedy's election in 1960 cause a surge of Mexican-American appointments in Washington to help form his government? The answer is *no*! Did Kennedy bring about national awareness of the presence of this invisible ethnic group called Mexican-Americans? A big, fat *no* is the answer. True, celebrations of his election among these young ex-GIs were described as "*a gritos y sombrerasos*" (shouts and hat-tossings). But afterwards, the Mexican-Americans who had been deeply involved in the "Viva Kennedy Clubs" of his presidential campaign stood around in circles asking each other, "Now what?" They learned the answer: Nothing. Nothing happened.

The Kennedy group and its New York media followers focused their attention and efforts instead on Mexican-Americans working in the rural and farm areas, achieving the very laudable goal of unionization with Cesar Chavez. Then, the tragic November 1963 death of President Kennedy caused the elevation of Lyndon Johnson to the presidency. His incumbency to complete Kennedy's term saw huge changes, with the enactment of civil rights laws in 1964. These laws improved the lot of Blacks almost immediately, but not Mexican-Americans—not yet, anyway. They stayed in the back pews to pray and hope in silence.

The Mexican-American civil rights movements of the 1960s were known by these terms: *La Causa* or *El Movimiento*. They were diffused and unfocused. The

League of United Latin American Citizens (LULAC) had been founded in 1929 in Laredo, Texas. The founders were primarily Criollos who had been educated leaders (lawyers, judges, and businessmen) and had not suffered the injustices of the Diaspora. They were, however, concerned that the hordes of Mestizos crossing the border into the United States during the 1910–1930 Diaspora should learn English, and they set about teaching them how to become "Latin American citizens." In 1965, the leadership changed the League's direction, however, and become more focused on the denial of civil rights for Mexican-Americans. That same year, the League elected its first Mestizo president, Al Hernandez, who was a Mexican-American lawyer. Another organization, the American GI Forum, had been established for the specific cause of fighting discrimination against Mexican-American ex-GIs. As Mexican-American migrants from South Texas settled down in the West and Midwest, additional chapters of the American GI Forum were established. A third organization, the Mexican-American Political Association (MAPA), was formed in California by lawyers and activists to increase participation by Mexican-Americans in the political process.

Organizations such as these had education and employment as top priorities, but the fact that Mexican-Americans were still classified as Whites was a big obstacle to improving the employment situation. In 1966, the University of California at Los Angeles issued its first mammoth report on its Mexican-American study project but did not include information on employment of Mexican-Americans. (The project's bibliography alone was over 100 pages long. The list of references demonstrates the disparate nomenclature for persons of

Mexican background: Spanish, Spanish-speaking, Spanish-surnamed, Mexican, Mexican-American, and Latin American.)

After winning election to his own first term in 1964, President Johnson continued to provide scant recognition of the young, restless, and demanding Chicanos out West. The Mexican-Americans in Colorado under Corky Gonzales were beginning to act out. In New Mexico, Reies Tijerina was challenging land grants and ownership.

By 1966, the problems in Mexican-American employment were becoming clear, and Mexican-Americans were beginning to emulate the success of the Blacks in drawing attention to their plight. Phil Montez, a psychologist who had been born and raised in Watts, a city a few miles southwest of Los Angeles, California, had just recently been hired by the U.S. Commission on Civil Rights and assigned as director of its Western Field Office in L.A. Almost as part of his job, he became the agent for developing organizations and events to advance the awareness of civil rights in the Chicano communities. His office became a Southwestern beehive for coordinating people, organizations, and events focused on the issue of employment disparities in the federal government.

Every other Saturday, Phil Montez and I, along with ten other Chicanos, met at Swalley's Restaurant on Olympic Boulevard in East Los Angeles to discuss how to advance the civil rights of Chicanos. We organized a plan to confront the newly established Equal Employment Opportunities Commission (EEOC) at its March 1966 hearings in Albuquerque, New Mexico, by designing a walkout. We chose Phil Montez to lead the protest and Armando Rodriguez, an educator, as its spokesman.

The protest was to complain that the EEOC had no Mexican-American member. Charles Erickson, former *Los Angeles Times* reporter and one of the twelve Chicanos at Swalley's, issued information to the press so that news of the confrontation could be widely disseminated. We also invited members of two other organizations, LULAC and the Political Association of Spanish-Speaking Organizations (PASSO). With their presence, the confrontation included a wider spectrum of activist civil rights membership. The walkout shouted to the civil rights community that a group called Chicanos wanted a place at the civil rights table. It alerted the nation and the Democratic Party in particular.

In response, Dr. Hector Garcia, a deeply partisan Democrat and close friend of President Lyndon Johnson, worked feverishly on his White House Texas connections to get Johnson to do something for the Mexican-American community. Eventually, he did. On June 9, 1967 (well over a year after the Albuquerque walkout), President Johnson nominated Vicente Ximenes as an EEOC commissioner. Ximenes had been born and raised in the small, segregated Texas town of Floresville, where his father had worked on the hacienda of the big landowner of the region, John Connolly.

Johnson also nominated his friend Dr. Garcia as a commissioner at the U.S. Commission on Civil Rights a year later in 1968. So, as President Johnson was exiting the White House, the hopeful loyal Mexican-American Democrats had achieved two appointments in the arena of civil rights. Out of the 3,000-plus appointments a president usually made in those years, one who grew up amid millions of Mexicans and Mexican-Americans finally made two! And the Mexican-Americans who were Democrats then heralded the feat. They still do today!

On the same day he appointed Vicente Ximenes an EEOC commissioner, President Johnson also authorized a new organization, the Inter-Agency Committee on Mexican-American Affairs. It was composed of the heads of five agencies: the Secretary of Labor; the Secretary of Health, Education and Welfare (HEW); the Secretary of Housing and Urban Development (HUD); the Secretary of Agriculture; and the director of the Office of Economic Opportunity. Their purpose was to assure that federal programs were reaching Mexican-Americans and to provide the assistance they needed. At the White House ceremony creating the new agency, President Johnson appointed Vicente Ximenes to two positions: chairman of the just-created Inter-Agency Committee and EEOC commissioner.

June 9, 1967, was a banner day. In one day, President Johnson created a committee, swore in a new EEOC commissioner, and named a chairman to a Cabinet-level committee. However, the Inter-Agency Committee on Mexican-American Affairs had a small budget. And it never met. Its chairman would later lament that he could never get hold of the committee's Cabinet members, but instead had to rely on contacts with lower-level bureaucrats.

Events would soon demonstrate a stark contrast between President Nixon and his men as compared with Kennedy and Johnson and theirs. The historical facts demonstrate that with Nixon, Mexican-Americans progressed, whereas under Kennedy and Johnson, they remained invisible. With the unexpected election of "that Nixon guy," Democratic Mexican-Americans went into shock. It became *our turn*, and we were ready.

President Richard M. Nixon was to make Mexican-Americans known and visible as real participants. His friend and Cabinet member Robert Finch, as Secretary of HEW, gathered a crowd of California Mexican-American talent and placed them in key spots at HEW, for example. One might say that Robert Finch led an "invasion" of Mexican-American talent into Washington the likes of which had never been seen before. These young Mexican-American professionals brought by Finch and others were mostly Democrats who had been brainwashed by Democratic liberals in higher education. Yet they wanted to make a difference in advancing "La Causa." It did not take a lot of time to cure them of their political immaturity, and almost all of them eventually registered Republican. One exception stands out. I placed Henry Cisneros in the White House Fellows Program—the first Mexican-American ever in that prestigious group. However, he refused to register Republican because he wanted to become mayor of San Antonio in the future (which he did in 1981).

In facilitating the arrival of eager young lawyers, Ph.D.s, and other professionals from 3,000 miles away to fill executive government positions, we did not overlook the pressing need for the employment of Mexican-Americans in the lower and middle levels of government, too. But there was a major obstacle. The enforcers of the Civil Rights Act of 1964 did not know Mexican-Americans. The actions of the U.S. Civil Rights Commission to count us in government employment did not start until four years later, in 1968. Moreover, the 1964 laws established a new agency in charge of minority employment, the EEOC. It was responsible for overseeing and enforcing the prohibition on employment discrimination. Each federal agency was required to establish an office to administer the civil rights laws, and the EEOC would watchdog each agency's personnel division. The Fourteenth Amendment would now be enforced, but did it include us? No! These offices focused on recruiting, training, and employing Blacks only.

The need for a "parallel" EEOC for Mexican-Americans was evident. So, in 1970, the CCOSSP drafted its own wonderful, gallant initiatives to increase government employment for Spanish-speaking people. There were some speed bumps, of course; after all, we had only just been counted, and the analysis of the data had barely begun by the end of 1970.

One of the speed bumps was the U.S. Civil Service Commission (CSC). The CSC functioned to increase the employment of African-Americans in the civil service of the federal government. Prior to Nixon's administration, Mexican-Americans were not included in the civil service—only in the military. To overcome this, three people at the Cabinet Committee formulated the "Sixteen-Point Program": Martin Castillo (who was then the CCOSSP chairman); John Bareno, CCOSSP executive director; and Merci Hernandez, CCOSSP personnel director. As best as I can reconstruct the history of this program from the evidence,[33] Merci Hernandez had developed a guide for equal employment opportunity training while working with the U.S. Air Force, probably in the 1960s. In 1969 and 1970, Merci Hernandez and Irving Kator, assistant executive director of the CSC, developed a list of actions for recruiting Spanish-speaking professionals for federal positions. This list became the basis for the Sixteen-Point Program. In essence it became an initiative for Mexican-Americans parallel to the EEOC rules, which at that time applied to Blacks only.

---

[33] John T. Bareno, "Enhancing Affirmative Action History," *La Luz*, December–January, 1980.

Unfortunately, the initiative remained dormant and unused. It was just another federal program in the books. As chief of the Mexican American Studies Division at the U.S. Commission on Civil Rights at the time, I should have been very aware of this initiative and program, but all I knew about it was that it was called the "Sixteen-Point Program." What further stymied its application was the fact that the leader of the CCOSSP left in November 1970. The CCOSSP lacked leadership and direction for nine months before my Oval Office meeting with the President.

At the meeting of the Cabinet Committee on August 5, 1971, President Nixon expressed deep frustration at the failure of his government to increase employment of the Spanish-speaking. He clenched his fist and his facial muscles tightened as he remarked, "A year ago, I announced the Sixteen-Point Program to assist Spanish-speaking citizens interested in federal employment, and you have been dragging your feet."

In our meetings that day, President Nixon exhibited the demeanor of a warrior who finally got what he had wanted. This was going to be his second chance to get his administration on the right track for the advancement of a people he had known since early life—a people who had been ignored, overlooked, and neglected. The President had proclaimed loudly and clearly that he wanted us still-forgotten and ignored Mexican-Americans to be included in mainstream American life. His goal was simple and his expectation clear: "Get it done!"

With the President's forceful impetus, genuine implementation began. In August 1971, the CCOSSP set out to get the whole U.S. government to count Spanish-surnamed Americans in its employment. We revitalized efforts to increase the employment of Spanish-speaking

Americans in government via the Sixteen-Point Program as well as by ordering EEOC to include us in their enforcement work. All of this was music to my ears as a leader in the Chicano civil rights movement. I considered that the children of the Mexican Diaspora of 1913–1930 had the constitutional right to be included in *all* segments of our government. After all, many of them were war veterans!

As the Cabinet's boss, only President Nixon could get its officers to cooperate with me, the CCOSSP chairman. I was at a level lower than they, but his support had a leveling effect. At the August 5 meeting, he added very significantly: "If any of you do not cooperate with Henry, he will be able to fire you!" This President, I realized, really gave a damn about us Chicanos.

And would you believe it? George Romney, Secretary of HUD, refused to cooperate with me on assigning Mexican-Americans to positions in the L.A. District Office and the San Francisco Regional Office. During my first visit to his HUD office for a photo opportunity, I complained to Secretary Romney that he was not being a team player with respect to the President's instructions. Secretary Romney responded, "I know full well what Nixon said. But I am running this department, and I will do what I think is best. And further, I realize what he said about your firing any of us who do not follow his instructions." My rejoinder was simple: I would report back to the President and see to it that Romney was fired. He was, and he was replaced by Jim Lynn.

Meanwhile, the nation's top newspapers were getting the drift that something big was happening. Scripps Howard News Service's Seth Kantor reported on August 14, 1971: "The Silent Minority Has a Voice." (He added that the President had told the Cabinet Committee, "You failed me. Do not do it again.")[34] Shortly afterward, the *Washington Post*'s Elsie Carper revealed: "Spanish-Speaking People's Committee Finally Implemented."[35] A writer for the *Los Angeles Herald-Examiner* noted: "New Era for Spanish Speaking."[36] And the print media with the largest Mexican-American readership in the country, the *Los Angeles Times*, weighed in with an in-depth story by Frank del Olmo.[37] At that time, Frank del Olmo was the most respected print reporter on Chicano and Mexican-American activism. His article, "Chicano Wants Involvement, Not Separation" appeared on September 13. The subtitle read: "Ramirez, Nixon Appointee seeks the Good Life for Mexican-Americans." Frank reported straight and factually—with only one error (which thankfully was near the end). He wrote that "the cabinet committee was created by Lyndon B. Johnson in 1967 as the Interagency Committee on Mexican-American Affairs." No wonder academic researchers have repeated the mistake.

Further, although the *Los Angeles Times* had so often given rough treatment to my boss, President Nixon, their hammering typewriter hit the nail squarely on the head in an editorial that opined: "Here in the Southwest we have a particular responsibility for the Mexican-Americans and Mexican Nationals. It is a group which only recently has

---

[34] Seth Kantor, "The Silent Minority Has a Voice," *Scripps-Howard News Service*, August 14, 1971.

[35] Elsie Carper, "Spanish-Speaking People's Committee Finally Implemented," *Washington Post*, August 26, 1971.

[36] "New Era for Spanish Speaking," *Los Angeles Herald-Examiner*, September 26, 1971.

[37] Frank del Olmo, "Chicano Wants Involvement, Not Separation," *Los Angeles Times*, September 13, 1971.

been listened to by the Anglo majority. It is a group only beginning to articulate effectively its goals, as well as its sense of outrage at the discrimination this people has suffered. It is a group whose patience understandably is wearing thin."[38]

The Spanish-language press in the United States and abroad was quite elated, expansive, and highly favorable about our work. The Cuban papers of New York and Miami were effusive with lengthy stories. The Mexican-American dailies and weeklies were skeptical, but supportive. The big exception was the papers catering to mainland Puerto Ricans, who dedicated their coverage to the noisy and unruly protest mounted in the offices of the Cabinet Committee several days after I was named chairman. The purpose of the protest was to oblige me to name a Puerto Rican as CCOSSP director. A few days later, Senators Charles Percy (Illinois), Abraham Ribicoff (Connecticut), and Jacob Javits (New York) demanded the same action of the White House. I complied. (From that day on, press, radio, and TV exposure were to be an active new ingredient in my life. I became a very public figure. I lived in a glass cage until 1974, when my family and I returned to the anonymity of life in Southern California.)

The Sixteen-Point Program led to tangible progress in 1973, nine years after the passage of the civil rights laws. After the famous dressing down in Navy talk that Commissioner Hampton received from the President himself in the first CCOSSP meeting, the U.S. Civil Service Commission undertook a special study to evaluate progress on the Sixteen-Point Program. Now that they had ethnic data, they had an object to study. As a result,

---

[38] Editorial, *Los Angeles Times*, August 23, 1971.

the agency recommended specific actions in January 1973. Federal Personnel Manual System Letter No. 713-18 said: "Each agency should appoint a Coordinator for the Sixteen-Point Program on the staff of the Director of Equal Employment Opportunity."[39] It was marked as high priority. In practice, however, agency personnel managers viewed it uncomfortably as a "me too" effort to piggyback on the hard-won advances of Blacks.

Another speed bump on the path to increasing the number of Spanish-speaking in government positions was outright discrimination. Certainly, the Kennedy brothers did not have many experiences with Mexicans as they were growing up in Boston. Lyndon Johnson, on the other hand, grew up knowing Mexicans but within a closed society that systematically segregated them. In Texas, Mexicans knew their place. Only light-skinned Mexicans, descendants of European Mexicans and/or members of the landed class, could interact on an equal footing with Texans, descendants of Europeans. Johnson's vote-getting methodologies were to throw beer and barbecue ranch parties to buy their vote, and he hoped they stayed bought.

Johnson may have wanted to assist Mexican-Americans more significantly, but he was hindered by the Washington team he inherited. It was composed of Italian, Jewish, German, and English Americans, who knew next to nothing about the downtrodden, uncounted, and ignored Mexican Mestizos. The Kennedy and Johnson teams knew a lot about Blacks, but not Mexicans. In fact, when Johnson established the temporary Inter-Agency Committee on Mexican-

---

[39] Federal Personnel Manual System Letter No. 713-18, January 23, 1973.

American Affairs, he assigned a European American, David North, to run it. That was the way the management of Mexicans was done in Texas. As an example, I was astounded to learn from our Mexican American Education Study questionnaires that it was common practice in Texas high schools to see that European American students occupied all student body offices, despite the fact that Mexican-Americans heavily predominated the student population (up to 90 percent). The school districts of Carrizo Springs and nearby Crystal City were prime cases. The European American landowners in those school districts would not permit Mexican student body officers to "lord it over" their offspring. No way.

Texas was not alone in this. Someone in the White House once asked me to visit Patterson High School in California. Patterson was a sizeable apricot and cherry farming community between Fresno and Sacramento. The well-connected city fathers had requested the President to visit their town; I was told that I would go as his representative instead. My special assistant, Mo Garcia, and I were gladly received by the mayor, the school district superintendent, and the high school principal, among others. But gradually our reason for being there was made known clearly: We were expected to diffuse the tension filling the community and calm the volatile high school student body. The Mexican-American students were protesting an unfair student body election. None of the Mexican-American candidates had won any student officer position, despite greatly outnumbering the Anglos. The school officials justified the election results by saying that so-called "citizenship grades" had disqualified the Mexican-Americans. The officials acquiesced to our suggestion to repeat the elections, and more equitable results produced tranquility. Mo and I drove out of town and stopped at roadside stands to purchase large bags of succulent black cherries, just recently picked from surrounding orchards.

Things were different in the eastern half of the country: There, the problem wasn't discrimination so much as just plain ignorance. In the years from 1968 to 1971, I became acutely aware that Americans living east of the Mississippi River did not know anything about Mexican-Americans. In Bethesda, Maryland, where my little family was growing up free from the trouble of discrimination, people did not know that we Mexican-Americans were supposed to be objects of discrimination—only that Blacks were. When we at the U.S. Civil Rights Commission needed to illustrate the first volumes of the Mexican American Education Study in 1971, Joe Mancias, a staff photojournalist, was dispatched to Southern California to photograph Mexican-American students. Not a single federal agency had a depository of this type of photography. After the Census Bureau released data on the Spanish-surnamed in late 1971, there was a rush to the Southwest to photograph Mexicans. With some luck, they might have taken pictures of signs that read: "No Dogs, No Mescans Allowed!"

During our frequent meetings, Robert Finch cautioned me to be constantly aware that official Washington did not know Mexican-Americans. He counseled me to be patient. Mutual acceptance and understanding would take time.

But the most mammoth speed bump impeding employment of Spanish-surnamed Americans was the lack of data collection by ethnicity. Neither I nor my Chicano cohorts who had met at Swalley's in East Los Angeles in the mid-1960s had known that there was actually no way the federal government could directly assist Mexican-American citizens, since it did not know we existed statistically. The local schools knew who we were; they segregated us. The local banks and real estate agents knew; they would not sell homes to us or let us buy in the "nice" areas of town. In southern Texas, where towns were divided by railroads or highways, the "Americanos" lived on one side, the "Mejicanos" on the other. But politicians in Washington were ill informed.

This bit of knowledge came in handy in the Oval Office, when President Nixon asked me how we were going to assist Mexican-Americans to gain employment. I suggested that the EEOC submit a plan for compelling businesses to gather data by ethnicity instead of just by race. I remarked to the President that if we could increase employment and augment promotions, now denied due to discrimination, we could improve the educational outcomes of Mexican-American students. I showed him how my study at the U.S. Commission on Civil Rights had demonstrated for the first time that the socioeconomic level of parents is the best predictor of student performance.

It was in my role as a senior research staffer at the U.S. Commission on Civil Rights that I had to review the methodology for a proposed study of federal enforcement efforts of civil rights laws, so I had become very familiar with what the entire federal government was doing to assure compliance. The proposed study under review included efforts on behalf of Blacks, but it bothered me that the study did not include finding out how Mexican-Americans were faring. It was understandable, since we were just then being counted in the census and agencies were not collecting data by ethnicity. However, with President Nixon's direct support, the Cabinet Committee was able to compel the entire federal government to count all Mexican-Americans, Puerto Ricans, and other Spanish-surnamed government employees and to publish the result. I knew that by being counted, we would be able to describe our situation and could provide programmatic solutions for advancing people's lives. Everyone could finally analyze the disparities in federal government employment.

So, federal departments and agencies began to implement their ethnic counts in 1971 and started using the term "Spanish-surnamed" instead of "Mexican-American." An outstanding example of how the new count by ethnicity was presented is contained in a March 1973 U.S. Department of Labor report. Table after table of numbers are presented in columns arranged like this.[40]

Total White / Total Negro / Spanish Origin: Total Mexican / Puerto Rican / Other

This represented a major improvement over the many, many years when the numbers were presented in the simplicity of two columns only: Total White and Total Negro.

It wasn't very long after the federal departments and agencies began to implement their ethnic counts and release their data that it provoked a strong reaction. On November 30, 1971, the U.S. Civil Service Commission released federal government employment data by race and ethnicity under the categories "Negro," "Spanish Surname," "American Indian," "Oriental," and "All Other." But when the country discovered that we were 6

[40] U.S. Department of Labor, "Manpower Report of the Department of Labor to the President and to the Congress," March 1973.

percent of the population and only 3 percent of federal government employment, all hell broke loose. Naturally, the Democrats faulted the President for the disparity. Soon more hollers and complaints resounded, with the gathering and publication of racial and ethnic data in other areas of government (such as housing and education). The Democrats commenced their attacks on the Sixteen-Point Program, claiming that it was a dismal failure. They did not want to acknowledge that first it was absolutely required to simply *understand* a situation before action could be taken to transform it.

However, I had anticipated their attacks. I gave talks, speeches, and radio and television interviews in which I repeated over and over where I saw the fault. President Nixon read about it in his early-morning news summary: "Ramirez, chairman of the Cabinet Committee on Opportunities for Spanish-Speaking People, said his group wasn't succeeding in employing Spanish-speaking in lower-level federal jobs and pointed to midlevel bureaucrats as the cause. 'It's one thing for the president to give an order,' said Ramirez, 'and [another thing] for his secretaries, agency heads and immediate lieutenants to heed it.'"[41] Some White House staffers were unhappy. For example, Ray Hanzlik, a new assistant to Counselor Finch, wrote: "At a time when we are working to stress the positive accomplishments, it goes without saying that these comments were not well received around here."[42] Their concerns made my job more difficult, but my reaction? Live and learn.

---

[41] President's News Summary, August 8, 1972. National Archives.

[42] Rayburn Hanzlik to Henry Ramirez, memorandum, August 9, 1972. National Archives.

Senator John Tunney, a California Democrat, hurled negatives in a November 11, 1971, report by Public Advocates, Inc., entitled "Federal Government Employment of the Mexican-American in California: A Classic Case of Government Apartheid and False Elitism." The question was, how did Senator Tunney and the Public Advocates organization know the statistical data on Mexican-Americans in California? The answer is, they did not—for it was not yet available. Further, when President Nixon had announced the Sixteen-Point Program the year before, it was for recruiting and hiring Mexican-Americans in the entire country, not just California. Chairman Robert E. Hampton of the U.S. Civil Service Commission reacted starkly to the report by Public Advocates, Inc.: "The report is misleading." (In Washington, when someone is accused of "misleading," it means that person is lying.) Chairman Hampton's five-page refutation of the report's scurrilous attacks against the President's efforts and the Sixteen-Point Program is devastating.[43]

Chairman Hampton responded again to defend the Sixteen-Point Program on March 29, 1972, this time to an inquiry by Congressman Robert McClory: "I am providing the following comments regarding the statement made by [Congressman Don Edwards, Democrat, California] concerning President Nixon's Sixteen-Point Program to assure equal employment opportunities for Spanish-surnamed persons. Contrary to Mr. Edwards' statement, the program has been taken very seriously by federal agencies. Contrary again to

---

[43] Robert E. Hampton to Senator John V. Tunney, "Federal Government Employment of the Mexican American in California," December 29, 1971. National Archives.

Congressman Edwards' statements, the Cabinet Committee on Opportunities for the Spanish Speaking is very highly regarded. There is, however, a failure on the part of some persons to recognize the progress that has been made by this administration in working toward the legitimate aspirations of the Spanish-surnamed group in federal employment."[44]

It is a shame just how utterly ignorant Congressman Edwards was. He was born in the Santa Clara Valley of California in 1915. He received his bachelor's and law degree from Stanford during the Depression, had served in the Navy, worked for a year with the FBI, and later became president of the Valley Title Company. While he was a student and a member of Stanford's golf team, I was on my knees picking ripe prunes and competing with yellow jackets in Edwards' neighborhood around San Jose, Santa Clara, Campbell, and the Saratoga Country Club's private golf course, where he hit the links. With my mother, five brothers, and five sisters, I lived in the apricot and prune orchards of the Santa Clara Valley, when from May to September we cut apricots and picked prunes from sunup to sundown every day except Sunday, when we went to Mass in San Jose. Did Congressman Don Edwards get to know us Chicanos, the seasonal migrant workers, while at Stanford? Or did he get to know us at his country club, at his church, or his real estate title company? I very much doubt it. His official comportment in Washington demonstrated that he did not. In fact, as the proceedings around Watergate

---

[44] Robert E. Hampton to Congressman Robert McClory, "Congressman Edwards' Statements on President Nixon's Sixteen-Point Program," March 29, 1972. National Archives.

developed, this congressman used his position of power to help destroy the Cabinet Committee.

Because of all the pressure Alex Armendariz was getting at the offices of the presidential campaign, he wrote a memo to Fred Malek, who was the presidential assistant in charge of White House personnel, to get top-level attention. It stated: "Underrepresentation of Spanish-speaking Americans in the federal government remains a critical campaign issue. Our political opponents are convincing the Spanish-speaking leadership that employment disparities can be alleviated by the president 'with one stroke of the pen,' i.e., by means of an Executive Order calling for more Spanish-speaking jobs." So, Alex Armendariz recommended an executive statement calling for aggressive recruitment of Spanish-speaking people in government.[45]

That started the ball rolling to draft an acceptable presidential memorandum on the Sixteen-Point Program. My efforts were met with a "try again." It was not until June 17, 1974, that Anne Armstrong, who had replaced Counselor Finch, approved an acceptable draft.[46] However, given the political situation at the time, the memorandum got no farther. I was to exit three months later; the President was soon to resign.

The Mexican-American spokesmen for the Democratic Party, and specifically Raul Yzaguirre, who headed the National Council of La Raza then, did not understand that it was simply necessary to count how

---

[45] Alex Armendariz to Fred Malek, memorandum, August 31, 1972, "Spanish-Speaking Federal Employment." National Archives.

[46] Henry M. Ramirez to Anne Armstrong, memorandum, June 17, 1974, "Presidential Memorandum on Equal Opportunity for Spanish Speaking People." National Archives.

many we were and where we lived. Evidently, those Mexican-American Democrats were convinced that everybody in the United States knew who we were, simply because they themselves knew. They had missed the fundamental fact that first, we had to be officially counted by *ethnicity*, and that is what President Nixon did. The Democrats could not reconcile themselves to this. They missed the boat.

In 1976, the National Council of La Raza publicized their report, "Cinco Anos Despues: A Preliminary Critique of the Sixteen Point Spanish Speaking Program Five Years after Its Creation."[47] It is probably collecting dust someplace, if any copies are extant. It was a pathetic attempt to discredit the successes of the Sixteen-Point Program. The National Council of La Raza had become an extension of the Democratic National Committee, the United Auto Workers union (UAW), and the American Federation of Labor and Congress of Industrial Organizations (AFL-CIO). It remains so today.

Despite the negative viewpoint of the National Council of La Raza, the much-debated and maligned Sixteen-Point Program was indeed successful. On July 26, 1974, Roy Fuentes, who was now working as a program officer at CCOSSP and auditing progress made in the initiative to increase the federal government employment of the Spanish-speaking people, sent me a memo listing the names, phone numbers, agencies, and addresses of

---

[47] Raul Yzaguirre, "Employment Tidbits: National Council of La Raza and IMAGE, a national organization of Spanish speaking government employees, released a report entitled 'Cinco Anos Despues: A Preliminary Critique of the Sixteen Point Spanish Speaking Program Five Years after Its Creation,'" *Critica* (October 1976), p. 7.

over twenty full-time bilingual and Spanish-speaking program coordinators.[48] It was the job of these coordinators to implement the Sixteen-Point Program. (Remember, following the recommendation of the U.S. Civil Service Commission, Federal Personnel Manual System Letter No. 713-18 had specified that each federal agency should appoint a coordinator for the Sixteen-Point Program.)

Within a year, Ed Valenzuela, president of the newly formed organization National Image, Inc., announced at their 1975 convention that the number of Spanish-speaking coordinators had increased from a mere fifty to a record number of a thousand. The increase from the figure reported by Fuentes in 1974 to the number released by Valenzuela only a year later is truly remarkable. The Sixteen-Point Program had taken off and was becoming systemic.

The legacy of the Sixteen-Point Program, its endurance and achievements, have been recognized. A quarter-century after its inception, Manuel Oliverez, chairman and chief executive officer of an organization formed to promote Hispanic professionals and executives in the federal work force, invited me to a historic luncheon on July 12, 1995. He wrote, "You, Chairman Ramirez, are one of the pioneers and visionaries, whose leadership and consummate professionalism gave the program its direction and vitality. We, in the Hispanic community, owe you a deep debt of gratitude. Accordingly, we will be pleased if you will do us the honor of accepting our invitation to be our special guest at the luncheon commemorating 25 years of the 16

---

[48] Roy O. Fuentes to Henry M. Ramirez, memorandum, July 26, 1974, "List of S/S Program Coordinators." Personal files.

Point/HEP program." (The Carter administration had renamed the Sixteen-Point Program to be the Hispanic Employment Program.)

One more revelation is needed to give credit where history demands it. In the 1920s, a Mexican family fled from the persecution of Catholics and their beloved Church in Mexico and came to settle in El Paso, Texas. A son, Carlos Esparza, started at the bottom at the U.S. Civil Service Commission; by 1971 he had risen to its higher echelons and was stationed in Washington. He knew the civil service laws, rules, and regulations by heart. Most important, he knew how to get things done the right way. He was the guy behind all the actions described in this chapter. Others got the credit, for they had the titles and publicity. Carlos just did his job. Today he is co-owner of a multimillion-dollar corporation that serves the outsourcing needs of government agencies, including the renamed U.S. Civil Service Commission, now known as the Office of Personnel and Management (OPM).

Of course, the Sixteen-Point Program/Hispanic Employment Program did not last forever. As Carlos explained in his own words in my previous book, *A Chicano in the White House: The Nixon No One Knew* (pp. 141–142):

The death knell for the Hispanic Employment Program started under OPM director Don Devine, a Reagan ultraconservative appointee, who in early 1983 abolished the office's newsletter, La Mesa Redonda. The newsletter was the key instrument for guiding program initiatives across the federal government. The program's demise continued under the administrations of George H. W. Bush and Bill Clinton. Major blows were dealt to the program during the administration of George W. Bush when several key instruments for facilitating the hiring of

Hispanics ended. They were bilingual certification and the use of crediting job-related cultural activities. Finally, the end of a court mandate (Angel Luevano v. OPM) that had enabled speedy and nonbureaucratic hiring of outstanding scholars was negotiated away in 2007. For almost 25 years this mandate had provided the most productive avenue for bringing talented Hispanics (and other groups) into government.

The era of employing Spanish-surnamed Americans was a success. Few people realize that we had to compete with our Black brothers, who had the direct benefits of hundreds of millions of dollars and thousands of persons to implement the legal imposition of nondiscrimination in employment, public or private. We at the Cabinet Committee knew, as did the President, that the Black community was the sole beneficiary of the recent laws and new employment commission. They were familiar to Washington, DC, and had been slaves; we had been only conquered and were invisible and unknown. As a result, we had to invent and implement our own employment program until we were counted and were able to be caught up with society.

I gave this statement before the Subcommittee of the Committee on Government Operations, House of Representatives, on July 23, 1973:

What the Cabinet Committee intends to ultimately accomplish is to institutionalize programs, policies, and mechanisms throughout the entire federal structure so that inclusion of the Spanish Speaking becomes an automatic function of government. By Inclusion, we mean bread and butter for the Spanish Speaking—recruitment, placement, promotion, contract compliance, procurement, and their right to acquire and receive an equitable share of government funds.[49]

This said it all. This is what President Nixon had wanted and had instructed.

---

[49] House Committee on Government Operations, *Opportunities for Spanish Speaking People*, July 23, 1973, pp. 1–13.

7. NIXON OPENS DOORS FOR "BROWN CAPITALISM"

So far, we've looked at several actions the Commander in Chief ordered be done for the advancement of Mexican-Americans:

- They would be **counted** in all segments of American society and no longer be invisible.

- They would be assured **equal opportunities** by the civil rights laws of 1964.

- They would be high-level **executives** in the federal government.

- They would have access to **federal employment**.

This chapter will present yet another area of advancement under Nixon: government **contracts and grants**.

Here again, we see the grand vision of President Nixon at work. As already shown, his vision caused inclusion of Spanish-surnamed Americans into the corpus of government. They became federal government executives, advisors, and employees with great opportunities for advancement. As supergrade decision-makers, they had the executive reins of authority. They hired people and awarded grants and contracts in substantial numbers and amounts.

Nixon's vision for minority empowerment was first articulated in two radio talks given in April 1968 under the title "Bridges to Human Dignity." He described two bridges that would move Blacks from welfare to dignity: the bridge of Black success and the bridge of Black capitalism. In his Quaker mentality, Nixon had the novel notion that people who can run their own businesses advance the American Way more rapidly and smoothly. And, when society discriminates against the powerless, government can and must lead the way. Linking those two concepts together, he put muscle and commitment into the economic empowerment of Blacks once he was elected.

Maurice Stans, Nixon's Secretary of Commerce, spoke about it at a Hofstra University conference that took place November 18–21, 1987. In his speech, he explained the situation faced by minorities at the time:

Prior to 1969, the federal government had no program to help members of racial or ethnic minorities to start a business and to stay in business. Help was possible for an applicant only if he or she qualified for assistance within one of the statutory activities of the Small Business

Administration. This approach was unavailing to the minorities, who would be in direct competition with the usually more qualified members of the White majority.[50]

To change that situation, President Nixon took three steps to translate his vision to action soon after occupying the Oval Office. First, he appointed Hilary Sandoval, a Mexican-American businessman from El Paso, Texas, as administrator of the Small Business Administration (SBA). Nixon charged Sandoval, together with Secretary Stans, to spearhead an initiative called "Black Capitalism." Second, he appointed Robert J. Brown as special assistant to the president on Black affairs; Brown's job was to liaison with the Black community. And third, after just a little more than a month in office, he signed an executive order to establish Black capitalism on March 5, 1969. Nixon did not wait for Congress to argue for the usual two years before legislation reached his desk for signature. This was Executive Order 11458: "Prescribing Arrangements for Developing and Coordinating a National Program for Minority Business Enterprise."

At first, Nixon's vision was directed primarily at the socially disadvantaged and economically denied American Blacks. They benefited immediately. Nevertheless, President Nixon was equally adamant about Hispanic business development and opportunities, and his original focus on Black capitalism expanded to include "Brown capitalism," although outreach to Spanish-speaking people evolved more slowly and developed later. Nixon now possessed the personnel and means for extending capitalism to both groups for the first time in U.S.

---

[50] Secretary Maurice Stans, "Nixon's Economic Policy toward Minorities," *The Sixth Annual Presidential Conference: Richard Nixon: A Retrospective on His Presidency*, Hofstra University, November 20, 1987.

history. Just as Robert Brown had toiled for Black economic empowerment, so also Hilary Sandoval worked assiduously as SBA administrator to improve the economic advancement of Spanish-surnamed Americans. He and Martin Castillo guided Benjamin Fernandez, a financial consultant, in his efforts to organize and lead the National Economic Development Association (NEDA).

While in Los Angeles in August 1970, Vice President Agnew announced the formation of NEDA as a new national organization to promote business development among the nation's ten million Spanish-speaking citizens. Funded by SBA and the U.S. Department of Commerce, NEDA successfully served tens of thousands of citizens and helped them become entrepreneurs, developing Hispanic capitalists—business people—in almost thirty urban areas.

Another business initiative that President Nixon started was the Office of Minority Business Enterprise in the U.S. Department of Commerce. The mission of this agency was to promote the development of minority business. It financed nonprofit organizations that in turn provided financial and managerial services to create entrepreneurs, thus serving as a gateway to capitalism.

I had discussed with the President the need for banks owned and operated by Mexican-Americans and other Hispanics. I visited the directors of the Office of the Comptroller of the Currency (OCC) and the Federal Home Loan Bank Board, the two agencies that chartered commercial and savings and loans banks. Both encouraged me to get Hispanics interested in this fundamental area of capitalism to organize and apply for charters. So, I discussed with Benjamin Fernandez the opportunities presented by the OCC and the Federal Home Loan Bank Board. As chairman of NEDA, he assisted people in applying for bank charters. By December 31, 1972, ten Hispanic-owned savings and loans associations had been established as well as ten commercial banks.[51]

In 1970, another program was initiated to generate deposits for minority banks from the federal government. The federal government receives large amounts of assets daily. For example, in Los Angeles alone, people form long lines to seek assistance from the Immigration and Naturalization Service, which therefore collects large sums of money that it must deposit somewhere. With this program begun under the Nixon administration, the deposits can be made at minority banks.

The Nixon administration also designed a vast injection of cash to go into poverty-stricken zones to turn citizens there into stakeholders. "Community Development Corporations" (CDCs) was the startling label given this program. The concepts driving its implementation held that people living in poverty could enjoy additional income if they were shareholders in local development corporations. Citizens in poverty made up one-third of the board of directors of these CDCs, and consultants provided technical assistance to these new boards on how to conduct and transact business. Some of these CDCs grew to become powerhouses that are still functioning today. For example, The East Los Angeles Community Union (TELACU) is huge.

President Johnson's Office of Economic Opportunity (OEO) was his way of helping lift people out of poverty. This agency became famous for dispensing huge chunks

---

[51] Raymond D. Chavez, Federal Home Loan Bank Board, to Armando P. Lopez, Economic Development Administration (U.S. Department of Commerce), April 1973. National Archives.

of cash; in the process, it became a target in political speeches. President Nixon appointed Donald Rumsfeld to run it, who hired Richard Cheney as his key assistant. Bringing an entrepreneurial approach to the War on Poverty, they funded TELACU with millions of dollars of seed money for business ventures. They did the same for CDCs in the Imperial Valley, Oakland, and Fresno, California. CDCs in other cities such as Phoenix, Denver, Albuquerque, El Paso, and San Antonio were equally well endowed.

Finally, the most enduring legacy in both Black and Brown capitalism was inclusion in government purchases. President Nixon instituted completely new ways for the government to conduct business with Black and Brown companies. The SBA increased lending to minority firms in the hundreds of millions of dollars. It also administered the tremendously successful 8(a) program. Under this program, Nixon required every government procurement center to increase federal purchases from minority-owned and controlled companies from almost zero to hundreds of millions of dollars. Three years after the start of Black and Brown capitalism, the SBA reported the following on March 1, 1972, to the Cabinet Committee on Opportunities for the Spanish-Speaking People (CCOSSP): The number of Spanish surnamed-owned companies in the 8(a) program was 173. Black-owned firms numbered 1,872. Since inception of the program in 1969, the total dollar amount of contracts awarded to companies owned by the Spanish-surnamed was $16,059,870 and $118,049,600 to companies owned by Blacks. It is important to note that prior to the creation of NEDA, no Hispanic companies had entered into the 8(a) program. It is safe to assume that the work of NEDA and

CCOSSP brought Hispanic men and women into the 8(a) world of government contracts.

It is a historical fact: President Nixon introduced capitalism to Spanish-surnamed citizens. The Spanish-speaking people participated in it successfully and in huge numbers. It is such a shame that the Latino press derided this fantastic accomplishment. It almost appeared that Spanish-surnamed writers wore socialism on their sleeves and held capitalism in opprobrium.

For example, the *Los Angeles Times* hired a top-rated reporter, Ruben Salazar, in the sixties. In August 1970, he covered the launching of a brand-new Nixon effort to bring capitalism to the barrio. He wrote: "By the end of the day, thanks to the great coverage the vice president gets from the news media, the whole nation knew of the formation of the National Economic Development Association or NEDA." Then, he just had to sarcastically and satirically add, "In the barrio Chicanos immediately started calling NEDA, *NADA,* which in Spanish means 'nothing.'"[52] I question rhetorically: Was this statement really uttered by some human being in the barrio? Was Mr. Salazar inventing news or was he actually recording facts? Was he venting some personal anguish against capitalism? Would he have preferred Chicanos grow up in the socialist Marxism of his birthplace, Mexico? Did he not know that in Socialism, there is no Santa Claus? He had been a reporter in Saigon, where he covered a war Communists had started in South Vietnam. Was he impressed with what he observed of Marxist methodologies and ideology?

---

[52] Ruben Salazar, "The Mexican-Americans NEDA Much Better School System," *Los Angeles Times,* August 28, 1970.

Remember, Mexican Mestizos and indigenous had been landless, uneducated, and powerless peasants since the Spanish Conquest. For generations they had lived under a feudal system; the landowners with all their privileges were almost all European in this system. Those landowners were not Chicanos; they were *gachupines*.

From 1910 to 1930, a massive migration of almost two million poor and rural Mexicans took place—the Mexican Diaspora. These *campesinos* (peasants) came from the ranchos and haciendas of Mexico's interior and rode boxcars *al Norte*, fleeing their little hamlets for the cities and farms of the United States, the land of the free. They knew nothing about capitalism. They were the country's migrant workers. They arrived in California to pick crops or work in the sugar beet fields of Colorado and Kansas. They found themselves in Chicago and scattered around the Great Lakes. But they became the parents of the Chicanos for whose commonwealth I struggled and toiled; their young men went off to war in Europe, the Pacific, and some even into India. These were the restive young World War II vets for whom President Nixon made capitalism a new reality.

8. NIXON ATTENDS MASS AT THE WHITE HOUSE

During my meeting in the Oval Office on August 5, 1971, President Nixon had said that he believed Mexican-Americans were such law-abiding and family-oriented people because of their Catholicism. He lauded the leadership that James Cardinal McIntyre, archbishop of Los Angeles, exercised over his Spanish-speaking flock. It was precisely at that moment that I pointed out to him the fifth point on my three-by-five note card: "Include us in White House activities to create a national awareness of the conditions of Mexican-Americans." He nodded in agreement.

One specific action I recommended to further that fifth point of my vision was to include Mexican-Americans in a White House Sunday service. I put forth this recommendation in the study I had done for Robert Finch in January 1971, "An Overview of Spanish-Speaking Affairs for White House Perspectives."

Shortly after his first inauguration in 1969, President Nixon initiated the practice of holding Sunday services in the East Room of the White House. A Quaker himself, he invited Rev. Billy Graham, a Baptist, to officiate the first Sunday service, and a rotation of different religious denominations followed in the semi-regular services held for White House staff members and invited guests. But until this point, a Catholic Mass had not been held.

As it turned out, my idea dovetailed nicely with a similar idea already in the works. Sometime in the spring of 1971, the office of Counselor Robert Finch initiated action to consider including San Antonio's Bishop Patrick Flores or Boston's Archbishop Humberto Madeiros in a White House Sunday service. A few months later, G. G. Garcia, who worked at the Cabinet Committee on Opportunities for Spanish-Speaking People (CCOSSP) at the time, wrote a memo to his boss, John Bareno, who was then the CCOSSP executive director, reporting on a phone call he'd received. The memo reads:

Just returned from a trip to Texas. While there, he [Carlos Villarreal] talked to Bishop Patrick Flores. Bishop Flores seemed very pleased that Villarreal would take the time and trouble to visit him.

The Bishop expects to spend much of the summer visiting migrant workers wherever they may be—in the fields. He believes that the Church must be concerned about those who are not well off.

Bishop Flores expects to visit Washington in the Fall. When he does, he would like to meet with a group of the Spanish Speaking members of the Nixon Administration. He will probably be here in November, and hopes that a gathering can be held at that time.

Villarreal hopes this can be arranged, and that Bob Finch can be a part of the gathering.

Meanwhile, it seems advisable to go ahead with the proposal that [Archbishop] Madeiros of Boston be proposed to hold services in the White House on a Sunday.[53]

Carlos Villarreal was the administrator of the Urban Mass Transportation Administration, an agency of the U.S. Department of Transportation now known as the Federal Transit Administration. He was from Brownsville, Texas, and a close friend of Archbishop Madeiros, who had been bishop of Brownsville from 1966 to 1970. Bishop Flores was the first Mexican-American bishop in the United States, ordained in May 1970; he served as auxiliary bishop to Archbishop Furey of the San Antonio Archdiocese.

When I took over as chairman of CCOSSP, I advocated for the selection of Bishop Flores in my discussions with Robert Finch, precisely because he was the first Mexican-American bishop. Archbishop Madeiros had immigrated to the United States from Portugal as a teenager; that he spoke fluent Spanish was only incidental for the purpose of including Mexican-American culture via a White House Sunday service.

Sometime in October 1971, a young attorney named Doug Hallett visited me in my office. He identified himself as a staffer for Chuck Colson, the White House political director. After assuring me that his visit would take only a few minutes, he related that he had been assigned to review my study. He added that he had reformatted it for distribution to White House staff on a "need to know" basis and that he had put my recommendations for action into proposals for the

---

[53] G. G. Garcia to John Bareno, memorandum, "Telephone call from Carlos Villarreal," July 6, 1971.

executive branch. One of those proposals was about the Sunday service. He asked me what I would recommend now that I was CCOSSP chairman. I responded that I would have to discuss the matter with my boss, Robert Finch. His reaction was fast and firm: "From here on," he remarked, "you tell Chuck through me what you want *to do*. And Finch, you tell him what you *have done*." As if to clarify the new White House lines of power, he added, "Chuck has breakfast with 'the Old Man' almost every day." I understood. I now had a new White House boss. One was for relating history; the new one was for making it.

In view of the new realities, I strongly advised that a White House Sunday service with hundreds of Spanish-speaking guests was a must. Hallett quickly responded, "You will hear from me very soon." And I did.

By November 3, 1971, there was hustle and bustle. The President had approved a Catholic Mass in recognition of the cultural heritage of the Spanish-speaking people! It was the first time Mass in Spanish had ever been held in the White House. A date had been selected, and Archbishop Madeiros would be officiating. (Apparently Carlos Villarreal and Robert Finch had chosen him instead despite my advocacy for Bishop Flores, the civil-rights activist, Chicano prelate.) I was told to develop a list of 500 names of key Spanish-speaking leaders. They would each receive a memento containing a picture of the new U.S. Treasurer, Romana Banuelos (first Hispanic treasurer of the United States), seated next to a smiling, relaxed President Nixon in the Oval Office, together with a one-dollar bill autographed by her. (A little side note: The ink on the signed dollar bills faded with time!) Invitations flew out, causing a flurry of phone calls and travel plans from California, New York, Texas,

Miami, and elsewhere. Parties and receptions to accompany the festivities in the White House were arranged. Some of the invitees would also attend a CCOSSP advisory council meeting on the day following the Sunday service.

On Sunday, November 14, 1971, President Richard M. Nixon and his wife joined the invited congregation at the first White House Sunday service for the Spanish-speaking people, a Mass celebrated by Archbishop Madeiros. Former President Lyndon B. Johnson and his wife also attended. Mr. Nixon and Mr. Johnson flanked Archbishop Madeiros in the reception line (Figure 8). The Supreme Court justices attended, as did the Joint Chiefs of Staff, members of the diplomatic corps (especially from Latin America), and Spanish-speaking members of Congress. Thus, all three branches of government participated in the Mass celebrated by Archbishop Madeiros. It was truly awesome and historical for the White House to host so many Mexican-Americans, Puerto Ricans, and Cubans. We wanted to share our euphoria about this exciting first with the world.

Figure 8. After Mass in the White House, my wife, Ester, and I greet Archbishop Madeiros in the receiving line with President Nixon and former President Lyndon B. Johnson. Although hardly visible in this photo, our daughter, Carol, is to Ester's left and our son, Michael, is at her right. *(Courtesy Richard M. Nixon Library)*

We looked for newspaper accounts that would breathlessly inform the American public of this momentous event. Alas, the women and men who report White House activities deemed it instead to be a nonevent. I had assumed innocently that they would, almost *ipso facto*, inform the American public and develop awareness of the national presence of the Spanish-speaking with favorable newspaper coverage. Instead, what a disappointing surprise it was to look for articles the following Monday. The Associated Press (AP) report in the *Philadelphia Inquirer* led with a photograph of President Johnson, Archbishop Madeiros, and President Nixon, partially cropped, with the caption: "After-Church

Discussion is Held in White House." The AP report focused on the Johnsons as it recounted:

> Former President and Mrs. Lyndon B. Johnson came back to the White House Sunday as guests of President and Mrs. Nixon for worship services and joined in the reception line afterward. They shared receiving lines, the two presidents and the archbishop in the State Dining Room, while Mrs. Nixon and Mrs. Johnson shook hands in the newly refurbished Red Room. Among the 300 guests were a number of Spanish-speaking representatives, who were on hand for a meeting on Monday of an advisory council of the Cabinet Committee on Opportunities for the Spanish Speaking Peoples.[54]

The reporter who wrote this to inform the English-reading public was either stupid or malicious. Most of the *500* Spanish-speaking leaders who were invited were able to attend. Therefore, the number of Spanish-speaking guests present was considerably higher than 300—it was between 400 and almost 500. For the sake of clarity and accuracy, the reporter could have given a more precise count of the service or reception attendees.

It is so interesting how biases and prejudices can be nuanced with a few neatly placed words. Beyond a shadow of doubt, writing of this type characterized the mean-spirited persons that "reported" what they actually wanted to *narrate* about the Nixon era. The AP reporter, for whatever undecipherable reason, just did not get it. I find it amazing that the reporter apparently did not learn (or care) that this was a historical first—i.e., that there

---

[54] "Johnsons Visit Nixons," *Philadelphia Inquirer*, November 15, 1971.

were so many Mexican-Americans, Cuban-Americans, and Puerto Ricans at a White House Sunday service.

To top it all off, one wire service filed their story on Saturday, November 13, before the event even took place—as if it were contemporary with the Sunday service! My outlook—that human beings used pencils, paper pads, and tape recorders to faithfully record an event—was becoming more and more cynical. Reality-twisting became the norm.

On the other hand, the most respected Spanish-language newspaper, *Diario las Americas* (headquartered in New York City with circulation in the United States and Latin America), covered the event with their own correspondent. I translate his lead paragraph:

> The very presence of the Catholic Archbishop of Boston, Monsignor Humberto S. Madeiros, as well as that of the Hispanic crowd to the Mass officiated by the distinguished prelate, in the chapel of the White House, represents a moral triumph for the Hispanic American population of the United States.[55]

Later, the article went on to state:

> At the end of Mass, Archbishop Madeiros stated that being the first Spanish-speaking prelate to officiate at a White House religious service constituted for him "a very high honor, and that he saw with deep satisfaction the presence of so many Spanish-speaking persons at the service."[56]

---

[55] "Muy Significante Para el Pueblo Hispano de E.U. un Acto en la Casa Blanca," *Diario Las Americas*, November 15, 1971.

[56] Ibid.

The story covered forty column inches, and its tone and tenor reflect honest and authentic reportage. What a difference!

Of particular interest is the manner in which the largest, but not most respected, Spanish-language newspaper handled the story. *La Opinion* of Los Angeles, still in print today, serves the most heavily populated Spanish-speaking area in the United States. It tends toward left of center; its pages are peppered with official Mexican government press releases. And for world news, it relies heavily on translated United Press International (UPI) handouts. It presented the White House religious event with a photo and ten column inches commencing on page one. The caption on the photo of Mr. Johnson, Archbishop Madeiros, and President Nixon reads "En la Casa Blanca" ("In the White House"), and the story headline translates, "Mr. Johnson on a visit in the White House." The continuation column on page two is headed simply "Mr. Johnson."[57]

Why did a newspaper like *La Opinion* obfuscate the reality of the event? Just from its area of circulation in Southern California alone, more than fifty Mexican-American leaders traveled to Washington for the White House service. I know how many leaders were there, because I reviewed the list of invitees and saw them at the White House. Yet *La Opinion* wrote: "About a hundred Spanish-speaking persons showed up among the other invited guests. The Spanish-speaking guests were really there for a Monday meeting of an advisory council." Not only does the writer gloss over the fact that among the

---

[57] "Mr. Johnson de visita en la Casa Blanca," *La Opinion*, November 14, 1971.

"other guests" were none other than Supreme Court justices, members of Congress, chiefs of the military, and members of the diplomatic corps, but the writer also misrepresents the number of Spanish-speaking guests and why they were there. Contrary to the story's headline, the Sunday service was not for the controversial ex-President Johnson. It was the first time Mass had been celebrated in the White House chapel in Spanish, and it was well attended. Above all, the event celebrated national cultural inclusion.

An interesting sidebar to this account of how *La Opinion* handled its reportage of such a singularly significant event for a predominantly Catholic group occurred after I returned to private life. Its owner and publisher, Ignacio Lozano, had been one of my presidential advisors to the Cabinet Committee, and around 1978, we had lunch at my request. I figured that it was time for him to explain the strengthening left-wing orientation of his paper. He explained that his daughter was now in charge, and as a young person she had some idealistic notions.

At that time, *La Opinion* was carrying wire releases on a daily basis that cast favorable light on the Sandinistas in Nicaragua. I said to him, "You and I know they are Communists working with the Russians and the Castro Cubans. Why not describe them accurately for what they are—Communists, instead of the phrases your paper uses—'left of center'?" He blithely responded, "We do not know if they are Communists. We do know, however, that they are left of center." To me, that answer explained all there was to know about why faulty reportage of the first Spanish Mass in the White House chapel occurred.

A further oddity in the newspaper accounts is reflected when comparing the AP report in the *Philadelphia Inquirer* side by side with that from UPI in *La Opinion*. The AP version reads, "The Johnsons were on a brief visit to Washington after stopping in Charlottesville, Va., to visit their daughter and son-in-law, Mr. and Mrs. Charles S. Robb." An examination of the UPI's sentence shows it to be a very close translation of the one in the AP story. The entire UPI story, in fact, seems to be translated from the AP story. There is one big difference, however. The AP story said there were 300 guests, but the UPI version in *La Opinion* only mentioned 100! As a result, the focus on the Johnsons, as presented in the *Philadelphia Inquirer*, is even more pronounced in *La Opinion*! The Catholic Mexican-Americans in Southern California were ill served indeed.

La Opinion ends its version by giving the impression that the "about a hundred" Spanish-speaking invitees just happened to be part of the crowd at the White House Sunday service. And that among them were some representatives of national Spanish-speaking organizations who just happened to be in Washington to attend an advisory council meeting on employment opportunities for the Spanish-speaking. The last paragraph in the AP story in the *Philadelphia Inquirer* accurately named the advisory council as that of the Cabinet Committee on Opportunities for Spanish-Speaking People, but *La Opinion* did not even deign to name it at all.

How interesting that Ignacio Lozano, the publisher and owner of *La Opinion*, was conspicuously absent from the Monday, November 15, 1971, advisory council meeting! Why was he not there? He never told me, and I did not ask.

9. I USE MY POSITION TO URGE THE VATICAN TO ELEVATE HISPANIC BISHOPS

To advance the national awareness of and improve the conditions of Spanish-speaking people, I perceived that the Catholic Church could and should play a vital and transformational role. I did not, however, have a plan for doing anything about that. I had done no reading or research on the matter, nor had I discussed it with my staff or included the topic in my study for Counselor Robert Finch in the winter of 1971.

Nonetheless, it is true that over the years I sometimes caught myself reflecting on the uniqueness of a bishop's position. From time to time, I imagined in what ways my life would have been different if I had acceded to the wishes of my own archbishop. He wanted me to study theology in the major seminary in Burgos, Spain, and possibly go to Rome for further studies after ordination. I did not accept the offer, however, precisely because of the discrimination I had endured from Spaniards. From early childhood, I had learned about the relationship between Spaniards and the Mestizos and indigenous Mexicans. It was a matter of superior to inferior. I was convinced it would be absolute hell to endure discrimination in the country itself that was the font of those prejudices.

Indeed, the effects of discrimination were the reason I abandoned my ordination studies. I knew quite well that acts of discrimination are endemic to man's nature. Original sin took care of that, and Catholics did not enjoy immunity. As I progressed toward the goal of ordination, there came a moment of after-dinner relaxation with a cigar in the company of Monsignor Benny Hawkes, chancellor of the Archdiocese of Los Angeles and the cardinal's right-hand man. We were taking our ease at Saint John's Major Seminary in Camarillo, California, in the student store.

"Henry," he confided, "you know what happened to Father So-and-so and Father So-and-so?"

"Yes," I responded in a prudent tone. I had known both of them. They were holy men assigned to Mexican parishes in East Los Angeles. They had been seminarians in the classes ahead of me.

Monsignor Hawkes continued, "They got too deeply involved as leaders of something new in East L.A. They became public leaders of the Chicanos against discrimination. They forgot that they were supposed to say Mass, hear confessions—you know, be priests! We get no problems from the Spanish priests about discrimination against the Mexicans. They do not go public. But you are a Mexican, and people will want you to be a leader in that arena. Let this be a word to the wise. Keep in mind where those two other guys are now: one in Chicago, the other in New Orleans. You will have to be a nice parish priest and not get involved."

I knew then and there that I would have to work to save my soul outside, in the secular world. I abandoned my studies and returned home.

I had lived away from home for almost ten years, save for summer vacations. The first few days of my return were utterly devastating, disorderly, and truly traumatic. The people in my parish church, my neighborhood, and my town did not know how to greet me. They had questions written all over their faces. My pastor ensconced me in his private study and scolded me vehemently for being so dumb as to leave a well-defined and successful career path. All my teachers, as well as the hierarchy, he stridently reminded me, had expected me to complete my studies with ordination to the priesthood. He tried mightily to get me to return to the seminary immediately. "Don't you know," he bellowed, "you have been selected to be the first Mexican-American bishop for our archdiocese?" But these words had no impact on me. *How did he know that?* I thought. It made not one scintilla of a difference in any case. My decision was definitive and irrevocable.

My pastor was right, as it turned out. Years later, in March 1971, my former classmate Monsignor Jack Urban took me to the common room at the rectory of Saint Basil Catholic Church in Los Angeles after dinner. Timothy Cardinal Manning was watching TV there. As the news program showed the ordination to bishop of another classmate at the cathedral that morning (Father Juan Arzube), the Cardinal turned to me and said, "Doctor, that ordination was supposed to have been conferred on you. Years ago, I had selected you." I first met Timothy Manning in 1945, when he was a monsignor and an assistant to Archbishop Cantwell. He once gave me a ride to school out in West Los Angeles from downtown. I was a freshman, and he was a young priest with a very heavy Irish accent. He was what we called an "FBI"—a foreign-born Irishman. There was something memorable about that ride; it would reappear in my mind often over the years. He was a very holy man. It was nice to know of his confidence in me, but my life had taken a very different path.

Not many months after that conversation in the common room, I became chairman of the Cabinet Committee on Opportunities for Spanish-Speaking People (CCOSSP), and not many months after that, a singular and significant event occurred in November 1971. I invited two bishops to dinner at our home, something I had never done before. Bishop Juan Arzube and Bishop Patrick Flores were in Washington to attend the annual meeting of the U.S. Conference of Catholic Bishops (USCCB). Of course, I knew Bishop Arzube from our classes together while at Saint John's Major Seminary, and I had met Bishop Flores on my frequent trips to San Antonio. I had no particular or pressing reason for wanting to spend a relaxing evening with these two remarkable and holy men. However, they had expressed a desire to meet with me.

I have no written notes of what transpired that evening, so I write here over thirty-five years later from recall. I remember that Bishop Arzube wanted to discuss Father Ralph Ruiz; I did not know at the time that Father Ruiz had founded the first civil rights organization of Mexican-American priests, called *Padres Asociados para Derechos Religiosos, Educativos, y Sociales* (P.A.D.R.E.S.).[58] I

---

[58] Rev. Ralph Ruiz, *P.A.D.R.E.S.*, Our Lady of the Lake University:

recall that Bishop Flores responded to Bishop Arzube's interest at great length. We probably discussed the emerging civil rights struggle that we called "*El Movimiento.*"

I know for sure that the bishops did not ask me why I left the seminary so late in my studies. If I had been asked, I would not have revealed to them that the embryonic Mexican-American civil rights struggle had made me confront the certainty that I would be called upon to define and articulate matters of discrimination against Mexican-Americans publicly. The administrators of the archdiocese were not receptive to that type of discussion in any media. Monsignor Hawkes had made it clear I could not be a civil rights leader for the Mexican-American community as a priest, so I had had to make a decision.

That decision to leave the seminary put me on a career path that eventually led me to Washington, and then to the position of chairman of the CCOSSP. My meeting with the bishops further stirred some thoughts I'd been turning over in my mind. As the months went on, I realized I was uniquely situated to define a new direction for meeting the temporal and spiritual needs of Spanish speakers. It was time for them to have Spanish-speaking shepherds again, as they'd had prior to the conquest of the Southwest under President James K. Polk, when Spanish-speaking bishops had served the area. After the American army conquered half of Mexico, German-American and Irish-American bishops were assigned to take over. It was now time to make some badly needed corrections.

San Antonio, Texas, 1970.

On June 16, 1972, I issued this press release in English and Spanish:

> Dr. Henry M. Ramirez, director of the Presidential Cabinet Committee on Opportunities for the Spanish-Speaking People of President Nixon, thinks that the Catholic Church should act quickly to designate more Spanish-speaking bishops in North America. "With ten Spanish-speaking bishops, the Church could have a large impact on the life of the Catholics of the Southwest of the country," Dr. Ramirez said. He added: "A big number of the Spanish-speaking Catholics in the United States (estimated at 25 percent) live in that area. Actually, there are only two Hispanic American bishops in the American Catholic hierarchy: Juan Arzube, Auxiliary Bishop of Los Angeles, California and Patrick Flores, Auxiliary Bishop of San Antonio, Texas. Also, there is the Spanish-speaking Archbishop of Boston, Massachusetts, a native of the Azores Islands, Portugal."
>
> Dr. Ramirez, who studied for the priesthood before embarking on careers in education and civil rights, added that the Catholic Church "has to recognize that she can play a big role in the social betterment of the Spanish-Speaking, since she knows their problems and has ways for providing solutions."
>
> Dr. Ramirez was born in Walnut, California into a family of eleven children. He spent every summer during his youth as a migrant farm worker. He relates that he and his family, from time to time, worked as peons, gathering all that fell to the ground, peaches and nuts. After he graduated from Saint John's Seminary in Camarillo, California, Dr. Ramirez received his master's degree in education in 1960 from

the University of Loyola in Los Angeles. "While working as a public school teacher and administrator, I was called a militant many times by my colleagues, since I was trying to make systemic changes to the schools based on my Christian faith." Dr. Ramirez explained that he worked to involve the Spanish-speaking teachers in outreaching to the community, so that they could become more aware of the special needs of said community. Before he became director of the presidential committee, whose members include the Secretaries of Agriculture, Commerce, Labor, Treasury, Health, Education and Welfare, among others, Dr. Ramirez was in charge of the Mexican American Studies Division of the Commission on Civil Rights. As chairman of the committee, Dr. Ramirez is responsible for directing the group toward the goal of assuring that federal programs are reaching the Spanish-Speaking and working for their benefit.

As a Catholic, Dr. Ramirez is interested in what the Catholic Church is doing to maintain the Christian faith in the American people. While recognizing the scarcity of Spanish-speaking priests, Dr. Ramirez added that "the Catholic barrios of the Southwest do not have Masses, or sermons, or confessions in Spanish...everything is in English."

He also added that: "Bishop Patrick Flores, a personal friend, was reprimanded by his superior, Archbishop Furey, a German American, solely for giving a sermon in Spanish when he was a parish priest." Bishop Flores, upon being questioned, confirmed this story in San Antonio, Texas, adding that similar incidents had "occurred many times because some priests believed that preaching in Spanish was prejudicial to their congregations."

"Catholic schools," he said, "give many Spanish-speaking persons an integral quality education. Otherwise, they would have to attend public schools without receiving a Christian education."

Dr. Ramirez, who has three children attending Catholic schools, praises the work of the Catholic schools.[59]

Five months after my office distributed that press release calling for the appointment of at least ten Spanish-speaking bishops, I received two visitors at the Cabinet Committee offices in November 1972: Ada Pena and Paul Sedillo. Ada Pena operated a travel agency and was the wife of Eduardo Pena, a high-ranking employee at the Equal Employment Opportunity Commission as well as a member of the Catholic University of America's board of regents. She was an active Roman Catholic and very involved in the national affairs of the League of United Latin American Citizens (LULAC). Paul Sedillo was the national director of Spanish-speaking affairs at the USCCB in Washington.

The purpose of their visit was to discuss the effects of my press release and the need for the elevation of Spanish-speaking bishops of Mexican, Puerto Rican, and Cuban ethnicity. They listed a series of reasons for the need for spiritual leadership and its concomitant effects on daily living. Their rationale made abundant sense. Sedillo further explained that his experience at the

---

[59] Cabinet Committee on Opportunities for Spanish-Speaking People, President Nixon's Advisor Speaks about the Need the Catholic Church Has to Ordain More Spanish-Speaking Bishops in the U.S. [press release], June 16, 1972.

headquarters of the USCCB had convinced him that the European American bishops and the Catholic hierarchy were naive about the country's growing number of Spanish-speaking Catholics. He added that they lacked experience and knowledge of the linguistic and cultural characteristics and temporal issues affecting Spanish-speaking people.

Sedillo was careful and cautious in his references to these dedicated and holy men. In response to my question of why they had presented the matter to my office, they responded with excellent justification. The government of the Church is monarchical; parish priests had no leverage on these matters, and laypeople had even less. The process to appoint a bishop involves several steps and ultimately comes from the pope: First, the leadership of the Church hierarchy in a particular nation submits a list of prospects to the pope's representative (called the apostolic delegate or papal nuncio). Nuncios are vested with both political and ecclesiastical powers; colloquially, they are papal ambassadors. The nuncio, after consultation with the hierarchy of the nation, selects a number of final candidates, which he then sends to the pope, who makes the final choice and appoints the new bishop. Back in November 1972, the apostolic delegate in the United States was Archbishop Luigi Raimondi. At the time of Pena and Sedillo's visit to me, Archbishop Raimondi had only approved of one Chicano bishop: the auxiliary bishop of San Antonio, Bishop Patrick Flores. As a result of their visit, I committed to a course of action that would take me to see the apostolic delegate. But first, I conferred with Secretary of State Henry Kissinger and noted his approval.

Later that month, Ada Pena and I visited the nunciature (the official name for the embassy of the Holy

See, the sovereign government of the Vatican) on Massachusetts Avenue in Washington's Embassy Row neighborhood. I approached the meeting from the perspective that I, the highest-ranking Mexican-American appointee of a sovereign nation, was conferring with the delegate of the sovereign of the Holy See. This was a feat no layman, parish priest, or bishop without protocol could do.

We were escorted to the study of the Most Reverend Luigi Raimondi. He was very generous with his time as he patiently and attentively listened to my presentation of why the Spanish-speaking people needed bicultural and bilingual shepherds. We both explored the issue of why there were only two Spanish-speaking bishops in the Southwest—one a Mexican-American (Bishop Flores), the other an Ecuadorian-American (Bishop Arzube)—and both only auxiliaries. We delved into comparing how the Church had rapidly established an indigenous hierarchy in Africa, but in the United States, the European American bishops seemed reluctant to submit recommendations of Spanish-speaking priests for elevation to bishops. The matter of the large loss of souls to the Protestant organized religions was also covered.

I quickly deduced from the direction of the archbishop's remarks and observations that he, too, along with the rest of official Washington, had been unaware of the emergence of a formerly uncounted and unknown American population: the Mexican-Americans.

The visit ended with proper formalities but with some clearly stated disagreements. At my strong suggestion that he energize the American hierarchy to submit names of Mexican-American, Cuban-American, and Puerto Rican priests from which he would select ten to send to Pope Paul VI, he balked and replied that the Holy Spirit would add Spanish-speaking bishops in due time. At that pontifical elaboration of the workings of the Third Person of the Holy Trinity, I quickly expressed my admiration for the efficacy of the Holy Spirit's actions in Africa. The Church in Africa was by and large already administered by Black cardinals, archbishops, and bishops! I insinuated that here in the United States, Irish- and German-American bishops were impeding the work of the Holy Spirit in areas populated by Catholic Chicanos. I gracefully but firmly stated that I would send a White House cable to His Holiness reporting on the meeting and its inconsequential outcome. He assured me that he, too, would dispatch a cable with his version.

Several months later, on March 5, 1973, Archbishop Luigi Raimondi was recalled to Rome and replaced by Archbishop Jean Jadot. Interestingly, Archbishop Raimondi did not invite me to his going-away party at the nunciature, although he did invite the other and now-famous Chicano appointees of President Nixon.

Shortly after Archbishop Jadot's arrival, his office called ours with an urgent message to meet as soon as possible. His invitation was warm and generous; he asked me to bring my wife and family. We met at the nunciature on November 15, 1973, where we were given a tour of the residence. We visited the lovely chapel, and then he and I proceeded to his study. His first words were that he had called me to meet with him because Pope Paul VI had told him, "Make sure you speak with Dr. Ramirez and inform him that the Holy See will proceed to elevate Spanish-speaking bishops as soon as possible." His Excellency stated that the Pope was aware of my correspondence. I was elated!

Then he topped it off. He asked for names of my former seminary classmates who should be considered for elevation. I recommended Father Henry Gomez of Los Angeles and Fathers Gilbert Padilla and Francisco (Paco) Long, both from Tucson, Arizona. I also recommended that Auxiliary Bishop Patrick Flores of San Antonio be promoted to ordinary (i.e., a bishop completely in charge of his own diocese). Further, I strongly recommended that some of my former classmates *not* be considered for promotion, since they were lacking in sensitivity toward Chicanos. They were already on the fast track— monsignors working in the chancery offices in Arizona and in California—but none of them did become bishops.

Immediately following our meeting, I sent this cable to His Holiness, Pope Paul VI:

On behalf of distinguished Spanish-speaking Catholic laymen in the United States we want to inform you of the cordial and productive conference we had recently with His Excellency Archbishop Jadot. The meeting with the Apostolic Delegate was held in his office in Washington, DC. We discussed areas of mutual interest, stressing the need for enhancing the presence of the Spanish-speaking and Spanish-surnamed in the American Catholic Church. We were most heartened by His Excellency's response to the creation of a climate in which the needs of the Spanish-speaking could be realized, particularly the appointment of more indigenous clergy to the positions of Bishops and including the Spanish-speaking laity in appropriate Church matters. We look forward to continuing this fruitful dialogue for the good of the Church and its members.

Respectfully yours,

Henry M. Ramirez
Chairman

In his seven years as apostolic delegate, Archbishop Jadot was responsible for several appointments of Spanish-speaking clergy:

- Father Gilbert Chavez of San Diego, California, was ordained auxiliary bishop of San Diego, California, on June 21, 1974.

- Father Robert Sanchez was ordained archbishop of Santa Fe, New Mexico, on July 25, 1974.

- Archbishop Aponte was elevated to cardinal of Puerto Rico in 1973.

- And Bishop Patrick Flores was promoted to ordinary of the Diocese of El Paso in 1978 and later, to archbishop of the Diocese of San Antonio.

Upon the ordination of Archbishop Sanchez in Santa Fe, religion writer John Dart wrote for the *Los Angeles Times*, "It was becoming embarrassingly clear to the Catholic Church five years ago that Spanish-speaking Catholics had grown to 25% of the U.S. membership but not one bishop had a Hispanic background. The most typical American bishop called Ireland his home or his ancestors' home."[60]

---

[60] John Dart, "Spanish-Speaking Bishops Gaining in U.S.," *Los Angeles Times*, July 27, 1974.

Commentators could have noted that prior to the 1970 census, no one in this country knew how many Mexican-Americans there were. The White House did not; Congress certainly did not know, either. In addition, those in the media responsible for forming public awareness and opinions did not know. In the context of a national "know-nothing" about Mexican-Americans, the religion writer of the well-known liberal paper could have written more objectively and less sarcastically. No one was embarrassed; there was no reason for embarrassment. There was, however, reason for elation. The Church was going in the right direction. The German-American and Irish-American bishops, under the guidance of the apostolic delegate, would now begin to recognize these formerly uncounted Catholics. And, most important, the European Catholic Church that had been transplanted to the United States was now going to merge with the Spanish-speaking Catholic Church that was started in this hemisphere in Anahuac in 1531 with the apparitions of the Mother of God, Our Lady of Guadalupe.

In 2009, the *National Catholic Reporter* noted upon Archbishop Jadot's death at age 99 that "Paul VI was very much aware of the fact that previous apostolic delegates had been pawns in the hands of the powerful kingmaker American cardinals."[61] But his apostolic delegate Archbishop Jadot was "not in the mold" of his predecessors. He immediately let the New York, Chicago, Saint Louis, and Philadelphia cardinals know things would be different. During his tenure as apostolic delegate, which lasted until 1980, he opened the door to the elevation of Spanish-speaking clergy to the rank of

---

[61] John A. Dick, "Cleric Who Shaped U.S. 'Pastoral Church' Dead at 99," *National Catholic Reporter*, January 21, 2009.

bishop. He was an outsider and successfully changed the progression and promotion of only Europeans.

The Vatican had acted.

10. NIXON WANTS AMNESTY FOR THE UNDOCUMENTED

Sometime after the presidential inauguration of 1973, perhaps in March, I was in my office doing uneventful chores when the private phone line rang. It received calls only from my wife and the White House. My reaction was always happy when my wife called, but if the call came from the White House, I received it with nerve-wracking urgency. This time, the caller calmly informed me, "This is the White House operator. Hold the line for Counselor Finch. He will be on the line soon."

Then, with a soft and gravelly voice, he identified himself: "This is Bob Finch." After I acknowledged him, he proceeded in a monotone, "I am on Air Force One, seated next to the President." A vivid picture formed immediately in my imagination of the two of them pensively reclining in aisle seats. I was so excited that, contrary to my routine procedure of logging every phone call daily (even if only cryptically), I wrote nothing and recorded the conversation only mentally. What a shame! Nonetheless, the balance of the conversation remains engraved in my memory.

Finch continued, "We just left San Clemente on our way to San Francisco. The President was ruminating over his successful reelection and expressing his joy over the huge Mexican-American vote he received." (Just days before, I had received a signed and framed personal thank-you letter from the President dated February 1, 1973, for my help getting him reelected.) "And, he was recalling your Oval Office meeting of August 1971—and specifically the spirited discussion both of you had over the Mexican-American vote. So, he told me, 'Call Henry for three highly significant suggestions, recommendations, or ideas he can think of that I, the President, can and should do to demonstrate my appreciation and gratitude to the Mexican-Americans for their outstanding and historical, first-time-ever vote of almost 30 percent!' He wants to do something of such proportion and magnitude that he will be remembered by the Mexican-Americans in a manner akin to their affection and remembrance for President Roosevelt."

"How much time do I have?" I asked.

"Take a few moments," Counselor Finch replied. A fleeting thought raced through my mind: *Pressure cooker time*. I ordered all my brain cells to work at hyperactive speed. Like a sports car's tires when the accelerator is floored, my intellect fired into action, spinning and screeching madly while gaining purchase. In my mind, I tried to flip through some community needs and quickly rank them on a scale of importance based on my own life experience.

To this day I know not why, but my very first thoughts raced to a garage on Ninth Street in Pomona, California. I imposed a tranquil and controlled tenor of voice while I described to the President my vivid memories of trips to Elias's garage. Elias was my old bachelor uncle, and my brother, Chalo, and I went there for our monthly haircuts. I recalled for the President my uncle's constant lament that he could not visit his hometown of Salamanca in Mexico, not because he couldn't afford to do so, but because he lacked official papers: "*Pero yo no tengo papeles.*" When he had entered this country at El Paso in 1923, *papeles* were not required. Now that he was retired from the Kaiser Steel Mill in Fontana, California, he had the money to travel but could not visit his birthplace and teenage home. I always pitied him, mentally shrugging my shoulders (being only thirteen years old, that's all I could do).

However, my dad, Pascual, Elias's older brother, had traveled several times to Mexico, visiting family, cousins, and pals in diverse cities. (The 1910 Revolution and the 1926–30 *Cristiada* war had emptied Salamanca and scattered its population.) As a result, he enjoyed a constant stream of correspondence with people in Mexico, and he would regale Uncle Elias and their other brothers, Rosendo and Alfonso, in detail about his visits "back home." My father was lucky: He had a "border pass."

My recollections simply tumbled out as I remarked that situations like my uncle's were commonplace and could easily number in the hundreds of thousands. Since I worked at the rectory of Sacred Heart Catholic Church in Pomona, California, from 1944 to 1953 filling out forms for baptisms, Holy Communions, confirmations, marriages, funerals, and such for thousands of families from all the nearby towns, I personally came to know hundreds of Mexican-Americans who shared the same shattered aspirations. "*No tengo papeles.*" The expression ached with unfulfilled longings, haunted by fleeting memories of youth. For many people, dreams and hopes of visiting their birthplace faded and vanished with advancing years. I wondered aloud how we could ameliorate that state of affairs.

Counselor Finch snapped at that and stopped me. He said, "The President likes that issue. He does not need to hear about any other ideas. He wants you to flesh it out. Get consultants to advise you. Get it staffed out. Get your congressional relations staffer to start working on it. At the University of Connecticut there is an expert that can help you."

I was stunned! And the next statement from Finch made me sit up straight: "The President wants to give them amnesty. Get moving! And that's an order. Give us some paperwork as soon as possible." And just like that, the phone conversation ended.

By this time, however, the Democrats, the *Washington Post*, and others were busy stirring up the pot that would become known as the Watergate break-in. I learned about how John Dean, counsel to the president, had foiled the FBI from checking his office files several days after the break-in at the Democratic National Committee's campaign offices on June 17, 1972. Nixon's presidency clearly was becoming endangered. However, I proceeded to do what I had been ordered to do.

First, I immediately summoned my close and trusted staff to share with them the phone call from Air Force One: my personal secretary, Mercedes Flores; my speechwriter and personal assistant, Mo Garcia; my spokesman and chief of information, E. B. Duarte; and my chief of congressional relations, Robert Brochtrup. (For this book, I interviewed Mercedes, Mo, and E. B. all separately and in detail about this event. Since I had no paperwork on it, I needed to get their memories. It was remarkable; they all remembered what I had shared in my office.)

That phone call with Bob Finch defined a novel and entirely unexpected direction for me as chairman of the Cabinet Committee on Opportunities for Spanish-Speaking People (CCOSSP). I had no experience with the issue of immigration. In fact, in February 1973 my cup was already overflowing; I had no interest in adding this area. The election result of almost 30 percent of the Mexican-American vote going for a Republican set the hair of the Democrats on end. How could they have lost nearly a third of the Mexican vote? They were going to come after me, and they would be looking for blood.

Besides, the immigration of my parents, siblings, relatives, and friends was history that had taken place prior to my birth; I had no direct experience of it myself. I was curious and perplexed on the subject, to be sure, but their stories left many unanswered questions. Although they conversed frequently about it, few answers to the questions of why, how, where, when, and who emerged, and those that did were troubling. It was not until years later, when I read the four volumes of *La Cristiada* by Jean Meyer that my curiosity about the immigrations of the 1920s was partly satiated. By then, I had traveled extensively in Mexico, conferred with hundreds of people, and read many books on the subject. I learned that Mexico censored and controlled information and knowledge through its very secret police system created to work just like the secret police in Communist countries. Called the *Direccion Federal de Seguridad,* this secret-police system was a font of invisible tyranny. President Vicente Fox dismantled it immediately upon taking power in Mexico in 2001.

Nevertheless, under Counselor Finch's orders, I was to add another dimension to the mission of the Cabinet Committee, which was viewed with new awe and respect and had a good reputation for getting things done. We would now focus on the people *sin papeles* (without official documents). I did what I always did when faced with a new challenge: I took time out to acquire intelligence on this new-to-me issue: immigration, migration, illegal aliens, undocumented workers, those of no legal status, and "guest workers."

I began with my own life and connections to people *sin papeles*, retreating for a time to research, read, consult, and recall events and pertinent experiences. I began to introspect about everything. I thought about my parents' house, which had electricity, gas, and running water and a separate garage and small barn on an acre of very tillable and rich, loamy soil at 1235 West Grand Avenue in Pomona, California. Purchased in 1939, this property had another feature: It was a block away from *La Iglesia del Sagrado Corazon* (Church of the Sacred Heart), which in the early 1930s my father had petitioned Bishop Cantwell to build.

Prior to 1939, our family, with its eleven boys and girls, had lived at 105 North Gordon Street. My father had been an employee of the Southern Pacific Railroad Corporation; as a railroad maintenance worker, he had toiled in the areas of Long Beach, La Puente, Walnut, Spadra, and Pomona, California. Mr. Ahern was the area superintendent in charge of the railroad work in all of those towns. He and his wife were very devout Irish Catholics from the Old Sod; they arranged for my parents to occupy their spacious "executive house" (something the railroad provided for its area superintendents) rent free from 1929 to 1939. What a blessing! The house was quite roomy and had all utilities.

Mr. Ahern also had a little side business about three-quarters of a mile away. In the barrio we called Celaya, he owned a spiffy white house with a separate building in the front yard that faced the corner of Hamilton and Monterey Avenues. That building was a little grocery store catering to the barrio's Chicanos. Our grandmother lived in that barrio, along with three of her sons, her widowed daughter with her daughter, and the son of another one of her sons who had died in Kansas during their Diaspora.

My memories of the years between 1934 and 1939 are vivid, rich, and pleasant. Downtown Pomona was but a few feet from our house. Its streets and stores were my recreational backyard. I made friends with the shopkeepers and was intrigued with their work. I asked zillions of questions, as the curious young are wont to do. As already mentioned in Part II, Chapter 1, I came to know Roy O. Day, the publisher of the local newspaper, the *Progress Bulletin*, at a young age. As of May 25, 1973, he was still writing personal, confidential letters to his "Dear Friend and President Richard Nixon" on my behalf.

However, in 1939, we had to move from Gordon Street because the city of Pomona was realigning the track of the Union Pacific Railroad Corporation to widen First Street. Up to now, the tracks had occupied half of the street. It happened that the house on Gordon Street had been built between the tracks of two railroad companies, Union Pacific on the south side and Southern Pacific on the north, only about forty feet away from either. While we lived there in that house, somehow we had become immune to the sounds of steam locomotives and grinding iron wheels pulling a hundred freight cars and a caboose. But now the house would be demolished to allow the Union Pacific tracks to move out of First Street.

My parents were very content and busy at our new home at 1235 West Grand. My father, despite an inoperable knee injury, made sure we worked every square inch of its land. (Land ownership? For the first time in my father's life, he owned land! In Mexico, poor people could not own land.) We raised hogs, pigeons, rabbits, chickens, and goats—for cheese, milk, meat, eggs, and cash. We harvested chiles, tomatoes, and sundry vegetables and fruits for canning, consumption, and sale.

We were at church frequently. My father was the choirmaster and president of the local Mexican Nocturnal Adoration Society. I was the perpetual altar boy and, after age fifteen, the clerical assistant at the rectory. I filled out forms and distributed bulletins door-to-door to Mexicans in two barrios (Celaya and Silao) and to houses in between. I got to know the names and faces of the churchgoing Catholics, the fallen-aways, some of the converts to Protestantism, the few retail businesspeople, and the handful of educated and privileged offspring of former landowners in Mexico (*gachupines*: Spaniards)—as well as a few rabidly anti-Catholic Jacobin Masons.

In 1941, the Second World War started. Chicano boys were drafted. Their parents hustled to Los Angeles to confer with the Mexican consul to seek exemption from military service. They pointed out their sons were born in Mexico and were Mexican citizens. They were aliens in the United States. But legal or not, it didn't matter. They had been working in the citrus groves picking lemons, grapefruit, and oranges, and now they were going into the army.

In 1942, a bilateral agreement between Mexico and the United States brought other Mexicans to pick the citrus. We began to see them attending Sacred Heart Church and shopping in downtown Pomona as well as at fiestas, celebrations, and dances. Their hats, shoes, and clothing made them stand out. These new arrivals were neither immigrants nor migrants. They were contract laborers working for a specific, limited time. Upon contract termination, they returned to Mexico. And, very often, they came back again for another contract. They were called *braceros* ("arms"); the agreement was called the Bracero Program and lasted until 1964.

The United States became addicted to the cheap, bountifully available Mexican labor. And, as it is so often stated, laws frequently have unintended consequences. Just as the Teutonic peoples of the Dark Ages (the 400s to the 800s) learned via the excellent Roman highways that winters in Spain, the Riviera, and the Po River Valley were highly desirable and migrated there to remain, the four-million-plus Mexicans of the Bracero Program learned that the winters in California and Texas were nice—and the dollar even nicer.

In the late forties and early fifties, I began to notice the presence of former *braceros* at Sacred Heart Church. They had moved into the barrios and were joining organizations in the church. And they were asking for forms to be filled out at the rectory to prove with church documents that they had been baptized, made their First Communion, and been confirmed. If they wanted to marry, they also had to prove with a letter from their church in Mexico that they had not been previously wed. It was my job to help them out.

In the early 1960s, *braceros* began to return to the United States with their families *sin papeles*. From their days as *braceros*, they personally knew the owners of the horse stables, flower ranches, cattle ranches, and so on. These owners were only too willing to fill out U.S. Department of Labor forms affirming that they had found healthy and reliable workers for their job vacancies. The Labor Department routinely approved these requests, forwarding them on to the U.S. Department of Justice, Immigration and Naturalization Service (INS) for the issuance of "green cards." As a result, millions of Mexicans became legal residents of the United States. The illegal migrants became immigrants. The semi-permanent became permanent.

Vast numbers of prospective workers *sin papeles* continued to cross the border into the United States. In 1954, INS implemented a program called "Operation Wetback" to catch hundreds of thousands of Mexicans crossing rivers illegally every year. Yet, their number kept increasing. In the Oval Office, President Nixon had asked my opinion on what we could do to curtail the illegal flow. I responded that if in twenty-five years, Mexico might finally get tired of its dictatorial and socialistic government and move toward capitalism, industry, and a reformed judicial system, this might supply the jobs that would keep people in the country. His throw-away response was, "Let us see in twenty-five years."

After several months of research, I realized that my parents had immigrated during the first serious exodus from Mexico. My mom and dad were urban dwellers who read a lot and were well informed on the current affairs of the time. They boarded the late-night train out of Salamanca in 1922, and became part of the Diaspora.

Nothing had ever before caused people from Central Mexico to leave the only world they knew, to move to a strange land with a different language, a different religion, and different attitudes—and worst of all, a country that had, in the memory of their grandparents, invaded theirs. The Diaspora was the very first wave of Mexicans to depart from El Bajio for the North.

The second wave of departures came by way of the Bracero Program (albeit intended as temporary) and was also occasioned by war. The *braceros* were here to replace the sons of the first wave who had been sent to fight in World War II. Their motivation for coming to the United States was economic—a pure and simple bid to improve their standard of living. The pattern of migration showed that the relatives of the workers in the Bracero Program also wanted the good life the U.S. dollar could provide— not only in their poor hovels in Mexico but even more so in the United States itself. The contractually regulated flow of human labor became a torrent, with or without legal papers. Awareness, personal knowledge, and quick, convenient means of transport and communications caused a new surge of illegal aliens. The world got much smaller.

To discover the extent of illegal immigration, research would have to be done and my congressional liaison would have to dialogue with congressional staffers. Also, the Office of Information would have to be prepared to handle requests arising from our increased activities regarding the immigration situation and our efforts to develop conditions for presidential amnesty. I conferred by phone with the consultants from Connecticut that Finch had recommended, yet my appointment logs do not record meeting with them in Washington. I am unable to recall any specific actions I took to advance their work or even if they were given a personal services contract by the executive director. It was a murky, chaotic, and disorderly time. The President and his inner staff were implementing policy directions for the next four years; since it was right after reelection, it was also a time of transience for political personnel in all agencies, and many were replaced with new faces trying to get their bearings.

I personally visited with the executive director of the House Appropriations Committee to present my ideas for counting illegal immigrants. I suggested that the matter would become nationally troubling in the near future. I asked him to add $50,000 to the U.S. Department of Justice budget for designing and field-testing a protocol. Later, I was informed that such a contract was duly awarded to Century, Inc.—a company owned by David North, the former Johnson-appointed executive director of the Inter-Agency Committee on Mexican-American Affairs. I was also informed when he completed the contract.

Sometime in the summer of 1973, I returned to the Rayburn House Building to ask the chair of the House Appropriations Committee, Rep. George Mahon, for $1.5 million for the INS budget. (The executive director of the House Appropriations Committee was sitting beside him.) The money became available on July 1, 1974, to be deployed according to the protocol designed and tested by Century, Inc.

Meanwhile, Robert Brochtrup, my congressional liaison, quietly held one-on-one conversations with congressmen who represented populations that were 10 percent or more Spanish-surnamed. They discussed the Air Force One phone call and the CCOSSP's preliminary efforts to come up with recommendations and suggestions for actions leading to amnesty. But we were overwhelmed by the black cloud of the Watergate break-in created by a corrupt Democratic Congress.

Nevertheless, President Nixon did not forget the matter of the phone call. Eight months later, in November 1973, an imposing figure dressed in proper, dark business attire strode into my office with a firm gait. My secretary introduced General Leonard Chapman, former Commandant of the U.S. Marine Corps, and departed, closing the door behind her.

General Chapman had come unannounced but on the specific instructions of President Nixon. He was to work with me on regularizing the status of so many Mexicans who still lacked proper documentation, even a simple border pass, after being in the United States for a long time. Again, I was startled. Even with all the issues related to Watergate swirling around, Nixon had not forgotten. The general declared that the President had appointed him INS commissioner and had instructed him to work with me on immigrant amnesty. "Where do you suggest we start?" he asked me. To myself, I thought, *"This is marvelous! I, an ex-army corporal, working with a retired four-star general on the President's instructions! Can this get any better?"*

But in answer to General Chapman, I confessed that I still did not have a firm grip on how to comply with the President's request for "some paperwork." I had responded to the Democrats' Watergate investigations, subpoenas, documents, and harassments; done research on the current status of immigration; searched for ways to identify the size of the problem by counting the number of illegal aliens; and initiated congressional contacts. I probably should have simplified the task by addressing our efforts at people in situations akin to my uncle's. But reality dictates that when the concept of amnesty is discussed with respect to immigration, the task is no longer simple.

I had sought the pulse on illegal immigration as reflected in newspapers between 1971 and 1973 and reviewed with General Chapman my search of the literature gathered through a daily newspaper clipping service. We had found only a few articles; immigration was not a big issue on the minds of Americans in that era. However, I did find an interesting editorial in the *News-Examiner* of Connersville, Indiana about illegal immigration of "wetbacks." The story ended, "Finally, in co-operation with U.S. authorities, Mexico is tracking down and arresting 'coyotes'—the recruiters responsible for the wetback traffic. The Mexican Justice Department has already jailed 200 of these animals."[62] It was a real puff job. The entire article could have been prepared by some public relations firm. The American public was not yet aware of the growing lines of people walking out of Mexico and into *El Norte*, seeking the American Dream of prosperity.

But a sign of things to come showed up in Chicago. The *Sun-Times* carried a story in April 1973 that said, "The Immigration and Naturalization Service district director denied Monday that his agents use harassment tactics on Mexican-Americans in their search for illegal aliens."[63]

I related to General Chapman my efforts to educate myself on the current state of affairs and attempts to crystallize opinions on what we could do about this potentially vast, growing problem. We could take any possible presidential actions now, looking toward congressional legislation of amnesty for longtime

---

[62] Editorial, "Mexico Has Decided to Dry Up the 'Wetback' Problem," *Connersville (Indiana) News-Examiner*, April 1, 1972.

[63] Dennis B. Fisher, "Immigration Aide Hits Harassment Charges," *Chicago Sun-Times*, April 3, 1973.

residents who had demonstrated that they were solid citizens. I suggested that the general invite me to address his district directors when he introduced himself as head of their agency, so I could outline my recommendations for them (and I did). I also told the general how we planned to count illegal aliens and told him about the $50,000 questionnaire and the $1.5 million to implement the actual field count. We remained in touch over the months.

Toward the very last days of my tenure at CCOSSP (definitely after the new fiscal year started in July 1974), the INS received its money from Congress. I got General Chapman (now known as "Chappie") and Joe Reyes, owner of an 8(a) firm, to have lunch at the swanky Sans Souci Restaurant close to the White House. We discussed how INS could award Reyes a contract to count illegal aliens.

A year later, I was in my office at 3600 Wilshire Boulevard in Los Angeles. E. B. Duarte, then a special assistant to Chappie at INS, called me with the news that Reyes had just secured that contract. I have tried without success to learn its findings. Leonel Castillo of Houston, who was appointed INS commissioner in 1977, terminated the Reyes contract on the advice of his staffer Arnold Flores. I have not been able to learn how much work Joe Reyes was able to perform, but it is a fact that no illegal aliens were counted for the record. What a shame!

The issue of illegals had been thrust on me; as a Mexican-American leader, I was expected to know something, but I lacked hard intelligence and research on the problem. Yet I had to come up with some solutions. In the beginning of 1974, I formed these notions, opinions, and solutions: The children of the first big wave of Mexican refugees who fled from persecutions in the 1920s (of which I was one myself) were no longer the labor pool for picking agricultural products; we had been replaced by the *braceros*. Their children, in turn, were now the agricultural, manufacturing, construction, and service business labor pool. They were the new illegals and were coming in huge numbers, especially from southern Mexico (which might be called that country's "Appalachia"). Their physical appearance and behaviors were quite different from those of prior waves of Mexicans. They were more Indian, more indigenous.

After the Air Force One phone call, I was under the gun to come up with something significant for the President to sign and do. The migration problem kept cropping up; matters were beginning to boil under the surface. In February 1974, on a trip to a conference in San Diego, I spoke with Frank Saldana, a reporter for the *San Diego Evening Tribune*. He got some of my thoughts in print: "Exploitation of illegal aliens could be stopped if the current work force could be stabilized, a federal official says. 'It would stop the turnstile approach to the problem created by the needs of employers,' said Henry M. Ramirez."[64]

On March 6, 1974, Pat Flores, a reporter for the *San Antonio Express-News*, also interviewed me. He wrote: "Ramirez said his committee will propose amnesty for countless illegal aliens in the U.S. 'Those illegal aliens who have been here for years, established roots, and are law abiding, should receive amnesty from deportation,' he said. Ramirez said support for this recommendation 'has

---

[64] Frank Saldana, "Solution Offered to Alien Problem," *San Diego Evening Tribune*, February 21, 1974.

been well received' in Congress."[65] This interview shows we were trying to get the amnesty proposal to become a reality even as the dark clouds of Watergate crowded the skies.

As I had predicted to General Chapman, the migration of illegals from Mexico did grow and become a highly publicized international issue. Six months after the February 1974 interview I gave Frank Saldana, General Chapman himself was featured in a *Seattle Daily Times* article entitled "Flow of Illegal Aliens: A Gusher."[66] And in the *San Diego Union*, General Chapman elaborated on the severity of the problem with detailed specifics, estimating the number of illegal aliens at six to seven million.[67] A *New York Times* headline around the same time was: "Chavez Seeks a Halt to Nation's 'Worst' Influx of Illegal Aliens."[68] In Fresno, California, Cesar Chavez, president of the United Farm Workers of America, demanded that the U.S. Border Patrol crack down on illegal alien workers. I was to learn years later that the Democratic National Committee, together with George Meany, president of the AFL-CIO, was utterly opposed to any amnesty, in concert with their new Mexican-American ally, the National Council of La Raza, headed up by Raul Yzaguirre.

---

[65] Pat Flores, "Migrants Get Gas Need Pledges," *San Antonio Express*, March 6, 1974.

[66] Bruce Johansen, "Flow of Illegal Aliens: A Gusher," *Seattle Daily Times*, July 23, 1974.

[67] "'Growing Daily': Alien Smuggling Problem Cited," *San Diego Union*, July 15, 1974.

[68] "Chavez Seeks a Halt to Nation's 'Worst' Influx of Illegal Aliens," *New York Times*, July 23, 1974.

Those two months of June and July 1974 marked a change in reportage from previous quiescence. The issue began to explode. The drumbeat began in Mexico, which protested the ill treatment of its workers in the United States, demanding improvements and denouncing the wholesale hunt for undocumented workers.[69,70,71,72,73,74,75] On the U.S. side, editorials began to appear. One California newspaper complained of "More Illegal Entry" and opened with "The illegal, alien invasion continues unabated...."[76] It was picked up by the *News-Courier* in Alabama[77] and the *Dispatch* in Tennessee.[78]

A very nasty article appeared in a Spanish-language Chicago newspaper, *El Nacional.* Its headline translated:

---

[69] "Convenio entre Mexico y Canada sobre braceros," *Mexico (DF) El Nacional,* June 18, 1974.

[70] "Nuevo tratado sobre braceros," *El Sol de Leon,* June 19, 1974.

[71] Editorial, "Trabajadores, migratorios," *Mexico (DF) La Prensa,* June 21, 1974.

[72] "Nada respeto a los braceros en la mision a EU," *Mexico (DF) Novedades,* June 23, 1974.

[73] "Que Washington realiza una caceria de mexicanos 'ilegales' para deportarlos," *Mexico (DF) Novedades,* June 23, 1974.

[74] "Anuncian en Denver que expulsaran a veintiocho mexicanos ilegales, *San Luis Potosi El Heraldo,* June 23, 1974.

[75] "Mexico protesta trato de E.U. a sus trabajadores emigrantes," *San Salvador La Prensa Grafica,* June 24, 1974.

[76] Editorial, "More Illegal Entry," *Hanford (California) Sentinel,* July 9, 1974.

[77] Editorial, "More Illegal Entry," *Athens (Alabama) News-Courier,* July 9, 1974.

[78] Editorial, "More Illegal Entry," *Cookeville (Tennessee) Dispatch,* July 11, 1974.

"Ramirez Acquires Entry for 32,000 Cubans. Dirty, Traitor: Henry Ramirez." The article went on to state, "He is working on getting parole for the immigration from Spain of refugees from Fidel Castro's Cuba."[79] Some Mexican-American journalists in Chicago disliked what I had done on behalf of Cubans who had fled to their ancestral motherland, Spain, and discovered they would be much better off in the United States. I had worked with my presidential advisor, Manuel Giberga, and Attorney General Richard Kleindienst, who was also a member of the Cabinet Committee, to get parole status for these Cubans. Perhaps some Mexican-American reporters were influenced by the Chicago opinion-makers (a la Saul Alinsky and other hardline leftists) and consequently had a strong dislike for Cubans who fled Fidel Castro's "island paradise"?

That phone call from Air Force One in early 1973 certainly opened a Pandora's box of ethnic emotions, legal issues, and international tensions in the mid-1970s. But by that time, I was on my way out of Washington, DC, and into the private sector, seeking anonymity and a tranquil life for my family back home in California. Immigration would become someone else's hot potato.

However, these and other efforts somehow or other culminated in the enactment of the Simpson-Mazzoli Act in 1986, which granted amnesty to more than 300,000 illegal alien Irish and about two million Mexicans. It would be a nice touch to give Nixon some credit for starting the ball rolling. It does take years for ideas to grow and become actualized.

---

[79] "Ramirez Consigue la Entrada a 32,000 Cubanos," *El Nacional*, January 11, 1974.

11. NATIONAL HISPANIC HERITAGE WEEK

"Include us in White House activities to create a national awareness of the conditions of Mexican-Americans." That was the fifth of the visions on my three-by-five card, and the White House Sunday service detailed in Part II, Chapter 8 was part of its actualization. This chapter will present another part: National Hispanic Heritage Week.

When I suggested that the White House should include Mexican-Americans in its cultural activities, I pointed out that the Washington area—unlike the Southwest—was not familiar with Mexican-Americans. For that reason, before I was appointed chairman of the Cabinet Committee on Opportunities for Spanish-Speaking People (CCOSSP), I wrote my fifty-page study, "An Overview of Spanish-Speaking Affairs for White House Perspectives," on what Mexican-Americans should expect from the administration.

First, my study reviewed the need for official recognition of the Spanish-speaking and suggested that they be identified by ethnicity in all government data tabulations. (This was done; see Part II, Chapter 3.) It also suggested the following actions: that the administration invite Spanish-speaking community leaders to a White House Sunday service (done); that the White House hold a meeting with members of Congress to discuss issues relevant to Spanish-speaking communities; and that it recognize the issues of farm labor.

Sometime later, I was able to acquire a copy of my study. It had been altered substantially. One copy was a fifty-two-page document marked "CONFIDENTIAL" that had totally converted my study into a political strategy and tactical report. Someone at the White House political shop had inserted a line after each area of concern that suggested a presidential action that could be approved to take or disapproved. In retrospect, for this former migrant worker, I am deeply impressed and gratified to realize that my study on Mexican-Americans achieved presidential oversight.

Later still, upon reviewing the chronology of White House activities with regard to Mexican-Americans initially, and later on with respect to mainland Puerto Ricans and Cubans, I realized that the mid-1970 arrival of Robert Finch in the West Wing initiated the White House's outreach to this new group, the Spanish-speaking. In August 1971, Washington did not really know what we Mexican-Americans looked like because there were only a few of us around, although this state of affairs changed permanently soon after.

How truly unlike what I faced in Pecos, Texas, in July 1951! Several seminarians and I were motoring to Mexico City from Los Angeles. We had departed from

Albuquerque that morning, and by the time we were passing through open cotton farms in that very, very hot country approaching the city limits of Pecos, it was well past lunchtime, and we were famished and thirsty. We were so happy to spot a sign advertising "The Best Hamburgers" at a roadside restaurant ahead. We found the restaurant and parked in its vast parking area surfaced with gravel (it obviously catered to motorists and truckers).

Quickly, we made for the entrance. But just as quickly, a glance at a sign posted at the steps made me come to a halt! Discrimination in California was subtle and oblique, but here, it was the "Texan way"—open, overt, and in your face. My mind raced back to my 1938 and 1939 seasonal migrant days in San Jose. While cutting apricots in open-air sheds and on our knees picking prunes lodged on clod-cluttered earth, I had met European Americans from Texas, Arkansas, and Oklahoma. We called them Okies. My mother did not permit us children to associate with them. She admonished us in Spanish that they were barbarian-like and somehow pagan, odd and unacceptably different.

Now I had come face to face with living history. The scrawled sign read: "No Mescans, No Dogs, No Niggers." With great celerity, my mind told me, "*European Americans in Pecos probably know what Mexicans look like. They will not hesitate to recognize me as the genuine article: a Mexican. And then they would have to deny me a greasy hamburger and a Coke.*"

They did identify me but not my classmates (who had names like Bob Hempfling); however, my cohorts left as hungry and thirsty as I was. I quickly assured them that this was an opportunity to offer our mortification for the suffering souls in Purgatory. Maybe we got one or two souls an early release. We resumed our journey toward Laredo. Had we taken a photograph of that scandalous sign, this chapter would be better illustrated. But we scurried out of there in such haste that the brand-new, black, four-door Buick sedan with four portholes left tire marks and a billowing cloud of dust raised by its screeching wheels.

I ruminated on that emotional event. If I had attempted to purchase food, I would simply have interfered with the social norms and behaviors of the descendants of recent slave owners. These European Americans possessed certainty of their White "superiority." The European American residents of Pecos, Texas, were still abiding by the vestigial effects of the invasion of this former part of Mexico by President Polk's minions 100 years earlier.

This kind of behavior continued in Texas as I later went on to become a professional researcher and civil rights government official. For example, in 1968, I interviewed an El Paso elementary school principal for the Mexican American Education Study. I was amazed to hear her solemn, yet delicate statement: "My job is so demanding. It is so difficult to bring these little 'mescan' kids up to our superior culture." I grimaced, with upraised eyebrows. As another example, in 1969, I documented that the trustees of the Pecos school system bused children so that Whites could go to new facilities almost fifty miles away in Zaragoza, while the Zaragozan Mexicans were brought in to the old buildings in Pecos.

By this time in my life, the world of "superior" and "inferior" cultures, with consequential acts of discrimination, was no longer a source of surprise or annoyance. I had been schooled on human interactions and relationships derived from class differences almost from the moment I arrived at the age of reason. As a teacher, I vigorously battled a related disorder that impeded student achievement: It was the negative self-image that so penetrated the psyche of Mexican Mestizos.

In 1971, creating national awareness of the Spanish-speaking was a must. Nothing prior in recent political history had been done about this national need. John F. Kennedy had not developed a strategy to include Mexican-Americans in American society. Bobby Kennedy, with his Viva Kennedy Clubs, had not even promised to count us! The Kennedys did make a national concern out of the unionization efforts of Cesar Chavez, the rural leader of a few Mexicans working in the vineyards around Fresno, California. Lyndon Johnson's memory was only jogged in the last days of his presidency as he recalled his elementary school teaching days in a Mexican-American school in Cotulla, Texas; it was only then that he decided that he had to do something. Sadly, I add that the VIPs of the emerging world of Mexican-Americans did not write about our great need to become known by being counted, either. Neither academics nor Mexican-American union bosses pointed out this deficiency, and neither did leaders like Dr. Hector Garcia nor elected representatives such as Congressmen Don Edwards (D., California) or "Little Joe" Montoya (D., New Mexico).

People can rightly state that the Civil Rights Act of 1964 profoundly diminished discrimination and credit President Johnson for it, but the law was enacted to benefit Black Americans. We had to struggle to be included, because at first, we were not even seen. For instance, Jeffrey Miller, at the U.S. Commission on Civil Rights, was assigned to study the enforcement of civil rights. He designed methods to measure how much discrimination had diminished by 1971—but only with respect to Black Americans. Given the limits of his methodology, I was able to convince the six commissioners that they approve of Miller's work only if it included the impact on the Spanish-speaking as well. The struggle to assure incorporation of Mexican-Americans and other Latinos into civil rights efforts continues even today.

Besides counting us, I also worked on other ways to develop national awareness of Mexican-Americans. About a month after President Nixon appointed me chairman of his Cabinet Committee, I wrote a memo to Counselor Finch about commemorating Mexico's Independence Day (September 16) as a step toward developing the national awareness Mexican-Americans so badly needed. In my memo, I proposed having the Mexican ambassador and a five-member delegation of Mexican-Americans visit the President in the Oval Office on September 16, 1971. I pointed out it would be a fine opportunity for photographs and for the Spanish-speaking people to see once again the Nixon administration's interest in them. I wrote to explain further:

The pictures and the meeting would reinforce the President's declared policy of boosting the importance of Spanish-speaking people in America. It would make the Mexican-American people feel that the President really does care about them, a point which must be very clearly demonstrated between now and November of 1972. I would appreciate your considerable persuasive powers behind this proposal which could be of great value to the Spanish-speaking people and to the Administration.[80]

---

80 Henry Ramirez to Counselor Finch, memorandum, September 3,

It is true that with respect to commemorating Mexico's Independence Day, Congress had already acted three years before. The Ninetieth Congress approved Public Law 90-498 on September 17, 1968, authorizing the president to issue an annual proclamation designating the week including September 15 and 16 as "National Hispanic Heritage Week" and called upon the people of the United States, especially the educational community, to observe it with appropriate ceremonies and activities. This action of Congress brings thoughts both negative and positive. Congress acted admirably, but what took it so long to become aware? Furthermore, President Johnson did not issue the proclamation that Congress authorized.

It was President Nixon who first signed a proclamation about National Hispanic Heritage Week (Figure 9), and Vice President Spiro Agnew read it publicly on September 16, 1973 (Figure 10). (Fifteen years later, President Reagan expanded National Hispanic Heritage Week to be National Hispanic Heritage Month.[81]) I submitted a list of 200 potential recipients to receive copies of the first presidential proclamation of National Hispanic Heritage Week.[82] This singular act of proclaiming a week dedicated to raising awareness and appreciation of Hispanic inheritance, culture, history, and

---

1971, "Proposed Action by the President to Commemorate Mexico's Independence Day of September 16, 1971." National Archives.

[81] Press release, Office of the White House Press Secretary, September 13, 1988, "Remarks by the President at the Signing Ceremony for Hispanic Heritage Week."

[82] Henry Ramirez to Fred Slight, memorandum, September 7, 1973, "Names for Hispanic Heritage Week."

arts caused spectacular advances in awareness of the Hispanic people in the United States.

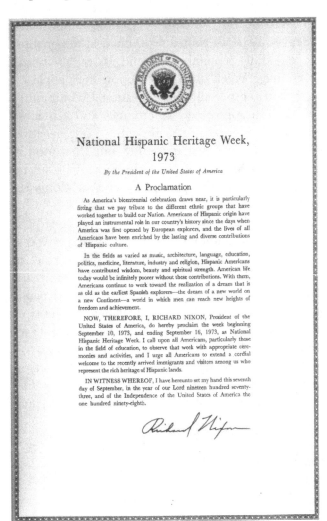

National Hispanic Heritage Week, 1973

By the President of the United States of America

A Proclamation

As America's bicentennial celebration draws near, it is particularly fitting that we pay tribute to the different ethnic groups that have worked together to build our Nation. Americans of Hispanic origin have played an instrumental role in our country's history since the days when America was first opened by European explorers, and the lives of all Americans have been enriched by the lasting and diverse contributions of Hispanic culture.

In the fields as varied as music, architecture, language, education, politics, medicine, literature, industry and religion, Hispanic Americans have contributed wisdom, beauty and spiritual strength. American life today would be infinitely poorer without these contributions. With them, Americans continue to work toward the realization of a dream that is as old as the earliest Spanish explorers—the dream of a new world on a new Continent—a world in which men can reach new heights of freedom and achievement.

NOW, THEREFORE, I, RICHARD NIXON, President of the United States of America, do hereby proclaim the week beginning September 10, 1973, and ending September 16, 1973, as National Hispanic Heritage Week. I call upon all Americans, particularly those in the field of education, to observe that week with appropriate ceremonies and activities, and I urge all Americans to extend a cordial welcome to the recently arrived immigrants and visitors among us who represent the rich heritage of Hispanic lands.

IN WITNESS WHEREOF, I have hereunto set my hand this seventh day of September, in the year of our Lord nineteen hundred seventy-three, and of the Independence of the United States of America the one hundred ninety-eighth.

Figure 9. President Richard M. Nixon signed this proclamation on National Hispanic Heritage Week in September 1973. *(Courtesy Richard M. Nixon Library)*

Figure 10. Vice President Agnew read the proclamation of National Hispanic Heritage Week on September 16, 1973. From left to right: Joseph Juarez, chairman of the American GI Forum; Pete Villa, president of the League of United Latin American Citizens; Phillip Sanchez, ambassador to Honduras; Manual Lujan, congressman (R., New Mexico); Dr. Henry M. Ramirez, chairman of Cabinet Committee on Opportunities for Spanish-Speaking People; Jose Juan de Olloqui, Mexican ambassador to the United States; and Vice President Agnew. *(Courtesy Richard M. Nixon Library)*

The concern over the national void of awareness of Mexican-American matters had now been shredded. President Nixon is to be credited for this accomplishment; sadly, under pressure wrought by frenzied Democrats, he departed from the presidency a few days before he would have also signed the second proclamation in September 1974. Instead, President Ford signed the second proclamation.

While I reached out to advance the nation's awareness of the Spanish-speaking people, the White House Communications Office had to join us in the effort. I was delighted to know that Counselor Finch and the communications director, Herb Klein, accepted my assignment of Carlos Conde to the Communications Office. Fluent in Spanish, Conde was instrumental in delivering information to the media in Spanish and English—another first! The other member agencies of the Cabinet Committee also soon began to issue information to Spanish-language publications.

I knew that I would be the definer and articulator of our efforts to inform Spanish-speaking Americans, especially on what the federal government was doing to reach out to them and to assure them of their equal opportunities. Our information newsletter, *Hoy*, performed remarkably well. My knowledge of European classics and humanities, coupled with my experiences with ethnic universality in Catholic school education, equipped me to weigh, understand, and perceive other points of view and opinions. The experience of being the only Mexican-American student in all my classes endowed me richly with a catholicity of cross-cultural understanding. By the time that President Nixon appointed me to oversee matters of the Spanish-speaking people, I was acutely aware of the sociopolitical effects of race, ethnicity, and land and business ownership.

Just as England had established colonies known as New England, the Spanish crown, represented by a viceroy, ruled *Nueva Espana* (New Spain), which stretched from South America to Oregon. Indigenous peoples were the original inhabitants of the part of New Spain that became the southwestern United States after war with Mexico. Many of their offspring became Mestizos and Catholics beginning in the 1500s. Miners from Zacatecas, Sonora, and Guanajuato arrived in what is now Colorado, New Mexico, Arizona, and California in the 1600s. Workers from Acapulco, Mazatlan, and Guadalajara helped the Jesuits and Franciscans build the California missions and their facilities in the 1700s. Other workers from the interior of Mexico, who tended horses, mules, cattle, and sheep, also accompanied the Spanish. They were to become known as cowboys and mule-train drivers. These were the people who came to live in the Southwest—as described by Professor Julian Zamora in his 1966 book, *La Raza: Forgotten Americans*. Some had lived in the Southwest for generations, dating from even before the United States existed as a country.

By 1974, awareness of the role and presence of the Spanish-speaking people in our country had been heightened significantly.

What role did the legislative branch play in this? Credit must be given to two House members, George H. W. Bush (R., Texas) and Edward Roybal (D., California). They persuaded Congress to vote for legislation to establish the CCOSSP by law. That happened in 1969. I spoke to Martin Castillo, the first chairman of the Cabinet Committee about this.[83] He and Bush shared much in common, including service as fighter pilots. Ed Roybal and Martin Castillo's father had both been born in Belen (a suburb of Albuquerque), New Mexico. As a registered Democrat prior to his presidential appointment as chairman, Castillo had supported Congressman Roybal. The blend of personalities, commonalities, and careers of these three men wrought a historic outcome through the subsequent work of the CCOSSP.

However, the newly formed CCOSSP did not hold a single meeting for twenty months. It was supposed to be a well-behaved agency that didn't make waves. The

---

[83] Martin Castillo, interview by author, Los Angeles, CA, September 4, 2010.

Democrats up on "the Hill" entertained no concern about it, and the Republicans in the White House did not know what to do with it. In its infancy, the small, new-kid-on-the-block agency created to assure Mexican-Americans their rights and opportunities struggled like a little orphan under "benign neglect."

But with a reelection campaign on the horizon, Nixon knew that energizing the CCOSSP as a full-fledged Cabinet Committee became imperative; he himself took charge and infused it with support, direction, and energy so that when I took over as chairman in 1971, we were able to accomplish great strides for the Spanish-speaking people of the United States.

Before November 1972, most members of Congress (like most Americans) did not really know who we Spanish speakers were. But when Nixon got over 30 percent of the Spanish-speaking vote, elected officials woke up to a new reality. Acutely attuned to the instrument of their elevation—the vote—they hustled to learn about us. With that success, we were on the road to having our political power known and recognized. Spanish-speaking Americans—formerly invisible, forgotten, neglected, and unknown—would now be courted for their vote for the first time in history.

President Nixon truly accomplished much for Mexican-Americans and other Spanish-speaking Americans through the CCOSSP.

However, the makers of history have indulged in actions of omission. The writers for the well-known newspapers have exercised profound ignorance of the realities revealed in this book. The relatively new method of informing us through pictures, voice, music, and moving actions by means of television has not drawn aside the curtain of public ignorance of who we, the Spanish-speaking people, are!

Instead, the methods of informing the public have been used to defame a truly great, visionary president of the United States. The industrious "debunkers" of history are legion. I have read, listened to, and know of many of them. It would not serve goodness to name them. God knows who they are.

Thus, this book is for people who want to know the truth of history. Nixon accomplished great deeds for the poor, illiterate, hard-working, Catholic Mestizos of the Diaspora from Mexico and their descendants. Congress added Cubans, Puerto Ricans, and other Spanish-speaking people, and they, too, have benefited greatly!

PART III

1. WHAT WAS UNKNOWN

The great strides Richard M. Nixon accomplished for Mexican-Americans (as well as other Spanish-speaking Americans), which have been summarized in the preceding chapters, helped many of them reach places in American society that their forefathers could not have conceived. However, these presidential actions were not mere political calculations designed to win votes. They arose from the personal interaction Richard Nixon had with Mexican-American families he knew in his younger days, particularly the families at Leffingwell Ranch and Murphy Ranch in East Whittier, California. His admiration for them and their values, principles, and way of life inspired and motivated him to direct the government to build bridges to the American Dream for Mexican-Americans. He wanted to do something for them, and he did.

But who were those Mexican-Americans that Nixon had encountered? While each person certainly has a unique story, some commonalities stand out. The roughly

200 Mexican-American families at the Leffingwell and Murphy Ranches, like so many other Mexican-Americans in the United States at the time, had arrived fairly recently in a wave of immigration during the first decades of the twentieth century. This was the Diaspora of two million Mexicans. Most of them were Mestizo; most of them were illiterate and of humble origin. It would be the children and grandchildren of these Diaspora survivors that President Nixon would assist, but curiously, these younger generations by and large knew little of the reasons for their families' departure or the story behind it. It is a tragic history, not well known. But because of the experiences of a young man in East Whittier, himself of humble origin, who came to be this country's thirty-seventh president, the unknown group has become known, and little by little, their story is revealed, too. This part of the book gives voice to the Diaspora survivors and witness to their hardships.

Hardships indeed they suffered! Recall the political situation in Mexico leading up to the Diaspora, in which seeds of bloody, violent upheaval were sown: After Mexico became independent from Spain in 1821, power in the country was concentrated in the hands of the relatively few Criollos. Although they made up only ten percent of the population, this educated class of intelligentsia controlled everything. They soaked in ideas popular in Europe at the time—principles of the French Revolution as well as concepts of new European philosophies promulgated by intellectuals such as Marx and Nietzsche. In addition, the eighteenth-century Age of Reason (the Enlightenment era) continued to influence educated people to reject the use of Faith and adopt Reason alone to explain all knowledge and promote godless materialism. They mocked the illiterate, uneducated, poor, and very devout Mestizos and Native Mexicans *(indios)*. They ridiculed the people filling the churches for believing in Heaven, Hell, Satan, and God Himself. After all, the celebrated scientific methods could not prove the existence of God!

In this toxic brew of thought, the viciously anti-Catholic Mexican Liberals (Masons, Positivists, Jacobins, and others), under the principal leadership of Benito Juarez, gained power by mid-century and launched *La Reforma*. They passed *Las Leyes de Reforma*, also known as *Las Leyes de Lerdo* (1856); ratified a new constitution (1857); and made Benito Juarez president in 1861. Both the Lerdo Laws and the constitution contained measures intended to disembowel the Catholic Church and eradicate its "mythology." However, Porfirio Diaz, who rose to power in the 1870s, checked the enforcement of those anti-Church laws. Under his firm rule, he only permitted Liberals to protest and "bark without biting," and Mexico enjoyed a period of relative calm while Porfirio Diaz strove to attract foreign investment and modernize the country in the direction of capitalism.

Porfirio Diaz governed for decades. However, still fomented by philosophies developing in Europe (now adding the Bolsheviks/Communists, Socialists, and their ilk), the *La Revolucion* ignited by Francisco Madero in November 1910 successfully toppled the Diaz government. Following Porfirio Diaz's exile in May 1911, Mexico sadly descended into a period of chaos as multiple players wrestled for control. Madero did not last long, and things went from bad to worse, as one dictator followed another from 1913 to 1930: Venustiano Carranza, Alvaro Obregon, and Plutarco Calles each outdid the other in terms of horrific atrocities committed against the Catholic Church and her faithful. (Pancho Villa and, to an even lesser extent, Emiliano Zapata were never real players in the transformative actions of the three dictators but certainly contributed to the chaos and destruction.)

In the civil strife that followed in the wake of Porfirio Diaz's exile, warring factions raided towns, haciendas, ranchos, and homes to get everything and anything of value to finance and support their grab for power. They also wanted food, clothing, lodging, and women. Procurement was performed at the point of a gun. Under these conditions, Mexico dissolved into disorder and lawlessness. The large population of Mestizos and *indios,* who had been living in a stable (though unjust) feudal economy and who (being illiterate, uneducated, and uninfected by European philosophies) had not participated in any government, suffered greatly. (Parenthetically, when Mexicans in Pomona, California, were asked if they had voted when they lived in Mexico, the responses came quickly with a smile and a chuckle. What? Vote? In Mexico one does not vote. The politicians become presidents, senators, etc., without the need for voting. Elections were a farce.)

Few eyewitness written accounts exist from the period (remember, ninety percent of the population at the time was illiterate and, of course, censorship was practiced vigorously); it has only been recently that the violence in Mexico during the years 1910–1930 has become more generally known. However, I will draw from several sources to sketch a picture of the conditions faced by Mexicans in the early twentieth century.

One of the most valuable sources is Jean Meyer's multivolume work, *La Cristiada*. In it, he documents a host of atrocities in Carranza's war against the Catholic Church. Carranza's military would enter towns and get the keys to the Catholic churches, then methodically imprison, kill, and rape, and in a final act of desecration, convert the churches into horse stables and places of banquets for the soldiers. Meyer makes it abundantly clear that the struggle was *not* a revolution, but a war against the Catholic Church. He writes, "As Carranza got power, he resurrected the obstinate opposition of Liberals, of their anticlericalism, that had existed for more than a century in Mexico.... All of the anticlericals merged with Carranza, and the Church became an object of singular persecution."[84]

All over Mexico, Carranza's troops committed one sacrilege after another. Meyer's examples include:[85]

- **Queretero**—On July 29, 1914, the Carrancistas closed all but two of the churches. They held the priests (forcing one, Father Sousa, to join the army), closed the schools, burned the confessionals in the public square, and made a police station out of the seminary.

- **Leon, Guanajuato**—They arrested the diocesan administrators, expelled religious orders, and exacted ransom for the bishop.

- **Irapuato, Silao, and Celaya, Guanajuato**— They killed a priest in Silao and forbade confessions in the other two cities.

- **Aguascalientes**—They removed the statues and

---

[84] Jean Meyer, *La Cristiada, Vol. 2* (Mexico: Siglo XXI Editores, S.A. de C.V., 1973), pp. 68–69.

[85] Ibid., pp. 76–82.

confessionals from the churches. Then, on August 14, 1914, Governor Fuentes threatened death to all priests who dared to celebrate Mass.

- **Zamora**—The soldiers of Joaquin Amaro plundered the bishop's offices. They also forced the very elderly archbishop of Durango, who had fled there, to sweep the streets with the priests.

- **Morelia**—Members of the Salesian order were expelled. However, this action provoked a serious riot, and the decree was revoked on October 17, 1914.

Meyer writes, "The Constitutionalists [i.e., the army] of Carranza took over the buildings and properties of the Church, they exiled the bishops, some they imprisoned together with the priests and nuns, they voted for persecutorial law and decrees, all the while offending the people with their sacrileges and executions of priests."[86] Is it any wonder that devout Catholics, predominantly Mestizo peasants, were against the Revolution? Spontaneously they took up arms and organized as guerrilla fighters, becoming known as *"Cristeros."* In a neat turn of public relations on the part of the government, however, they would come to be blamed for this period of violence and destruction: history rewritten.

The historian Jose Rojas Garciduenas points out that Carranza was not the only one causing turmoil during the years of power struggle in Mexico. Pancho Villa, along with his men *(Division del Norte)*, also roamed the countryside and did his share of stealing, killing, and

---

[86] Ibid., pp. 68–69.

pillaging. Carranza, his former partner in the so-called revolution, did not interfere. Garciduenas writes of Villa's April 1915 arrival in Salamanca, Guanajuato (the hometown of my parents): "One of Pancho Villa's generals, Rodolfo Fierro, encouraged his men to sack the town of Salamanca. A few days later, the governor of the state of Guanajuato arrived in Salamanca, arrested a number of middle-class persons from neighboring towns, made them appear in court, and without any procedures, sentenced each one and had them shot immediately."[87]

The persecution renewed its brutality in 1924. In Jalisco, under Governor Jose Guadalupe Zuno, government officials announced that only six churches would be tolerated by the state. In addition, they closed Catholic schools in La Barca, Atotonilco, San Gabriel, Lagos, Talpa, and Villa Guerrero.[88] Governor Zuno was sending a clear message that he wanted all Catholics to desert their lands and homes. And many did. Jean Meyer writes, "There remained but two options, that of exile or that of war. And, so it was. In 1926, the government reported that 476,000 had emigrated to the North. The emigrants would say: We flee for much more than just misery."[89]

Probably the government's report underestimated the number of Mexicans fleeing the country; we know (thanks to the 1930 census that counted Mexicans born in Mexico) that eventually two million crossed the border to build new lives in the U.S.—this was the Diaspora. Jean

---

[87] Jose Rojas Garciduenas, *Salamanca: Recuerdos de mi tierra guanajuatense* (Mexico: Editorial Porrua, S.A., 1982), pp. 228–229.

[88] Jean Meyer, *La Cristiada, Vol. 2* (Mexico: Siglo XXI Editores, S.A. de C.V., 1973), p. 145.

[89] Ibid., p. 192.

Meyer cites a newspaper, *La Gaceta de Guaymas,* which reported a vivid image of the flood of emigrants: "The third-class seating in all the trains that pass by Guaymas [a city in Sonora] to the border are so full of passengers that not even in the aisle seats was space available to hang a hairpin."[90] Countless others in those brutal years 1913 to 1930 either were killed in the waves of violence and persecution under Carranza, Obregon, and Calles or died en route to the border.

Of the Diaspora, Jose Rojas Garciduenas recounts: "The peasants and some workers (skilled) emigrated to the United States. The young men of middle class also left for the United States or Mexico [City]; if over there they prospered, their families would follow them.... Many of us did not return to live in Salamanca."[91]

But for much more detail about the deluge of Mexicans crossing the border, I vigorously recommend reading *Investigation of Mexican Affairs,* a compilation of hearings held by the U.S. Senate Committee on Foreign Relations from 1910 to 1920, published by the Government Printing Office in 1920. It contains thousands of pages of sworn testimony that document the utter corruption, cruelty, and thievery going on during those years. Oddly, the prevailing American view of Mexican affairs has seemed to ignore this corpus of material, instead being content to portray Porfirio Diaz as the "bad guy." While Diaz was far from a perfect leader, where is the acknowledgment that Carranza, Obregon, and Calles were even worse dictators? The U.S. Senate hearings document involvement of Communists, the ugly

---

[90] Ibid., p. 192.

[91] Jose Rojas Garciduenas, *Salamanca: Recuerdos de mi tierra guanajuatense* (Mexico: Editorial Porrua, S.A., 1982), p. 13.

military invasion of Mexico by President Wilson, the war to eradicate the Catholic Church, the expulsion of American Mormons and investors (mines, railroads, agriculture, and the oil industry), and more.

The hearings included a wide range of perspectives. A representative of President Wilson, M. Silliman, testified, "Generally all admit that the worst thing in Mexico, besides prostitution, is the Catholic Church, and that both have to go."[92] Offering a very different perspective, Mother Elias of the Most Holy Sacrament (Madre Elias del Santisimo Sacramento) testified, "As soon as they entered into a city, they would get the keys to the churches...they would take the ciboriums and empty the consecrated hosts into the horse feeders...they would place the priestly vestments on the backs of horses...they would shoot at the tabernacles...they would burn the confessionals...they would drink out of the chalices...."[93]

The Senators heard much more sworn testimony given by witnesses who, once they spoke, could never return to Mexico. Here are some examples from the mountainous evidence:

- Wallace Thompson, editor of the *Mexico Herald*, an English-language daily newspaper in Mexico: "The Carrancistas routinely take possession of haciendas and strip them of all—food, animals,

---

[92] Senate Committee on Foreign Relations. Investigation of Mexican Affairs: Preliminary report and hearings of the Committee on Foreign Relations, United States Senate, pursuant to S. res. 106, directing the Committee on Foreign Relations to investigate the matter of outrages on citizens of the United States in Mexico, 1920, p. 2657.

[93] Ibid., p. 2649.

and anything of value."[94]

- Henry Lane Wilson, U.S. ambassador: "There is a great number of Mexicans from the class of the Criollos in the United States and also from the class of skilled workers who today are scattered throughout the southwest of the United States. They are all in search—simply stated—of life. They have arrived even as far as Kansas City. They are the intellectuals, the land owners, the middle class, and a lot of peasants. They now number more than one million."[95]

- Melquiades Ortiz, labor contracting agent: "During the past month, I shipped 150 Mexicans. They say there is nothing to do in Mexico. They have no work. They are indigent."[96]

- Mr. Rix, labor contracting agent: "Last month I sent 300. They come looking for work, with deep hunger, with only the clothes on their back, they possess nothing. The vast majority come from the interior [of Mexico]. I have processed thousands and thousands. They cannot write their own names. They are honest and peaceful. They know nothing about the world around them. But, yes, there are a few that are well educated and come from the high class; for them there is nothing I can do. From here, San Antonio to Laredo, for

---

[94] Ibid., p. 2943.

[95] Ibid., p. 2298.

[96] Ibid., p. 2142.

every 50 or 100 yards, you will encounter groups of 5 to 10 persons."[97]

- M. L. Osborne, labor contracting agent: "In various ways they find out there is work in the United States. During the war, we sent six to seven thousand to Pennsylvania, to New York, to Michigan, and other places in the north.... They said conditions in Mexico are terrible.... They say they grow corn and plant, but when they mature, the Carrancistas come and steal all. And that no one can complain, because if one complains, they kill them. They are innocent people, ignorant, and they know nothing. The very first cents they earn, they immediately send to their wives. All of them intend to bring their families and friends as quickly as possible. Most of them are from Jalisco, Michoacan, and Guanajuato. I have sent 75,000 to the North."[98]

- Roscoe C. Burbank, Garza Labor Agency: "In February we shipped 1,200 men, women, and children. They come in bunches from the same town or pueblo."[99]

- George Agnew Chamberlain, a retired Foreign Service officer, who had been the consul general for Consular Services in Mexico City: "The immigration, the Texas Rangers, and others

---

97 Ibid., p. 2146.

98 Ibid., p. 2153.

99 Ibid., p. 2148.

estimate that between El Paso and Brownsville in only three weeks, 50,000 persons from Jalisco, Michoacan, Colima, and Guanajuato have crossed the border."[100]

At one point, Albert B. Fall, chairman of the Senate Committee, announced, "The Committee has been getting telegrams and correspondence informing it of a real exodus of Mexicans, workers from the rural parts of Mexico, and specifically from Jalisco, San Luis Potosi, Michoacan, Aguascalientes, and that now daily thousands are arriving on this side. And, because the number in this Exodus has increased so immensely, Carranza wants to stop it by means of the military."[101]

Carranza may not have staunched the flow of Mexicans across the Rio Grande as he intended militarily, but he or his followers and successors did manage to hide the story. In my research, I obtained information on a study performed at the National Archives of Mexico by the staff of the Treasurer of the Mexican Railroad Workers Union that aimed to shed light on how two million people traveled from El Bajio to the United States on empty railroad boxcars. The study states, however: "Unfortunately, the documents that describe and quantify the migration to the north **remain lost** [emphasis mine]."[102] How convenient. The real story of a national tragedy clearly was censored.

I learned about the censorship practices of the

---

[100] Ibid., p. 2879.

[101] Ibid., p. 2135.

[102] Manuel Armando Marquez Gonzalez, "Los ferrocarrileros mexicanos en U.S.A.," Mexican Railroad Workers Union, September 15, 2015.

Mexican government and secret police from a confidant who worked very closely with two Mexican presidents and must remain anonymous. Just as the Communists impose secrecy and censorship even today, such was the standard for the Mexican Marxist-controlled war against the Catholic Church from 1913 to 1930. For years afterward, concealment of the truth continued under the Institutional Revolutionary Party (*Partido Revolucionario Institucional,* or PRI), which was the party in power. (The 1973 publication of Jean Meyer's book, *La Cristiada,* in Mexico City during the presidency of Echevarria was an exception to the rule. The publisher was a Marxist; Meyer in France had also been a Marxist. Thus, I guess he qualified for a waiver from censorship.) Seventy-one years of PRI control was broken in 2000 with the election of Vicente Fox Quesada as president. Fox ended the Marxist-style secret police, *La Policia Judicial Federal,* and government control of all newsprint. Step by step, the truth has been emerging. Now, it is my turn to contribute.

In recounting what Nixon did, this book tells how Mexicans came to be Mexican-Americans. It is hoped that this history will inspire Mexican-Americans to appreciate who they are and from where they've come. In this part, the true stories of fellow Mexican-Americans may also illuminate their own personal family histories—why their parents or grandparents (or even great-grandparents) were among the nearly two million poor, illiterate Mestizo peasants who suddenly abandoned their homes, extended families, friends, and way of life in Mexico to venture forth into what they knew to be religious freedom, safety, and work in *"El Norte."* This part relives memories of the Mexican Diaspora of 1913–1930, and the stories presented here share some similarities. These families felt cruelly forced to leave a centuries-old, familiar way of life, perhaps never to see or communicate again with loved ones left behind, to travel a thousand miles or more and start over. Why they did so are memories best forgotten, yet one purpose of this book is to document them nonetheless, lest horrible atrocities are again committed.

Hence, this series of Mexican Diaspora family stories covers families who left Mexico during the period 1905 to 1926. Ten "sons of the Diaspora" have agreed to share their stories here. I asked each to tell about when his respective *familia* abandoned their piece of Mexico, why they left, and how they got to the United States. Their revealing family histories are the climax of this book. They say it all.

2. THE DIASPORA STORIES OF TEN FAMILIES

Events in history can be tantalizing and fantastic, and we wisely treasure the stories and storytellers who pass them on to us. Think of the truly amazing story of the Jewish people preserved for us in Scripture. Or the history of the feats of the Romans, who left records of their extensive conquests and civilization. Closer to home, Francisco Javier Clavijero relates in *Historia Antigua de Megico* that the Aztecs migrated from the north to conquer the *Reino de Megico*. He was an unusual eighteenth-century historian in that he could understand the hieroglyphic literature of the Mexicans dating back to 1250 A.D. No one could equal his knowledge of languages, customs, wars, religion, kings, etc., of the people of Mexico—or as he wrote, "Megico." (The second syllable in the word Mexico was the euphonic *"she"* and not like the Germanic guttural sound of today; the pronunciation *"he"* was imposed by the Spaniards to please their Flemish king.)

In the spirit of the preserving history through stories, I now present ten stories of Diaspora families. The first is from Al Lemus, son of Mexican immigrants. I came to know Al quite by chance only recently; yet he is the vital link to Richard M. Nixon, because he is the one who provided a very significant photograph (see Part I, Chapter 7) that offers pictorial evidence connecting the Mexican refugees of the Diaspora to a youngster who later became president of the United States.

The Lemus Family: Their Diaspora and Nixon

On the website *Los Angeles Revisited*, there is an entry about Murphy Ranch in Whittier, California, by Elizabeth L. Uyeda.[103] The entry features a 1941 photograph of workers at the ranch. When I discovered it, I contacted the site's author, and she happily put me in touch with the owner of the photograph, Al Lemus. According to Mr. Lemus, his father is third from the right in the rear row. He further confirmed that the men depicted in the photograph participated in the Diaspora.

I asked Mr. Lemus about his parents' migration to California. He recalls his father mentioning the store in the Murphy Ranch area owned by the Nixon family, but the ranch was not in fact his father's original destination. His family had heard from a former neighbor in the hacienda where they lived, La Concepcion (or "La Consa," as it was called), that the Simons Brick Company in Southern California was hiring Mexican immigrants.

---

[103] Elizabeth L. Uyeda, "Murphy Ranch, Whittier, Cal.," *Los Angeles Revisited*, August 11, 2010, https://losangelesrevisited.blogspot.com/2010/07/murphys-ranch-whittier-cal.html.

His father worked for Simons for some time, then moved to Murphy Ranch until around 1944 when he left for a defense-related job in Los Angeles County.

As to why they left Mexico for the United States, Mr. Lemus only told me, "As far as I know, they left for a better life, in part to flee from the religious persecutions and [in part] in search of work." He does not know how the family traveled, but he did find a document entitled "Alien-Head Tax Receipt" issued in March 1918 for $8 by the Department of Labor, U.S. Immigration Service at Port of Laredo, Texas, pinpointing the time and place of the family's arrival. From there, his family made their way slowly to California. Their 1918 arrival in the United States makes sense, since it was then that Carranza was persecuting Catholics, and Pancho Villa was ransacking, pillaging, killing, and stealing at will. Is it any wonder the Lemus family abandoned the hacienda La Concepcion?

The Lemus family story illustrates an interesting point about the Diaspora. According to Mr. Lemus, many of the Murphy Ranch Mexicans were born in the areas around Penjamo, Guanajuato, Mexico. How did they know about work in Los Angeles from their tiny hovels in the haciendas and ranchos around Penjamo? Recall that ninety percent of the Mexican population living at that time were illiterate. Even if they had obtained a newspaper, of what use would it be? They could not read. Instead, the source of news was the railroad. It was the world of the Roman roads of ancient history repeated. The Atchison, Topeka, and Santa Fe Railway employed railroad workers in Mexico and brought them to work on their lines in the United States well before 1913. Many workers were hired from El Bajio, where the average pay per day was only thirteen cents. When they traveled back home, they regaled their relatives and friends with stories of life in *"El Norte"* where they earned a whole dollar per day! Thus, in the early years of the so-called *Revolucion*, families who had learned about life in the United States were the first to leave. The very poor and very isolated remained ignorant of the vent the North provided until later, when they faced two options: join the Cristero Army or flee. Their exits were predominantly suffered from 1924 to 1929.

Al Lemus now lives in Southern California. Since he has been an active and participating Catholic, he was elected by his fellow brothers as Grand Knight of his Knights of Columbus Council in East Los Angeles, California.

I am very grateful for Al Lemus's contribution to make known an unknown history. Once I learned how Nixon, as a young man, interfaced with the 200 Diaspora families who settled around Whittier and worked at the Murphy and Leffingwell Ranches, I finally gained a profound understanding of the *whys* of August 5, 1971, when I sat in the Oval Office and listened to President Nixon characterize in detail his experiences and deep knowledge of those families. I was able to conclude Nixon never forgot them, and as president, by golly, he was going to do something about their situation. And he did.

The Lomeli and Gomez Families

Marcelino Lomeli and his wife, Felicitas Avila, lived in La Barca, Jalisco, Mexico, as did their forefathers before them. For centuries, their ancestors had lived close to the shores of the biggest lake in all of Mexico, *El Lago de Chapala* (Lake Chapala). And for good reason: The land of that area was flat, pluvial, and very fertile. The temperate weather suffered no extremes.

So why did Marcelino and Felicitas depart from La Barca in 1905 and endure the hardships of moving to a strange land? Why did they leave behind family and friends? I inquired of three Lomeli grandsons as to why their grandparents departed Mexico. Neither Dr. Leo Lomeli, now a retired physician, nor his brother, Marcelino, an outstanding and successful professional horticulturist, knew the answer. Marcelino told me, "I asked what brought them to the United States, and Dad [Leopoldo Avila Lomeli, son of Marcelino and Felicitas] said he would tell me in time. He never did." Their cousin, Barney Barajas, a retired engineer, could not offer any details, either, although his wife, Virginia, did know of the Diaspora history of her family, who had also left Jalisco.

I theorize that the arrival of a new industry—the railroad—fundamentally changed daily living for families previously locked into an agricultural feudal society but now employed by the railroad company. They were able to start a new way of life. They enjoyed solid jobs with outstanding pay and reliable conditions. They could leave the fields owned by the Criollos permanently.

An aerial map of the lands where the Lomeli family lived displays huge stretches of flat, cultivated agricultural lands. This area was the bread basket of Mexico. However, given the chance, any bright, able-bodied young man would jump at an opportunity to leave *las milpas* (corn fields) and the care of animals for a much better life. Marcelino Lomeli was a participant in the revolution—the industrial one, not the shooting and killing one.

It is reasonable to find motivations in the necessities of life. Friends who had left La Barca revealed that in another Mexico, called "New," they were paid a dollar in Albuquerque instead of thirteen cents in La Barca. According to Jeffrey Marcos Garcilazo in his book *Traqueros: Mexican Railroad Workers in the United States 1870–1930*, Mexican railroad workers would return home at times from working in the United States and recount stories of good pay, good work, and orderly life in the North.[104] Perhaps the accounts of Marcelino Lomeli's friends who worked on the railroad in Albuquerque, New Mexico, were persuasive. However, Marcelino and Felicitas had another motive, besides: their children. They already had four (Leopoldo, 4; Sal, 3; Soledad, 2; and infant Elena). With a growing family, the Lomeli family chose to depart from La Barca and move to Albuquerque, New Mexico, in 1905 for better pay and a better life for their children. Therein lies the answer to the *why*.

Marcelino and Felicitas's eldest son, Leopoldo, came to the use of reason in the United States. He knew about Mexico from his parents and their friends. In 1913, the family moved from Albuquerque to Los Angeles, California. Leo chose the railroad industry for his lifetime work and retired as a high-level executive. His mother and father died while his siblings were still young. Consequently, he became the man of the house and raised them until they were able to take care of themselves. Once he had accomplished that, Leo moved to La Verne, California, where his employer, the Santa Fe Railroad, promoted him to station manager until he

---

[104] Jeffrey Marcos Garcilazo, *Traqueros: Mexican Railroad Workers in the United States, 1870–1930* (Denton, Texas: University of North Texas Press, 2012), p. 36.

retired. He established himself in that town, was appointed to the Park and Recreation Commission, and then served as councilman for twelve years. After marrying Esperanza Gomez, he built his own elegant house from adobe. Together, he and his wife raised an outstanding family of three boys.

Esperanza's parents, Marcelino Gomez and Jesusita (Maria de Jesus) Bernal de Gomez, also suffered and lived the Diaspora. Marcelino Gomez left Mexico in 1922. By that point, life in Jalisco had become untenable due to the civil strife stirred up by Pancho Villa and the dictators Venustiano Carranza and Alvaro Obregon, in addition to marauding gangs. Arriving in Claremont, California, Marcelino Gomez quickly found work and settled in. Two years later, on July 7, 1924, Jesusita crossed the border at Laredo, Texas, to join him. With her came two sons, Rigoberto and Ramiro. However, the couple's daughter, Esperanza Gomez (born in 1921), remained in Mexico with her grandmother until age 12, and then she, too, joined the growing Gomez family in Claremont.

Esperanza is my sister-in-law. I asked her what she could recall about life in Ciudad Guzman, Jalisco, under the dictatorial rule of Plutarco Elias Calles, who was president of Mexico from 1924 to 1928. Although she was but a young girl during Calles's rule, she lucidly related an incident from her school days. When told that the authorities were checking their school for signs of the "teaching of the Catholic religion," she and her classmates promptly hid their religion books.

This episode compels an explanation. Why did government officials search and haunt the school of little children? In 1917, President Venustiano Carranza adopted a new constitution that called for the crippling of the Catholic Church, if not its eradication. A few years later, President Calles went one step further. He issued about 140 penal laws effective July 31, 1926, known collectively as the Calles Law *(Ley Calles)*. Penalties were specific. Just a few examples will suffice. A priest wearing clerical garb in public was penalized 500 pesos (U.S.$250)—a steep fine, considering that a man might be paid only a dollar per day at that time! If a priest criticized the government, he was penalized five years in jail. Some states added even more laws. The state of Chihuahua permitted only *one* priest for the entire state.

So, understandably, the religion books of Esperanza and her classmates needed to be concealed from the eyes of government officials. (As an aside, the Calles Law was still on the books when I toured Mexico in 1953 with my classmates. We were all theology students who wore Roman collars and cassocks. We were aptly warned: "Not in Mexico.")

Clearly the Gomez family suffered under the dictators, and this suffering must have figured prominently in their drastic decision to leave Mexico. Why did Marcelino Gomez leave first? I heard his dramatic story when I was a young man courting his daughter. I often thought of the plight of the Ancient Mariner as my future father-in-law would tell his daughter to forget about going to the movies that night because he wanted to talk to me. I now wish I had written his story. On a goodly number of evenings, he engaged my attention into the wee hours with his soliloquys, speaking in complete confidence to me in the privacy available. Marcelino had been in the army of Venustiano Carranza as a military officer with many men under his command. His neighbors called him "El Coronel," and in time, the men close to him even referred to him as "El General." But at last, the time came when he could suffer no more desecration of

Catholic churches and persecution of the clergy, so he deserted the army and was chased. For hours, he would relate his pursuit by the military officers known as "the Black Hand" ("La Mano Negra"). He knew the ravines and canyons much better than those chasing him, however, and finally he reached Guadalajara. From there, he traveled north and eventually arrived in Claremont, California. I have often thought to myself that in the period of 1900–1930, Mexico lost the best and the brightest.

A little, but important sequel to our one-way chats is that on Saturdays my fiancée and I would go to church for confession. On one occasion, I asked Don Marcelino to accompany us. He acquiesced, but he pulled me aside and asked me privately in low voice, "Do you think God will forgive me?" I chuckled interiorly but grimaced seriously and assured him that Father Strange, our pastor, would understand and ask God to forgive. He was so happy after his confession.

My own parents packed up their bags in 1922 and boarded the evening train from Salamanca, Guanajuato, Mexico, to El Paso, Texas. My parents were well informed on what was transpiring in Mexico. As I grew up, I recall that my father would often speak with a booming voice to condemn the actions of all those he saw as wronging Mexico: Carranza, Obregon, Calles, the Communists, Masons, Socialists, and atheists.

Despite their hardships in leaving their homeland and starting anew, the Lomeli and Gomez families have done well in the United States. Both Marcelino Gomez and Jesusita's children and Leo Lomeli and Esperanza's children have excelled.

The Family of Father Frank Tinajero

From my window seat on the bus from Leon, Guanajuato, to Guadalajara, Jalisco, I was excited to see the towns I had previously only heard of come alive before my eyes. The Mexican parishioners at Sacred Heart Church in Pomona, California, had spoken of Leon, San Juan de los Lagos, Lagos de Moreno, San Miguel el Alto, and other towns along the route. And now, I—a 21-year-old college graduate—was traveling through the history of El Bajio, the huge central valley of Mexico. It was summer 1951.

If I were to make the same trip today from Leon to Guadalajara, I would not discover as much about the life of real people as I did then. Today, the buses are speedy and move on superhighways, bypassing the small towns. But back in 1951, I saw and learned much from the window of that old bus as it wound slowly along the route, carrying chickens, vegetables, fruits, and vendors besides passengers. On this early weekday morning, I enjoyed the sight of so many people walking everywhere. Cars? Hardly any at all. People walked to church, to market, or wherever they were going. But what I most vividly recall was the beauty of so many young women. I marveled at their beauty, despite being so poorly clad.

Today as I write the story of Father Frank Tinajero, I think about his ancestors born and raised in those lands I traveled through years ago. It seems so strange that I can visually recreate the pictures, the people, and the landscape of 1951 here on my computer by visiting YouTube. (Semiconductors have changed so much of life.)

Father Tinajero and I attended the same Catholic seminary in California together. The big difference is that Frank was ordained a priest, while I was not; I left priestly studies and commenced the life of a layman. Yet we have maintained our friendship over the years. Like my family, Father Tinajero's parents and grandparents were part of the Diaspora. I asked him to share why, how, and when they left the area of Mexico known as Los Altos de Jalisco to go north.

Father Tinajero's grandfather, Don Guillermo Gonzalez, was born in Teocaltiche, Jalisco, in 1885. In those times, when horses were used for moving about, people in Teocaltiche must have known about other nearby states. The state of Zacatecas was but two *leguas* (about five miles) west of town. The state of Aguascalientes was north of town a little further, about a day's horse ride away, and the state of Guanajuato was nearby on the east. Daily life around Teocaltiche had been uncomplicated for generations. Apart from the Criollo (European) landowners in this feudal economy, most of the inhabitants were devout Catholics who were raised where they were born, worked and got married, had children, and died in old age to meet their Creator.

However, by the time of Guillermo Gonzalez's birth, the world was changing. The Mexico of that period was facing two opposing forces: Christianity and the emerging anti-Christian Liberals. Yet while Porfirio Diaz held power in Mexico City, peace and law and order generally reigned in Mexico despite the rumbling thunder of a gathering storm. Guillermo found steady employment working for the railroads sometime in the early 1900s, which allowed him to travel to other states in Mexico where construction was underway. As a result, in the nearby state of San Luis Potosi, he met his future wife, Dona Piedad Rincon de Gonzalez. When both were 20 years of age, they married in Aguascalientes in 1905 and celebrated their new life in complete tranquility. Unfortunately, the peace was not to last.

As the violence unleashed in the 1910 Revolution roiled around the country, Guillermo continued working on the railroads in Mexico and later in western and central U.S. areas (Arizona, New Mexico, Kansas, Colorado, Illinois, and California). During that epoch, he would travel back and forth to Mexico, often with his growing family (he ultimately had the blessing of seven children, five of whom were born in Mexico, two in the United States; the fifth, Luz Maria, would become Father Tinajero's mother). The search for security for his family was, however, a constant pressure due to the scourge of ongoing tumult in El Bajio. Guillermo Gonzalez frequently found himself outrunning the persecutions, the torture and killing of priests, the denial of religious practice to the people, and the closing of churches.

At last Guillermo was able to obtain security and employment in Los Angeles. However, the stock market crash of 1929 and the ensuing Depression caused him and his family to return to Mexico. Mercifully, the government wars against the Catholic Church had ended by that time. His daughter Luz Maria (born in 1924 in Mexico) went back and forth between Los Angeles and Mexico, but in time, the whole family returned to Los Angeles "to begin a new generation that would finally settle down and set roots here in the United States of America," as Father Tinajero put it.

Life in a Diaspora is truly most difficult and demanding of heroism.

The Family of Julian Martinez

Julian was so privileged, at least in this sense: His father, Jim Martinez, always had time for his son's constant queries. Julian yearned to learn about the history of his family. Born, raised, and educated in Hutchinson, Kansas, Julian knew he was very different from his classmates.

Hutchinson had three societies: one Black, another Mexican Mestizo, and the third European (commonly referred to as "Anglos"). The Mexicans and their Mexican-American children lived across the tracks in the south part of town. They worshipped in their church, Our Lady of Guadalupe. In the summer, they could swim only on Thursdays when the pools were emptied and prepared for clean fresh water. If a trip to the movie house was in order, they would find their seats in the balcony, the only place they were allowed to sit. The nice restaurants had no seating at all for them, only take-outs. Haircuts? OK, but only from their own barbers.

It was precisely because of those conditions that in 1968 I selected a community (Garden City) in Kansas for testing questionnaires prepared by my staff at the U.S. Commission on Civil Rights, Mexican American Studies Division. It was necessary to refine the questionnaires intended for use in studying the schools of the Southwest under conditions similar to what we knew existed in Texas, California, Colorado, Arizona, and New Mexico.

Julian was no dummy. He was bright, with a high IQ, and he wanted to know. Why were Mexicans discriminated against? What was life in Mexico like? Why had his parents left their country? How did they get from the region of El Bajio in Mexico to Kansas? While Julian toiled in his father's business, Martinez and Sons Machine Shop, he constantly asked these kinds of questions and conversed with his father, who was able to provide answers. Julian told me: "My dad loved history. He enjoyed relating his life. He knew all the names [associated with] recent Mexican political history, especially those of Venustiano Carranza, Pancho Villa, and Porfirio Diaz, and to a much lesser degree, a few other names."

Jim's father, a former student for the Catholic priesthood, had immigrated the Martinez family to the United States in 1911. He was hired by the Atchison, Topeka, and Santa Fe Railway to work in Burrton, Kansas. Jim was barely four years old. He attended school and learned English. Life in an English-speaking, Protestant society was a bit uncomfortable, however. So, as often happened with recent immigrants, the family returned to Mexico four years later in 1915 to their little villa, Zaragoza, next to the city of La Piedad, Michoacan, along the River Lerma. But Jim Martinez would return to Kansas when he was seventeen and eventually be elected mayor of Hutchinson in 1970. He must have been quite a leader to overcome discrimination.

Julian provided me with newspaper clippings containing stories of his father's life in Hutchinson. Regarding the family's move back to Mexico, one clipping states: "[Jim] Martinez' father decided perhaps life would be better for his family in Mexico."[105] Whether misinformed or uninformed, that decision was ill-timed. Mexico was awash in violence in 1915 when the elder Martinez moved the family back home, and matters were only getting uglier in El Bajio—conditions that would last until 1930!

Julian hungered to know why his dad left his village in 1924 and returned to Kansas, and Jim explained the

---

[105] Julian Martinez, personal communication, June 11, 2017.

reason to his son. As Julian related the story to me, "Armed men would come by to take young men to the army. If they refused to go, they would be killed on the spot. My dad was seventeen. It was time to return to the safety of the United States."

Thus, Jim Martinez became a participant in the Mexican Diaspora. His trek back to Kansas was replete with struggles. Lawlessness was prevalent. He was robbed, beaten, and hospitalized. Finally, he made it to Hutchison, Kansas, and eventually became a successful participant in the American Dream.

And Julian? I came to know him when he worked as the assistant to Lee Atwater, who had successfully managed the presidential campaign of George H. W. Bush and was subsequently appointed chairman of the Republican National Committee. Julian was the first Mexican-American to work as assistant to the chairman.

The Family of Guadalupe G. Garcia

To appreciate the story of the Diaspora of the family of Mr. Guadalupe G. ("G. G.") Garcia, recall that three ethnic groups coexisted in Mexico: the Spaniards (Criollos), the indigenous (Native Mexicans), and those of mixed parentage (Mestizos). These three groups fill the pages of history.

The Spaniards enjoyed a positive self-image of themselves. After all, were they not the children of the *Conquistadores*? Were they not the owners of all one could see? Were they not the educated ones who could count numbers and read letters? Were they not the ones who could become Catholic priests and bishops, military officers, or government officials, and be in charge of all? Of course! Thus, they wrote laws that gave themselves legal privileges and standing. Yep. They put themselves first in line. But the Mexican Revolution of 1910 hit them hard, very hard! Jose Vasconcelos reflects on life as it was in 1905 in Durango, Mexico, prior to the outbreak of the Revolution in his book *Ulises Criollo*: "No one could have foreseen, as one observed the women seated in their corner of the world, so sure of their position in life, surrounded by ostentation, that a few years later some of them would be molested by the peasants at their properties, and by self-declared generals; the other women would have to emigrate suddenly to escape."[106]

How were the original inhabitants, the Native Mexicans, doing at the time of the Mexican Revolution? A simple answer: not well. They had been dismissed as "those Indians" for generations. Just a few examples will help show their plight. In the city of Durango, the capital of the state of the same name, *los indios* were not allowed to be present within the city limits after sunset in the early 1900s, according to Jose Vasconcelos. He adds that within Durango the population was almost entirely Criollo, but just outside the city limits, a purely indigenous population lived in conditions similar to those of the time of the Aztecs.[107]

And what about the Mestizos, the products of Spaniard men and indigenous women? In the Mexico of today, they are the predominant ethnic group. But at one time, being Mestizo was a strange novelty. Both the Native Mexicans and the Spaniards were confused, astounded, and profoundly taken aback when the Mother of Jesus arrived in 1531 on Tepeyac Hill (in what is now

---

[106] Jose Vasconcelos, *Ulises Criollo* (Mexico, D.F.: Editorial Universidad de Costa Rica, 2000), p. 244.

[107] Ibid., pp. 251–252.

Mexico City) with the face of a Mestiza! The Mother of God, a Mestiza? How could that be? In time that supernatural "error" was corrected; artists painted her as a holy, yet beautiful young Spanish lady. This brings out an important point about the plight of the Mestizos: The common assumption was that the more *"Espanol"* a person looked, the higher their status. Thus, in a Mestizo family with many children, the ones who had the lightest skin, lightest hair, and blue or green eyes were the *"consentidos"* (pampered) ones and caused no end of jealousies and struggles with their siblings because of their parents' favor. They were nicknamed *"El Guero"* or *"La Guera"* (slang for "blonde" or "fair"), and they could gain better jobs, becoming skilled workers or grocery store workers, for example, where public contact was necessary. The degree to which some Mestizos could be better off than others was a function of their proximity to European appearance. It was a given that superiority rested on being "white," and inferiority—as everyone knew—resided in the darker skin tone, *piel canela.* This caste system persisted even in the United States; as a youngster, I heard women admire newborns with expressions such as, *"Que bueno, salio muy blanquito!"* or the converse in a pitying tone, *"Que lastima, salio muy indio."*

I asked G. G. Garcia for information on his *familia* in order to write faithfully about their Diaspora. He forwarded a response written by his nephew, Michaelangelo Carmona-Renaud, who informed me that G. G.'s grandfather, Lorenzo Gutierrez, was born in the town of Guanajuato on August 19, 1885, to a Criollo family. When he was a young seminarian, however, Lorenzo was forced to flee Guanajuato after he came upon his sister being physically abused by her husband and, grabbing a knife, fought and killed his brother-in-law. He then traveled up to San Felipe Torres Mochas, about 75 miles away.

One may speculate about his journey and life in San Felipe. Why did he select that town? How did he get there? Did he know someone there? What did he do for income? Did he merge with the Mestizo populace and avoid the Criollo community, lest word get out to other Criollos with contacts in Guanajuato about where he lived in San Felipe? We do not know. Certainly, he must have worried about being discovered by his enemies, yet since he had been a seminarian studying for the priesthood, he probably found solace in the Catholic churches frequented by people of *piel canela*—Mestizos and Native Mexicans. Perhaps a sympathetic clergyman who traveled from San Felipe to Guanajuato served as a secure messenger to his parents to let them know how he fared.

While in San Felipe, he met a local girl of humble origins, Maria Francisca ("Panchita") Moncivais, born June 20, 1885, in a nearby rancho, El Terrero. Her parents were Jesus Moncivais and Marcelina Barrientos. After Marcelina died, young Panchita went to live in a convent (orphanage) in San Felipe. Lorenzo and Panchita got married at age 17, and, given the circumstances, Lorenzo avoided the inquiry his Criollo society would have imposed: *"De que familia viene?"* ("From what family does she come?") Their first child was born December 24, 1903, baptized with the name Delfina. Later, Delfina acquired another name, Josefina, upon receiving the sacrament of confirmation, and later still, she became the mother of G. G. Garcia.

During his first year of marriage, Lorenzo made a return trip alone to Guanajuato, disguising himself by growing a beard and mustache, lest he be recognized. His parents quickly welcomed him and locked themselves inside the home. The family had a meal together, but his anxious parents convinced him to leave before the authorities discovered his presence. Though their new daughter-in-law had remained in San Felipe, Lorenzo's parents already knew that their son had violated the strict caste norms observed in the correct Criollo society of the time by marrying a Mestiza. After all, these norms formed the basis of the system of domination imposed for centuries by the conquerors. Nothing new here. In the United States, the plantations of the South lived by the same strict rules.

However, Grandpa Lorenzo was a good man, true to his wife. He charted a new route for himself and his family, and that road would eventually take them to another country. Although the family did not know it at the time, he left the state of Guanajuato just before the seeds of violence sown by Benito Juarez and Lerdo de Tejada's anti-Catholic laws germinated in the hands of Mexico's uniformly anti-Catholic intellectual class. Very soon life in Guanajuato was to be traumatized, although no one knew in 1903 just how horrible the changes would be.

Even so, Lorenzo Gutierrez and his family were not untouched by the upheaval. The family's whereabouts in the period 1903–1913 are somewhat unclear. According to Mr. Carmona-Renaud, Lorenzo first moved his family to the city of Monterrey in Nuevo Leon, Mexico, where he found out that merchandise would get moved from Monterrey to the small village of Reynosa, just across the border from McAllen, Texas, and from there, it was shipped downriver to the port. Knowing he could find better work there, he moved the family to Reynosa. "He must have stood out among the locals," notes his great-grandson in his correspondence to me. "He was a typical *'Espanol.'*" Meanwhile, G. G. Garcia says that Lorenzo joined the Revolution in 1910 and was mustered out in 1912.

What is definite and clear is that *La Toma de Reynosa* (the Battle of Reynosa), which occurred on May 9, 1913, provided new directions for the Gutierrez family. The violence of war does have unexpected consequences. In this case, it prompted the Gutierrez family to cross the Rio Grande (called the Rio Bravo on the Mexican side) for safety and shelter. Mr. Carmona-Renaud describes that history: "Grandpa Lorenzo took his family and joined the exodus of families racing for the Rio Bravo to take shelter on the other side until the battle ceased. He had recently met Don Cristoforo Vela, owner of a pull-ferry across the Rio Grande. He helped them escape the battle on his *'challan'* (a raft) to the north side."

Many of the families who fled across the river set up camp in the brush around the small settlement of Hidalgo, Texas. However, Don Cristoforo invited the Gutierrez family to stay in his home. When the dust of the battle had settled, the family returned home to gather their belongings, then went back to Hidalgo and remained with Don Cristoforo Vela. They ended up staying on the northern (U.S.) side of the river, eventually establishing themselves in the nearby town of Mercedes, where G. G. Garcia grew up. At an early age, he fell in love with the local library and its books, which took him to faraway places in faraway times. Despite handicaps that would have dealt body-blows to others, G. G. Garcia overcame the obstacles posed by his status as a migrant worker, dire poverty, and overt discrimination and can proclaim he did his military duty and served honorably. He ascended educationally to attend the nationally prestigious

Georgetown University in Washington, DC, and stayed to work in the halls of Congress and for the nationally known newspaper, the *Washington Post*. Additionally, he was a candidate for the Senate of the Republic of Texas; he also helped the first Republican candidate for governor of Texas achieve success and became one of his top assistants. And not to forget, he was also a top assistant for the president of the United States with one of his Cabinet officers at the Cabinet Committee on Opportunities for Spanish-Speaking People. Wow! Back in Guanajuato at the turn of the century, G. G. Garcia's newlywed Mestiza grandmother and Criollo grandfather never would have imagined or even daydreamed that someday their grandson would achieve the American Dream in such a fashion.

The Family of Everett Alvarez

If today you met Everett Alvarez, you would be surprised. Nothing about him would suggest he has within him the stuff of heroes. He is not pretentious; he is humble. Humility demands truthfulness, and Everett knows the truth of his life. He has written his story in a book, *Chained Eagle: The Heroic Story of the First American Shot Down over North Vietnam*, which describes his experience as a prisoner of war for 8½ years (longer than any other flier in Vietnam). The godless, materialistic Communists forced him to endure a passion that reminds us of the Passion of Christ. Indeed, Everett remained steadfast in his faith during his ordeal.

I got to know Everett personally during the first months of the Reagan administration. After the wonderful election of Ronald Reagan as president in November 1980, I joined the Presidential Personnel

Team. I received word that Nancy Reagan wanted Everett to have a good position, and she got her wish: He became deputy administrator of the Veterans Administration. As we became more acquainted and I learned his family's story, I always found Everett to be cooperative, informative, open, and genial.

His family traces their lives to the depths of El Bajio, in Guanajuato and Jalisco, two states in Mexico deeply affected by upheavals and violence in the first decades of the 1900s. Christianity in El Bajio formed the values, principles, and way of life of strong people dating from the early colonial days of the 1540s. The people of El Bajio were very devout Catholics. They had no time for European ideologies; yet in time, those ideologies would ensnare them.

Everett's paternal grandfather, Senor Alvarez, was born in Teocaltiche, Jalisco. Based on the birthdate of Everett's father, Lalo, in Jerome, Arizona, in 1917, we can assume that his grandfather left Mexico sometime in the period of 1913 to 1916 and settled in Jerome to work in the mines. He met Beatrice Sanchez after arriving in Arizona and married her. However, following Beatrice's death, her family took over raising young Lalo. The family moved to Los Angeles first and eventually to Salinas, California.

Meanwhile, Everett's maternal grandfather, surnamed Rivera, and grandmother, surnamed Navarrette, were both from Huanimaro, Guanajuato. They departed with their little family on their Diaspora journey around 1915 and arrived at Colton, California. Grandfather Rivera knew his way around. He had worked on the railroads of Southern California and had been going back and forth to his hometown in earlier years. The Rivera-Navarrette couple gave birth to Everett's mother, Chole, in 1919 in Colton.

Lalo Alvarez and Chole Rivera met and wed in 1937 in Castroville, California, a town eight miles from Salinas. In late December of that year, Everett Alvarez was born in Salinas. In high school, Everett excelled in math. He was urged and helped to enroll at Santa Clara University in Santa Clara, California, where he received an excellent Jesuit education. He joined the Navy after graduation and became a pilot. When his plane was shot down in August 1964, he parachuted to the waters below and ended up in the hands of the North Vietnamese. After his horrid 8½-year ordeal of torture, starvation, and isolation at the hands of uncivilized adherents of European modern philosophies, President Nixon ended his years as a prisoner of war, and Everett retired from the Navy with the rank of naval commander.

How did he do it? What kept him strong and able to return with excellent mental health? In what way did Everett's Mexican heritage contribute? What did his parents and forefathers endow him with that enabled him to survive and gave him the traits and values of a true American hero?

We know (more or less) when Everett's grandparents left Mexico, probably traveling over a thousand miles by rail to arrive in the United States around 1915. As to why they abandoned their way of life to start again, consider the context. Profound changes were occurring in Mexico at that time. Their remote causes can be traced to Europe, as previously stated, and their proximate causes have key names that have already been pointed out: Carranza, Obregon, Calles.

Everett's grandfather's hometown of Teocaltiche and the surrounding communities in Jalisco suffered at the hands of the corrupt and murderous thief, Carranza. The area around the hometown of Everett's maternal grandparents, Huanimaro, was not spared, either; we have eyewitness accounts as evidence. Jose Rojas Garciduenas was born and raised in Salamanca, a town only a few miles from Huanimaro. In his book, *Salamanca: Recuerdos de mi tierra guanajuatense,* he gives us blow-by-blow accounts. I translate some key passages here:

1913 to 1918—Fighting among the Revolutionary factions affected the city and the whole region profoundly.

April of 1915—Francisco [Pancho] Villa leaves Salamanca with his trains and the entire *Division del Norte* to attack Alvaro Obregon in nearby Celaya. He was defeated and retreated to Chihuahua.

July 6, 1915—General Rodolfo Fierro, a Pancho Villa general, enters Salamanca with his troops and for a few hours proceeds to sack houses and stores. A few days later, Colonel Jose Sivrob, of the Carranza army, and appointed by Carranza as governor of the State of Guanajuato and its military commander, ordered the apprehension of a number of men from the surrounding areas, all from the middle class, and made them stand for judgment before him. Then he dictated sentences on each as it pleased him, with no judicial proceeding: no arguments, no proofs, no charges, and much less a defense. He ordered a dozen of them shot immediately by a firing squad in the city square.

1915—The whole countryside of El Bajio was enduring profound difficulties in getting food; [there was] lack of cultivation and irregular communications and business, since most of the trains were being used to transport troops and for other purposes of the civil war.[108]

In view of the lack of work and religious freedom, is it any wonder why Everett's grandparents left as quickly as they could?

The story of the Diaspora of two million Mexicans to the north must be made known. A few of the two million were Criollo landowners who were educated and prepared to cope with new environments. Most, however, were illiterate Mestizos, including Everett's grandparents. They are the type Nixon came to know in Whittier, California, and admire for their devotion to God, their faith, and their religion. Everett was blessed to have been raised and formed by these courageous and faith-driven forebears so as to become an American hero who bested the bestial Communists of his day.

The Family of Frank Gamboa

Was Pancho Villa the proximate cause of the flight of Francisco (Frank) Gamboa's forefathers to the north? It is reasonable to guess that yes, he was one of the instant causes. Of course, as with the Diaspora families already profiled, the clash of sectarian and Christian ideas in the world at that period in history was the fundamental and remote cause.

So how did Pancho Villa get involved with Frank's parents? And how did President Richard M. Nixon get

---

[108] Jose Rojas Garciduenas, *Salamanca: Recuerdos de mi tierra guanajuatense* (Mexico: Editorial Porrua, S.A., 1982), pp. 228–229.

into the picture? Both of these personalities played a pivotal role in Frank's life story, which is detailed in his book, *El Capitan!: The Making of an American Naval Officer*.

Before delving into those intersections, however, a bit of background is helpful to know. Long before Frank's ancestors crossed the Atlantic from Spain or Pancho Villa arose from the "beehives of mines" in the northern Mexican states of Chihuahua and Durango, that mountainous countryside was home to the Tarahumaras. These indigenous inhabitants were called "Tepejuanes" in the native language of Nahuatl, which means "mountain dwellers." Their harsh mountain homeland was rich in gold, silver, copper, and other minerals, but the Tarahumaras had no interest in those "rocks." In contrast, other people in far-away lands had a great and powerful interest—even love for—such "rocks." Possession of them could change lives. After Cortes and his men took control of Tenochtitlan (now Mexico City), Spanish explorers pushed farther and farther, establishing outposts to mine deposits of valuable minerals found in what are now the states of Hidalgo, Guanajuato, and Zacatecas. Later, in 1631, vast new findings were made in both Chihuahua and Durango. Is it any wonder Spaniards left Spain to come to the New World? There were minerals to be mined! First, the conquerors transported goods, materials, and people from Spain in and around Mexico; later, they became the owners of the land and mines.

Our story of Frank's life begins with some of the people who came from Spain. His maternal great-great-grandmother Patricia, born around 1830 in Burgos, Spain, married Juan Santellanes at age 16. Around 1847, the pair left Burgos to arrive in the mountains of Chihuahua and Durango, Mexico. They settled in the mining town of

Parral, Chihuahua, called the "Silver Capital of the World" by the king of Spain, where Juan Santellanes owned property. The couple were blessed with seven children, but when Juan died of smallpox, Patricia sold their home and property and moved to a small mining area in nearby Durango called Guanacevi. There she prospered by mounting a coffee shop catering to the miners.

Several years later, another Spaniard, Ignacio Rivera, arrived from Spain, and in time the widow Patricia married him. The newlywed couple returned to Burgos, where their daughter Felicita was born. Another daughter, Andrea (Frank's great-grandmother), was born in Madrid. While Andrea was still an infant, the family moved back to Parral, where the girls grew up. Felicita married a mining engineer by the name of Johnson, while Andrea also got married and had a daughter named Concepcion. In 1904, Concepcion married a miner, Juan Perez, from the town of Guanacevi; they were to become Frank's grandparents. Their daughter, Enriqueta (Frank's mother), was born October 26, 1910, in the town of Santa Barbara, Chihuahua, where gold and silver had been mined for years and years since the town's founding in 1567. But Enriqueta was born on the eve of great changes to the lives and fortunes of the families living in the mining towns of Chihuahua and Durango. Just a few weeks later, the Revolution would begin on November 20, 1910.

Under the presidency of Porfirio Diaz (1877 to 1911), Americans invested in Mexican railroads, oil, cattle, and mining. Mines in the area where Frank's relatives lived were owned and operated by American companies, including the mine managed and operated by Mr. Johnson from San Francisco, California, who had married

Enriqueta's great-aunt Felicita. When the revolution broke out, the Johnsons moved to San Francisco, and Felicita later became the bridge to safety and work in the United States for her kin.

Concepcion departed Mexico in 1915 and arrived in Watts, California, where her aunt Felicita had purchased a house. But she left behind her husband, Juan Perez, along with her daughter and mother. Why? As a miner, Juan Perez had a special skill that set him apart—and ultimately brought him to the attention of Pancho Villa. Juan had become an expert at explosives, having received training in that art in Parral.

Pancho Villa, meanwhile, had been living as a leader of thieving scoundrels. He had gathered a goodly number into what he named his *Division del Norte* and joined them to the revolutionary armed forces. What he needed was an expert demolition man, and he knew of one: Juan Perez. As Captain Frank Gamboa writes in his book, *El Capitan!*:

> Revolutionary general Pancho Villa learned that my grandfather was an explosives expert and recruited him to blow up trains and bridges for his army. In return, Juan and his family were provided a large comfortable home in the city (probably the property of a wealthy family who had fled to the United States). Because of Villa's frequent campaigns, my grandfather was away from home for extended periods so Enriqueta saw very little of her father.[109]

---

[109] Frank Gamboa, *El Capitan!: The Making of an American Naval Officer* (Herndon, Virginia: Fortis Publishing, 2011), p. 21.

But when Pancho Villa attacked a town just three miles from the Mexico-U.S. border, Juan Perez took the opportunity to leave Villa's army and headed toward California. In the process, he also disappeared from his wife and family. Nothing is known of his disappearance. As a result, Frank's mother and her grandmother lost their Chihuahua house, financial support, and military protection from Pancho Villa, causing desperate conditions for them. Fortunately, from afar in San Francisco, Felicita was able to arrange for their departure to the United States, where they were reunited with Concepcion in Watts, California.

In time, Enriqueta grew up, got married, and gave birth to Frank. As a young man, his dream was to become a U.S. naval officer, and here's where Nixon played a role. In order to accomplish his dream, Frank needed a recommendation to gain admission to the U.S. Naval Academy in Annapolis, Maryland. Nixon, then a U.S. senator from California, provided that recommendation, giving another example of his connection to the Mexicans of the Diaspora. Frank went on to graduate from the Naval Academy and eventually was promoted to captain of a warship. As the jacket of *El Capitan!* reads, he was the first Mexican-American naval surface warfare officer to command a major U.S. Navy warship.

Reflecting on the life stories of his ancestors, he writes:

They arrived in America with only their luggage and clothes they were wearing. But they had things of great value—ambition, ability, determination, and hope. Through dedicated perseverance and hard work, they overcame daunting challenges, established their homes in California, and created their new lives.[110]

God bless America!

The Family of Roger Arthur Campos

Bring your imagination to the awesome vista of the Grand Canyon in Arizona. It is so vast, so different from anything else, and so beautiful. Now place your imagination on Copper Canyon, an immense canyon system in Chihuahua, Mexico. It is longer, deeper, and narrower than the Grand Canyon and boasts views that are nothing short of spectacular. It was in the rugged countryside around Copper Canyon, in the states of Chihuahua and Sinaloa, that the forefathers of Roger Arthur Campos lived and worked.

The Spaniards arrived in the Sierra Madre Occidental mountains in the mid-1500s and by 1610 had built a fort, El Fuerte, in what is now Sinaloa, for protection from the indigenous peoples, the Zuaques and Tahuecos. It hadn't taken the Spanish long to discover gold (and other minerals) in the area, and the entire area around El Fuerte became so important for business, trade, and mining that in 1824 it was designated the capital of the newly created Mexican state of Sonora y Sinaloa (which then reached deep into what is now Arizona).

A very well-documented history of Roger's forebears researched and written by Jeannine E. Shanahan (the wife of Roger's cousin Jerry Shanahan) provides excellent information on their lives. The first paragraph of *La Vida* ("The Life") commences: "With much hardship his

---

[110] Ibid., p. 23.

grandparents, Francisco Ernesto Campos and Ana Marie Orduno de Campos, immigrated to the United States through the border of Andrade, California, in 1918 to escape the war in Mexico. They had six children and raised their family in California."

That says in a nutshell when and why Roger's grandparents left Mexico, but there is much more to the story of Francisco and Ana. Francisco's mother, Rosa Espinoza de Campos, was born on August 30, 1847, high in the mountains in the little mining town of Yecorato, Sinaloa. She married Placido de Campos, but following his death, Rosa moved to Lluvia de Oro ("Rain of Gold"), another little mining town in Sinaloa located in the remote mountainous region atop the now-famous Copper Canyon. Not surprisingly, Rosa's son Francisco became a gold miner, but eventually he traded the mines for agriculture when he moved to the vibrant and growing town of Los Mochis, Sinaloa. His wife, Ana, was a teacher who kept a diary.

Francisco and Ana's first child, Arturo Rogelio Campos (Roger's father), was born on September 5, 1913, in Los Mochis. Located on a fertile plain in the foothills of the Sierra Madre range, Los Mochis was a bustling stop on the recently built railroad line that ran from Arizona to Guadalajara, Jalisco. It was a good place to raise a family—except for the effects of a revolution.

It was from the states neighboring Sinaloa that the revolution erupted in 1910. The very wealthy *hacendado* Francisco Madero ignited the fighting that quickly pitted people on one side or the other; he was soon joined by Pancho Villa, an illiterate Mestizo who had lived as a refugee from the law in the mountains of Durango, which borders Sinaloa to the east. Although the bloodiest scenes were suffered in El Bajio in central Mexico, Sinaloa experienced horrific violence as well. As Jeannine Shanahan noted, Francisco and Ana (with five-year-old Arturo) migrated "with much hardship" in the midst of this violence, seeking the best home they could find for their growing family.

From Andrade, California, where Francisco found work in a lumber mill, they journeyed to Reese, Utah, where he became a railroad worker. A year later, they were in the high mountain country in Westwood, California, and two years later, moved from there to Los Angeles for three years. But the mountains and plenty of work beckoned them back to Westwood, where Francisco (or Frank, as he was now called) worked until he retired.

Meanwhile, Arturo started his own married life. He met Marian Serembe Lang, and they got married in her hometown of Brooklyn, New York. The couple then moved to Houston, Texas, where Arturo started a corn-chip business. He and Marian had a son born in Houston, Roger Campos; two years later, the family moved to Modesto, California, where Arturo became a teacher at Modesto High School.

Arturo started another corn-chip factory in Modesto, too. His father, Francisco, now retired, moved to Modesto to help with the business as well as his brother, Francisco Reynaldo (Ray). Eventually the family business became one of the largest and most reputable tortilla factories in northern California.

Since the early 1950s, Modesto has become the place of gathering for the Campos family. Year after year, the Campos grandchildren have converged to celebrate Thanksgiving and honor their *abuelos* (grandparents). It is now a family tradition passed on to new generations of the Campos family.

And what of Roger, the grandson of Francisco and Ana? He went on to become a lawyer and was hired by President Nixon to work in the White House Office of Management and Budget. Then the U.S. Department of Commerce assisted him in forming a National Minority Business Association, of which he became the CEO. Upon Larry Hogan's 2014 election as governor of Maryland, Roger joined his cabinet, where today he serves as Maryland's first business ombudsman. He launched the first customer service standards for the management of the State of Maryland.

How wonderful to see the good that can arise from the ashes of ugly human behavior. Thanks be to God!

The Family of Charles Cervantes

It was the middle of summer, July 1919. How could he, eleven-year-old Ramon (who was to be Charles's father), understand why he, his five siblings, and his parents were selling their house and fleeing north? Ramon's parents, Jose Cervantes, a carpenter, and his mother, Aurelia, a teacher, were abandoning their lovely town of Yurecuaro in Michoacan, Mexico, and their extended families and friends. Why?

Only very tragic events could compel them to join a Diaspora to the north. Why else would the grandmother of Charles Cervantes, Aurelia Alvarez Hernandez, who had lived in the rich lands of Los Altos de Jalisco, want to abandon her world? Yet it was Aurelia, according to Charles, who decided to leave her highland homeland nestled in the beautiful mountains. Why else would her husband, Jose Ortega Cervantes, who had lived on fertile lands along the River Lerma, also agree to leave? That entire area was known for private ownership of small farms, and Aurelia had grown up on her father's small farm they called "Ranchito El Tecolote." The family was self-sufficient on the farm, raising hogs, growing corn, tending goats for milk and cheese and bees for honey. Then the Zapatista rebels passed through town, pillaging and plundering. Not long afterward, the anticlerical Plutarco Elias Calles had his Federal troops do the same—more pillaging and plundering, only this time under the authority of the federal government. Aurelia's father was not a combatant, but he did help and harbor those who were being persecuted because of their beliefs. The family had priests in the Dominican and Jesuit orders and were sympathetic.

Charles Cervantes, the grandson of Jose Cervantes and Aurelia Alvarez, conveyed to me that much of what he knows of his family history he learned from conversations with his father, Ramon. "[My father] would often volunteer his memories of his early life in Mexico with a wistful and woeful countenance," he wrote. Growing up in such a beautiful place as Ranchito El Tecolote was a rural paradise for him and his brother, Fortunato ("Nato")—until the violence and killings started.

Charles remembers his father, Ramon, recounting a story about hunting in the foothills of Degollado with Nato. The boys were hungry, so they sat underneath a tall shade tree and were eating their tortillas with beans when Nato noticed something hanging down to the ground from above. They looked up and saw two men hanged from branches. Their *"baba"* (saliva) had dripped to the ground from the mouths of the hanged men. Ramon and Nato were so frightened that they dropped their lunches and ran all the way back to the safety of Ranchito El Tecolote. It was not the only time they would see such horrific evidence of violence. Ramon told Charles stories of seeing men hanged from trees and lampposts by Calles's troops and how, when there was a lull in the violence, villagers would collect the bloated and putrid corpses, put them onto donkey-driven carts, and haul them to mass graves.

The Cervantes family doubtless hoped to find more security on the other side of the border. So, in 1919, they arrived in Texas, leaving behind a particularly chaotic time in Mexico. Revolutionary leader Francisco Madero had been killed, and the current president, Venustiano Carranza, was preparing for exile in France. Pancho Villa was still active in his game of raiding, stealing, and killing, but the following year (1920), he would retire to a ranch. In that same year, Carranza would be killed en route to Europe, and Alvaro Obregon would become the new dictator.

Once they were processed and photographed, the Cervantes family migrated into Texas with their border passes. However, they still faced challenges. They knew Spanish only; Texans knew English only. They were Catholics; Texans were Protestants. Things were so different! So, they returned to Mexico two years later in 1921, going back to their hometown, where they ended up renting the same house they had previously owned. Imagine their happiness and delight!

Sadly, however, the situation in Mexico had not improved in their absence. Under Obregon, the war that Carranza had been waging to eliminate the Catholic Church continued. He ferociously persecuted the Church and carried out atrocities and sacrileges from 1920 to 1924. In the midst of the violence, the Cervantes family left Mexico by train again in 1923 (the year Pancho Villa was killed), this time for good. Ramon was now fifteen. He understood why.

Returning to Texas, the family settled in Dallas. In time, Ramon married Olivia Rodriguez and raised a family of six. Charles was their fifth child. Recalling the successes and work ethic of his father, Charles told me, "My heroic father, Ramon, started as a dishwasher in Dallas, Texas, and became the executive chef of the Dallas Country Club, the Dallas Athletic Club, and the Preston Trails Country Club." Inspired by his father's own example, Charles succeeded in school and sports, achieving both election to the National Honor Society and top awards as a football quarterback. His education culminated in becoming a lawyer. In 1973, he was recruited to become attorney-advisor at the U.S. Department of Health, Education and Welfare (HEW) in Washington, DC. His career as an attorney has also brought him into higher circles of achievement, including election as trustee of the Fairfax County (Virginia) Public School system, membership in the Bar of the Supreme Court, and scholar-in-residence in Mexico.

Charles and I have discussed how the Mexican federal government in those years of violence denied the Catholic Church its freedom of religion and attacked its priests and nuns, killing many of them as well as many Catholic laypeople. When the movie *No Greater Glory* was shown in local theaters, Charles invited me to attend a showing. The movie relates the struggle of Catholic warriors against the Mexican dictators Carranza, Obregon, and the last and most cruel, Plutarco Elias Calles (1924–1928). Imagine the surprise and elation Charles experienced when he saw a railroad station with the name Yurecuaro in one scene of the movie. Charles blurted out, "That was our hometown!"

Charles Cervantes, son of Ramon Cervantes, has lived the American Dream beyond the wildest expectations of his forefathers. He is enriched today by knowing why and how his grandparents and their children, including his father, escaped the horrible disorder and lawlessness of Mexico in the years of turmoil, 1913 to 1930.

The Family of Francisco M. Vega

Our super senior member of the Diaspora—now at age 95—fled in a Model T! Was his diaspora different from the others? You betcha! Very, very few others in the Diaspora escaped in a car.

Francisco Miguel Vega's story starts in the historic city of Saltillo, Coahuila. Saltillo was the capital of the state of Coahuila and before that, when its domain was more expansive, it was also the capital of the territory of Texas and other nearby areas. Named for the Coahuiltecans, the indigenous people who lived in the area when the Spaniards arrived, Coahuila is now one of the Mexican states that borders Texas along the Rio Grande. Along with its neighboring northern Mexico states, Coahuila has shown an affinity for American matters, a tendency not uncommon among neighboring nations that share certain commonalities (think of Switzerland and its languages, religions, political patterns, commerce, and education). For example, during the Civil War in the United States, the governors of Coahuila and four additional northern Mexico states expressed a willingness to join the Confederacy to form a new nation in a letter dated September 27, 1861, addressed to Simon Cameron, Secretary of War, from Fort Fauntleroy, New Mexico.[111]

---

[111] *The War of the Rebellion* (Washington, DC: Government Printing Office, 1897), pp. 635–641.

Francisco Vega's home state has other historic connections. About forty miles due west from Saltillo is the town of Las Paras, which gave birth, wealth, and fame to Francisco Madero, leader of the Mexican Revolution of 1910 and subsequent president of Mexico. Another very wealthy neighbor of the Vega *familia* lived about sixty miles north of Saltillo in the town of Cuarto Cienegas. His infamous name was Venustiano Carranza, and he, too, would rise to rule Mexico thanks to the help of President Woodrow Wilson.

Of course, the family of Don Francisco Vega was totally uninvolved with Madero and Carranza and probably had no idea how the actions of these wealthy *hacendados* would affect them in Saltillo. But with the revolution and its aftermath came military actions, killings, thievery, and utter disorder. Against this panorama, the family of Francisco shuttled back and forth between Saltillo and Monterrey, a city about fifty miles away in the neighboring state of Nuevo Leon. "We had businesses and families," Don Francisco wrote to me recently, "and moved as the fighting came [our] way and to avoid the dangers to the families." Finally, in 1919, his family abandoned their prosperous way of life in Mexico and joined the Diaspora of two million other Mexicans to the north. To save their lives and start afresh, they crossed the border and came to settle in San Antonio, Texas: Francisco Vega, along with his grandmother, Maria de los Angeles Tapia viuda de Lopez; his mother, Sara Lopez Tapia de Vega; his father, Lazaro Nava Vega; and his aunts, uncles, cousins, and other relatives.

When his parents took him to register at the local public elementary school (named for the Confederate general John B. Hood), Don Francisco underwent an experience common to many Diaspora children: He was not allowed to use his proper name "Francisco," but instead the school official recorded his name on the registration as "Mike Vega." The family had no choice. It was either accept "Mike Vega" or he couldn't attend school, according to the official. Thus, there is no record of Francisco Vega receiving an education at John B. Hood Elementary School, or Washington Irving Junior High School, either. But upon entering Central Catholic High School in San Antonio, he insisted on using his given name. There was no objection, and so he continued throughout his life as Francisco M. Vega, or when feeling particularly thorough, Francisco Miguel Nava Vega Lopez Tapia.

Francisco Vega went on to serve in the U.S. Army. He worked at the headquarters under General Eisenhower in England and helped in the preparations for D-Day in Europe. He served honorably, married, and eventually made a home in Michigan, where he has prospered and enjoyed the American Dream.

EPILOGUE

In writing this book, I tried mightily to find the answer to *"Why?"* Why did I see so many Mexicans around me in my early life in Pomona, California? Why had so many left Mexico? Why did Mexico lose its best people in such an enormous wave of emigration? So many wonderful young Mexicans had abandoned life in Mexico—never to return or have knowledge of their loved ones left behind in their little *jacales* (shacks) in rural rancherias.

My research led me to delve deeply into the history of Mexico. I dug into the origin of the Mestizaje, an ethnicity generally unknown, with little written about it. I also justified my bachelor of arts degree in philosophy, applying it to readings of the major European philosophers and seeing how their concepts, conclusions, and calls to action changed the lives of my parents and grandparents—indeed, of all Mexicans.

I finally discovered the *why:* It was hidden in the nefarious conspiratorial causes of the Mexican Diaspora of 1913–1930. The most salient cause (and least known) happened in December 1913 in Veracruz, Mexico.

At that time, ardent intellectual followers of the

principles of Empiricism, the Jacobins, Marx, Nietzsche, Hegel, Socialism, and Masonry were to be found in universities and major cities. The Communists among them were the most organized, and their active working networks spanned across countries, including Mexico. A Mexican Communist, Gerardo Murillo, a.k.a. Dr. Atl, while working in Paris, France, supported the Madero revolution of 1910 but in reality was representing the interests and purposes of the Communist conspiracy. In nearby Switzerland, three men in exile from their homeland, Russia, were leading the international Communist conspiracy: Lenin, Stalin, and Trotsky. One may well deduce that Dr. Atl might have been in contact with them.

Dr. Atl returned to Mexico to carry on the conspiratorial aims of the three men in Switzerland. He gathered other Communists and fellow-travelers in Veracruz, Mexico, in December 1913 and made arrangements as explained in Part I, Chapter 5.

Historical facts and events substantiate my conclusion that the contract signed by Carranza's people and the Communists in Veracruz **caused** the Mexican Diaspora of 1913–1930. Look no further for more significant elements in the causality and in the *why*.

The Mexican Diaspora was the very first caused by the international Communist conspiracy. Sadly, it was followed by more around the world: Russians, Cubans, Vietnamese, and others have fled their homelands in the wake of Communist tragedies.

The tools of the Communists are: lies, misinformation, censorship, and utmost secrecy. That is why the truth of the Mexican Diaspora, the misrepresentation of the so-called Revolution, the horrors committed by the Mexican government and the Mexican army in their war against the Catholic Church, and the brutal persecution of clergy, nuns, and laity have remained hidden and occult. But the truth must be revealed.

We, the descendants of the Diaspora here in the United States, have much to appreciate. We offer our gratitude to the two million brave Mexican women and men who lived the truth of the Diaspora for their sacrifices. We also thank President Richard M. Nixon, always an ardent anti-Communist, for making sure we were no longer unknown or forgotten. And above all, we thank God for the opportunity we have to enjoy freedom of religion and the American Dream.